Traveling Companions

Traveling Companions

Feminism, Teaching, and Action Research

EDITED BY MARY BRYDON-MILLER,
PATRICIA MAGUIRE, AND
ALICE McINTYRE

Joe L. Kincheloe and Shirley Steinberg,
Advisory Editors

PRAEGER

Westport, Connecticut
London

Library of Congress Cataloging-in-Publication Data

Traveling companions : feminism, teaching, and action research / edited by Mary
 Brydon-Miller, Patricia Maguire, and Alice McIntyre.
     p.   cm.
 Includes bibliographical references and index.
 ISBN 0–275–98027–8 (alk. paper)
    1. Feminism—-Research. 2. Women's studies. 3. Action research. I. Brydon-
 Miller, Mary. II. Maguire, Patricia. III. McIntyre, Alice, 1956–
 HQ1180.T75   2004
 305.42'07'2—dc22   2003058152

British Library Cataloging in Publication Data is available.

Library of Congress Catalog Card Number: 2003058152
ISBN: 0–275–98027–8

First published in 2004

Praeger Publishers, 88 Post Road West, Westport, CT 06881
An imprint of Greenwood Publishing Group, Inc.
www.praeger.com

Printed in the United States of America

The paper used in this book complies with the
Permanent Paper Standard issued by the National
Information Standards Organization (Z39.48–1984).

10 9 8 7 6 5 4 3 2 1

We dedicate this book to the diverse communities who have informed, influenced, and enriched the fields of feminist and action research. May they, and we, continue to travel together in the hopes of creating a more just world.

Contents

Introduction

Patricia Maguire, Mary Brydon-Miller,
and Alice McIntyre

I have grown so attached to the image of the Traveling Companions and have found the meaning of that to be representative of so much about feminism and PAR. I thought of it in Belfast this summer when three friends came to participate in (the) photo-text project ...

We were all walking up Falls Road in West Belfast, at one point shoulder-to-shoulder.... As we looked at the murals and storefronts, we all seemed to be scattered, but traveling in the same direction.... At one point, I thought of the title of the book....

(Alice McIntyre, personal communication, 10/4/2002)

This book is a story by and about traveling companions. We, the contributors to this volume, are feminist and participatory action researchers, traveling companions, who hope to influence feminist scholarship to be more participatory and action-oriented, and participatory action research (PAR) to be more grounded in feminist theories and values. For years, our mutual destination has been that place of hope where activist researchers join with others to try to transform the world, not merely study it (Stanley, 1990). While we may have been headed in similar directions, rarely have feminist and participatory action researchers acknowledged each other as collaborators with mutually important contributions to the journey. Through the work presented in this volume, we hope to meet at the crossroads, share the stories of our travels, and widen the circle of traveling companions.

The journey of this volume began over 15 years ago. At that time, many feminist researchers were drawn to PAR as a counter-hegemonic approach to knowledge creation that challenged established approaches to research by emphasizing collaborative processes of inquiry, education, and action. In addition, many of us believed we could integrate the ideas of the 1960s women's movements and the theories framing feminisms into the various aspects of PAR.

Our initial enthusiasm was short-lived. In our attempts to engage in feminist-informed PAR, we found ourselves more often than not standing at the fork in the road: our feminisms going in one direction; PAR in the other. Rather quickly it became clear to us that some aspects of PAR, which was framed as a liberatory and transformative approach to knowledge creation, were as androcentric as traditional, positivist research (Maguire, 1987). This recognition raised the question: Just what would PAR liberate us from and just what would it transform us into?

The androcentrism that characterizes much of the work associated with PAR may have been understandable in the early years. As Anderson, Herr, and Nihlen (1994) note, many early action research traditions were associated with men. Similarly, the world of PAR had been—and to some extent, still is—dominated in visibility and stature by men, many of whom have been content to ignore feminisms or leave the "gender stuff" to women. The contributors to this volume have argued that the unquestioned masculinized worldview of PAR, and the discrepancies between liberatory theories and the participatory practices they espouse, prevent PAR's transformative possibilities from being realized.

Feminists' long-time annoyance with the androcentrism in PAR and commitment to proactively expand its theoretical base came to a head following the ironic marginalization of women and gender issues at the 1997 Cartagena World Congress on Participatory Action Research and Action Learning, Action Research, and Process Management (Maguire, 2000). Some have celebrated the Cartagena World Congress for formally initiating and intensifying the dialogue and solidarity among diverse action research schools, between young people and discipline old-timers, and among Third-World researchers (Fals Borda, 1998; Pyrch, 1997). Others have criticized it for its blatant marginalization of women and feminist issues in the planning process and the congress substance (Collins, 1997; Maguire, 1999; Wadsworth, 1997). The official congress history trivializes women's activist uprising at the congress as "happily spontaneous" (Fals Borda, 1998, p. 2). It was neither happy nor spontaneous. Indeed, precongress planning and decision-making structures and processes, organized and accomplished by a group of mostly men, functioned to silence and marginalize women and feminist concerns by simply excluding or ignoring them (Swantz, 1999; Wadsworth, 1999).

In response to the marginalization of women at the World Conference and in PAR, generally, a group of feminist activists and researchers decided to stop depending on "the ventriloquism of good but powerful men" (Wadsworth, 1999) and intentionally create spaces for and give attention to feminisms within PAR. This book represents one aspect of that "doing it" process.

The collective journey of the contributors of this book began in 1999. Funded by a small grant from the Society for the Psychological Study of Social Issues,[1] Mary Brydon-Miller, Pat Maguire, and Alice McIntyre invited a number of feminist researchers and practitioners of PAR to organize a working conference to "bridge the gap" between feminist scholarship and participatory action research. By exploring the intersections between the two fields, we hoped to contribute new perspectives and energy to both.

Jill Morawski (1997) contends that one of the greatest challenges for feminist scholars is "modifying the near environment in which researchers conduct their science, learn, teach, and judge the efforts of other scientists" (p. 677). An important aspect of modifying the near environment of the conference was our decision to create a process that was informed by many of the underlying principles of feminism and PAR. To this end, we developed a process in which the conference participants worked together to generate themes for the conference, as well as to write, individually or collaboratively, conference papers that reflected those themes. Participants were also invited to read and respond to one another's drafts prior to the scheduled conference. We hoped that by doing so the conference itself could focus more on deepening our dialogue about these issues and on developing the relationships that would sustain this dialogue over time.

Pat Maguire's colleague, Roy Howard, created an Internet Web site that allowed all the participants to discuss questions, share comments, and present aspects of their teaching and research on-line. Over the next seven months, participants interacted with one another through Web-based threaded discussions, developing themes, concepts, and rough drafts of conference papers—all of which became the fodder for the three-day meeting we held in June, 2001.[2]

Although the participatory nature of the conference planning was challenging—particularly because academics are so accustomed to more traditional, hierarchical conference structures to establish agendas, review papers, and present work—it was well worth the effort. The conference was developed collaboratively and reflected the issues and concerns that were salient to attendees. Many of these issues and concerns are discussed and explored in this book. In the presentation of these issues, contributors have experimented with new forms of narrative, incorporating storytelling and personal experiences to give voice and substance to our shared commitment to address issues that continue to mediate, complicate, enliven, and frustrate action-based feminist-inspired research aimed at eradicating social injustices.

A WORD ABOUT FEMINISMS AND PAR

Third-World feminists, Women of Color, indeed all "hyphenated" feminists have challenged the notion of a monolithic or universal feminist perspective (Behar & Gordon, 1995; hooks, 1989; Luke, 1996; McIntyre, 2000a; Mohanty, 1987; Spelman, 1988). In addition, many action-oriented feminist researchers have been frustrated by the lack of an articulated framework for translating feminist insights into concrete actions aimed at achieving social change. Although there are many feminist researchers engaging in inquiry-based research that mirrors feminisms' commitment to methods that shift power relations, challenge hierarchies, provoke alternative tools for examining social issues, promote participant collaboration, and contribute to positioning research as a site for social justice, few of them are framed within a PAR paradigm.

The contributors to this volume embrace an approach to feminist theory that accounts for the multiple positionalities of all women, and men, and "includes an analysis of power and the multiple ways people are oppressed and oppressing" (Brabeck & Brown, 1997, p. 23; see also Kemp & Squires, 1997) at the same time as it translates into concrete, tangible actions that improve the lives of everyday people.

The contributors have differing relationships to and definitions of feminisms and PAR and come to both fields with varied histories and work experiences. While few of us work within women's studies or feminist studies departments, we acknowledge a deep debt to those in women's or feminist studies who have carved out radicalizing spaces in universities to connect theory and practice and who have dedicated their research to improving the everyday lives of women and children. Raising critical questions, they have created compelling alternatives to how we engage the social sciences.

The contributors to this volume come from both resource-rich universities and university extension centers or programs in resource-poor communities. Of those contributors who work in the academy, many of us have moved from a variety of fields into education departments where we advocate for and engage in teacher action research or teacher inquiry. As advocates of participatory or action-oriented feminist research, all of us are sprinkled throughout fields often separated by the artificial discipline barriers of the social sciences. We have been building alliances with others in the university who are struggling to pry open the stranglehold of positivist research in their disciplines and organizations and engage in truly transformative knowledge creation processes (Greenwood & Levin, 1998; Tolman & Brydon-Miller, 2001). Similarly, we work with diverse communities of people outside the university who are also struggling to create spaces where they can transform local knowledge into actions that lead to community well-being.

For some of us, building alliances in the university and in local communities has been complicated by our experiences of and with personal and private marginalizations based on aspects of our identities: Muslim, lesbian, Jew, working class, Hindu, Pakistani-American, single in a couples world, woman/mother, nontenured or "justastudent." Likewise, each of us has been granted particular privileges based on various aspects of our identities: White, First World, heterosexual, middle class, married, university-educated, tenured, or parent. Each of us has been at the center and at the margins (see Finke in Maher & Tetreault, 1994). Our multiple identities, and the ways in which we are both the oppressed and the oppressing, are revealed in different ways throughout this volume and speak to the interdependency of privilege and oppression within feminist and participatory research processes (Dill & Baca Zinn, 1997).

Many of us seek to break the silences that exist in university systems where "official knowledge is promulgated and the given order maintained" (Heaney, 1993, p. 46). We concur with Heaney (1993) when he posits that universities devalue popular knowledge and retain a "monopolistic hold on the production and legitimatization of useful knowledge" (p. 42). Yet, we disagree with the premise that feminist research, PAR, and "the university" cannot share similar space.

For certain, the space is messy, conflictual, contradictory, complex, and controversial. Yet, the space can also provide university-based researchers with opportunities to link research with academic and community practices. By positioning ourselves as both feminist and participatory action researchers and members of a university community, we can bring to bear *inside* the university what we are attempting to bring to bear *outside* of it: namely, institutional and social change, the formation of alliances with others so as to undo systems of injustice, the creation of new ways of thinking and being, and an intentionality about collaborating with others in order to produce and construct knowledge that benefits *all* people. (McIntyre, 2000b, p. 28)

As we struggle to transform our near environments (Morawski, 1997), we carve out spaces for the next generation of activist researchers to do the same (see, e.g., Reid, 2002). Oftentimes, we are sought out by a graduate student who is desperately seeking affirmation for her/his efforts to attempt feminist-informed PAR or action-oriented feminist scholarship. Many of us were those students ourselves.

At the same time that we mentor the next cohort of researchers, we work across differences and continents to support one another as we continue to transform social science research, university teaching, and community inquiry and action. We do so at the intersection of our personal lives as daughters, sons, sisters, brothers, mothers, lovers, partners, and friends— people who set familial priorities that oftentimes clash with our responsibilities at work and our responsibilities to the participants of our projects.

For as important as it is for us to mentor students and be allies to one another, it is equally important for us to work diligently with many people living in the communities in which we work who labor with us to co-create humanizing spaces that nurture and value their everyday lives, their indigenous knowledges, and their contribution to our work in the academy.

TRAVELING COMPANIONS

Both feminist scholarship and PAR recognize that knowledge is created in the context of genuine human relationships and, further, that both knowledge and social action are created as the result of specific groups of people acting as subjects rather than objects of the inquiry process. In order for this inquiry process to contribute to true social change, research participants must have a meaningful voice in identifying the problems to be explored. Finally, knowledge creation always involves differences of power and privilege among those taking part in the process. Therefore, feminist researchers and practitioners of PAR attend to the dynamics and mechanics of participant/researcher relationships, working to recognize and reconstruct some of the inherent hierarchies that exist in those relationships by addressing the underlying causes of inequality.

Issues of power, hierarchies, and knowledge creation are but a few of the topics that are discussed, explored, critiqued, and questioned in this volume. Those issues are framed within the following three sections: (1) power and the construction of knowledge; (2) issues of status and relationships between communities and the academy; and (3) the ethical dimensions and particular meanings of feminist and participatory action research.

Part I: Power and the Construction of Knowledge

Feminist, postcolonial, and critical race theory all provide lenses through which to better understand the multiple identities of researchers and participants that are informed by gender, race, and other socially constructed positions. Oftentimes, these positions determine the extent to which people are privileged in society as well as the ways in which people use that privilege to effect change. Scholars within these theoretical frameworks have created new literary genres that reflect the importance of acknowledging subjectivity and authorial presence and embrace the use of narrative and storytelling as legitimate forms of academic writing (see, e.g., Behar, 1996; Delgado & Stefancic, 2000). The chapters in this first section reflect both issues of power and privilege and the experimental narrative styles of these theoretical frameworks.

Mary Brydon-Miller examines issues of power and privilege, providing insights into how they influence both our everyday lives and our work as academics and activists. In addition, she highlights the importance of narrative as a strategy for opening up spaces where the powerless can be heard, listened to, and valued for what and who they are.

Nimat Barazangi explores how Muslim women scholar-activists resist Westernized feminism and many forms of PAR as frameworks for social activism. The women's self-identification with Islam, the ways in which they construct and interpret knowledge, and their individual and collective worldviews complicate the notion that feminisms and PAR—as they are played out in particular countries and cultures—can attend to the multiple aspects of representation, voice, power, and privilege.

Kalina Brabeck extends the discussion of how to open up spaces for marginalized peoples by examining the literary genre of testimonio as an approach to knowing the Other that challenges Western notions of authorial presence, universal truth, and the autonomous individual. Brabeck suggests that testimonio offers insight into how First-World feminist and activist researchers can stand in solidarity with others in the face of social injustice.

Part II: Issues of Status and Relationships between Communities and the Academy

In the second section of the book we examine the shifting roles of researchers within the academy and within the community settings in which they work. The contributors in this section explore how their varied positions influence their ability to live out many of the underlying principles that frame feminist and participatory action research.

Alice McIntyre and M. Brinton Lykes explore the multiple positions and relationships they occupied—both individually and collectively—within the North of Ireland (McIntyre) and Guatemala (Lykes). As researchers and participants, friends and colleagues, they describe how they weave visual, oral, and written stories into texts whose authorship transcends false dichotomies and fixed notions of "us" and "them."

Based in large part on her research in Maori communities in Aotearoa New Zealand, Jill Chrisp explores the tensions researchers experience as they bridge the community-academy divide. Chrisp investigates the link between institutionalized gate-keeping processes that oftentimes benefit academics at the expense of the local communities in which they work.

In the last chapter of this section, Susan E. Noffke and Marie Brennan use their experiences as action researchers in the United States and Australia to explore the ways in which their research and activist projects have and have not reflected feminist agendas and frameworks. Through their individual stories and shared reflections, the authors identify the theories they believe will bring action research into useful intersections with the overall aims of social justice.

Part III: Ethical Dimensions and Meanings of Feminist and Participatory Action Research

Feminist and participatory action researchers propose a passionate commitment to social justice, democracy, and a critical examination of the moral implications of our practice. With this commitment comes a recognition that existing systems of conducting and evaluating research must be reframed if our scholarship is to be consistent with the values we espouse. In the final section of this book, we explore the ethical dimensions of feminist and participatory action research and consider the implications of and for both.

Patricia Maguire examines the challenges of exposing educational action researchers to feminist-informed action research in a university context. Maguire's work in a university classroom suggests that the way to feminist-informed Action Research is directly through feminism. Maguire draws on her students' voices in describing their increasingly more nuanced understanding of feminism and of educational action research and their growing commitment to incorporating this understanding into their own practice as teachers and counselors.

Angela Shartrand and Mary Brabeck explore the ways in which feminist ethics can contribute to a more ethical framework for conducting feminist research. The authors use recent work on feminist ethics to raise questions about the extent to which the American Psychological Association's code of ethics is grounded in assumptions that do not reflect collaborative, participatory, feminist, and/or nonpositivist research.

Davydd Greenwood suggests that there is a complex, organic relationship between feminism and action research. He explores how the two approaches are neither competitive nor complementary but wound together in a highly complex way that makes them both interdependent and, potentially, mutually sustaining.

In the final chapter, we return to the issue of ethics as explored by Rhoda Unger. Using her experiences as a well-established scholar and journal editor, Unger turns the spotlight on the tensions and contradictions inherent in publishing feminist scholarship. Unger suggests that gate-keepers, of which she is one, need to analyze and criticize their work as feminists and activist researchers so as to decrease the opportunities for naysayers in the academy who would prefer to "tear down the edifices [feminists] have built" (Unger, this volume p. 177).

CONCLUDING REFLECTIONS

Advocating for feminist-informed PAR from within the academy, and various other organizations, is not a career advancer. Many of us have been denied tenure, refused grants, skipped over for promotion, and fired for the work that we do. However, we want those new to or curious about the field of feminist participatory research to know that it is possible to survive as activist academics or academic activists. Indeed, many of us are thriving as deans, full professors, journal editors, and department chairpersons. Having achieved a significant amount of power within our institutions and our disciplines, we are committed to share and use that power to open spaces for others, change our institutions, speak out, and build and sustain spaces for politicized research and activism. While it is difficult, sometimes disheartening, and oftentimes challenging to stay true to the principles that guide activist research, teaching, and learning, the process of doing so is well worth it, for activist work, and activist research, are not events. They are processes "that we are living through, creating as we go" (Maguire, 1993, p. 176). The question for us then isn't *should* we engage those processes. The question is *how* and *when* will we do so (McIntyre, 2000b).

We hope this book captures the spirit of innovation, fearlessness, dedication, and determination that characterizes the fields of feminist and participatory action research. As importantly, the authors hope to reveal the significant ways in which feminism and PAR complement one another as approaches to research that are liberating, transformative, and that can— if we act with care and are honest—contribute to *new* ways of relating, *new* ways of constructing knowledge, *new* ways to confront privilege, *new* criteria for what is valued in society, and *new* directions for implementing research processes that lead to just social change (McIntyre, 2000b).

NOTES

1. Other conference support was generously provided by the Peter and Carol Lynch School of Education at Boston College and the Gallup Graduate Studies Center at Western New Mexico University.

2. The frontispiece of this volume is one manifestation of the fun and experimentation that we have experienced in working together. The quilt represented there was created from pieces of fabric that participants brought to the conference as a way of introducing themselves and explaining what they hoped to bring to the conference as well as how they hoped to benefit from the two-day gathering. The stories the participants told about themselves via their pieces of fabric focused on a host of experiences, identities, and events. We spoke about being mothers and grandmothers; about celebrating traditions and honoring memories; about friendships and the deep personal relationships we have developed within a variety of communities and within our birth families. We also talked about the long years many of us have been working together for change and how our life experiences underscore our commitments to democratic practice and social justice.

Some of the participants voiced concern over the use of a quilt to represent us, arguing that traditional women's art forms can reinforce the continued oppression of women in many cultures. Other participants embraced the notion of using a quilt to frame the conference because the quilt celebrates the creative and loving contributions of women throughout history. As a group, we acknowledged the range of feelings and responses about using a quilt as a way to represent us and by the conclusion of the conference had developed an overall representation that reflected our individual and collective life stories and our present and future aspirations.

After the conference, the individual pieces of fabric were sewn into a quilt by Mary Brydon-Miller's mother, Kibber Miller, and her mother's friend of many, many years, Caroline Stanhope. We thank them for their many hours of work and for the artistry with which they brought such disparate pieces together. In so doing, they provided us with a unique representation of the themes of this volume and of the people who contributed to it. The quilt has since accompanied us to conferences in Toronto, Canada, and Rotorua, Aotearoa New Zealand.

Thanks to the wonderful work of Roy Howard, the fabric pieces and accompanying stories can be viewed at http://www. wnmu.org/tc.html.

REFERENCES

Anderson, G., Herr, K., & Nihlen, A. (1994). *Studying your own school: An educator's guide to qualitative practitioner research.* Thousand Oaks, CA: Corwin Press.

Behar, R. (1996). *The vulnerable observer: Anthropology that breaks your heart.* Boston: Beacon Press.

Behar, R., & Gordon, D. (Eds.). (1995). *Women writing culture.* Berkeley, CA: University of California Press.

Brabeck, M., & Brown, L. (with Christian, L., Espin, O., Hare-Mustin, R., Kaplan, A., Kaschak, E., Miller, D., Phillips, E., Ferns, T., & Van Ormer, A.) (1997). Feminist theory and psychological practice. In J. Worell & N. Johnson (Eds.), *Shaping the future of feminist psychology, education, research, and practice* (pp. 15–36). Washington, DC: American Psychological Association Books.

Collins, K. (1997). *Report on participatory action research and action learning.* World Conference at Cartagena, Columbia, Latin America. Department of Social Work, UNISA, South Africa.

Delgado, R., & Stefancic, J. (Eds.). (2000). *Critical race theory: The cutting edge.* Philadelphia: Temple University Press.

Dill, B. T., & Baca Zinn, M. (1997). Race and gender: Revisioning the social sciences: Teaching and research in the academy. In M. Anderson, L. Fine, K. Geissler, & J. Ladenson (Eds.), *Doing feminism* (pp. 39–52). East Lansing, MI: Women's Studies Program, Michigan State University.

Fals Borda, O. (Ed). (1998). *People's participation: Challenges ahead.* Bogotá: FAIEP.

Greenwood, D., & Levin, M. (1998). *Introduction to action research: Social research for social change.* Thousand Oaks, CA: SAGE Publications.

Heaney, T. W. (1993). If you can't beat 'em, join 'em: The professionalization of participatory research. In P. Park, M. Brydon-Miller, B. Hall, & T. Jackson (Eds.), *Voices of change: Participatory research in the United States and Canada* (pp. 41–46). Westport, CT: Greenwood Press.

hooks, b. (1989). *Talking back: Thinking feminist, thinking black.* Boston: South End Press.

Kemp, S., & Squires, J. (Eds.). (1997). *Feminisms.* Oxford: Oxford University Press.

Luke, C. (1996). *Feminism & pedagogies of everyday life.* Albany: State University of New York Press.

Maguire, P. (1987). *Doing participatory research: A feminist approach.* Amherst: The Center for International Education, University of Massachusetts.

Maguire, P. (1993). Challenges, contradictions, and celebrations: Attempting participatory research as a doctoral student. In P. Park, M. Brydon-Miller, B. Hall, & T. Jackson (Eds.), *Voices of change: Participatory research in the United States and Canada* (pp. 157–176). Westport, CT: Greenwood Press.

Maguire, P. (1999). *E-Dialogue across distance: Post-Cartagena cyber-conversations: Feminists, feminisms, and action research.* Speech, 9th World Congress Participatory Action Research and the 5th ALARPM World Congress. Ballarat, Australia.

Maguire, P. (2000). Uneven ground: Feminisms and action research. In P. Reason & H. Bradbury (Eds.), *Handbook of action research: Participative inquiry and practice* (pp. 59–69). Thousand Oaks, CA: SAGE Publications.

Maher, F. A., & Tetreault, M. K. T. (1994). *The feminist classroom: An inside look at how professors and students are transforming higher education for a diverse society.* New York: Basic Books.

McIntyre, A. (2000a). Antiracist pedagogy in the university: The ethical challenges of making whiteness public. In M. Brabeck (Ed.), *Practicing feminist ethics in psychology.* Washington, DC: American Psychological Association.

McIntyre, A. (2000b). *Inner-city kids: Adolescents confront life and violence in an urban community.* New York: New York University Press.

Mohanty, C. (1987). Under western eyes: Feminist scholarship and colonial discourses. *Feminist Review, 30,* 1–88.

Morawski, J. (1997). The science behind feminist methods. *Journal of Social Issues, 53*(4), 667–682.

Pyrch, T. (1997). Letter from Cartagena. *Convergence, 30*(4), 18–24.

Reid, C. (2002). *"We don't count, we're just not there": Using feminist action research to explore the relationship between exclusion, poverty and women's health.* Doctoral dissertation. University of British Columbia.

Spelman, E. (1988). *Inessential women: Problems of exclusion in feminist thought.* Boston: Beacon Press.

Stanley, L. (1990). Feminist praxis and the academic mode of production: An editorial introduction. In L. Stanley (Ed.), *Feminist praxis: Research, theory, and epistemology in feminist sociology* (pp. 3–19). London: Routledge.

Swantz, personal communication, March 24, 1999.

Tolman, D., & Brydon-Miller, M. (Eds.). (2001). *From subjects to subjectivities: A handbook of interpretive and participatory methods.* New York: New York University Press.

Wadsworth, Y. (1997). *Report on the Cartagena AR/PAR Congress.* The Action Research Issues Association. Melbourne, Australia.

Wadsworth, personal communication, March 9, 1999a.

Wadsworth, personal communication, November 30, 1999b.

PART I

Power and the Construction of Knowledge

CHAPTER 1

The Terrifying Truth: Interrogating Systems of Power and Privilege and Choosing to Act

Mary Brydon-Miller

FOUR SCENES FROM THE LIFE OF A SHAPESHIFTER

Scene I: I can kill with one punch. I would never strike anyone for fear of causing death. Never injury, death. The terrifying truth of this statement has never been tested and is completely unjustified by any outward appearance or action. A middle-aged woman, average height and weight, graying hair, bifocals—my appearance masks my lethal nature and there are many who underestimate my power. I show restraint. I have learned to use words instead. With words I can protect myself without fear of actually killing my opponent. My victims often register horror and surprise at the vehemence with which I attack. They don't know how lucky they are to be alive.

Scene II: "He leads with his stomach," my friend says. It describes him perfectly. A big, loud man who occupies all available space as if we are unwelcome squatters on his farm. His voice alone overwhelms us—laughing or shouting, he controls even the air. After yet another disagreement he storms into my office, towering over me and clearly angry.

"If you have a problem you take it up with me. Why did you go to the Dean?" he bellows.

"Because I knew this was how you'd respond." Trying to keep my emotions under control, I can barely manage a whisper.

"Whaddya mean?" he demands.

"I mean I knew you'd come in here and try to bully me." I am trying to steel myself.

"Bully you?!" He sits down uninvited, blocking any possible exit. I feel a quiet node of panic forming in my chest.

"I'd like you to leave now," I say. He ignores me and continues to press me on our disagreement.

"I would like you to leave now," I say again, my voice sounding taut and barely under control. He continues to rail against me. Eventually I start to cry and tell him exactly what I think of him. Sobbing, I call him names and review each abuse. I have the sense he almost enjoys it, the Sturm und Drang of my furious tirade.

At one point I take a breath, exhausted. "I hate arguing with you," I say quietly, spent.

He looks puzzled, "I thought you enjoyed it."

I am incredulous. "Just because I don't back down, don't imagine I enjoy it."

When the Dean hears of the incident he tells me I use tears to get my way.

Scene III: Dr. Brydon-Miller, Gerontology Program Director. One of my favorite tasks is to drive through the Notch, into what they call the North Country, where I meet with a local elder activist group. One of the members of the committee is an older man who continues to wield a significant degree of control both locally and at the state level. He is intelligent, self-assured, and politically experienced. He is also a poor listener who tends to hold forth at meetings, making it difficult for others to take part. The staff person who chairs the meetings is at her wits' end trying to deal with him. Most of the other members of the committee are older women, women whose insight and experience I respect greatly, and it distresses me to see them silenced, so I am perfectly happy to be brought in periodically to facilitate a meeting. I understand why I am there and I understand my position. I am an expert, someone sanctioned by the authorities, someone with titles and connections. I am powerful and confident, professionally dressed, and I knowingly use these characteristics to control the meeting. I make a point of seating this man next to me, where he cannot make eye contact easily and so is prevented from taking the floor. I stand; he sits. When he does speak and goes on too long, I put my hand gently on his shoulder and suggest that we might hear from others, and he complies. I assign roles and tasks in such a way as to draw out competent, but more self-effacing members of the committee. I direct questions and support ideas proposed by the women in the group. I'm good—really good!

Scene IV: I walk out of the faculty meeting between two colleagues. I no longer remember what issue we had been discussing, but I had voiced an opinion sure to be unpopular with the administration. My colleagues, both people I consider friends, discuss my statement and prospects for a future at the institution—one attacking my position, one defending it. Both are male, both more than half a foot taller than I am. My defender is a professor of economics, lean and handsome, patrician looking. The attacker, a member of the business faculty, resembles an old boxer. I stand between them, beneath them, the object of their discussion, unable to enter the space within which the debate is taking place. I gaze up at them. Women are so often depicted gazing up at men in adoration. I gaze in fury. I will myself to grow. Almost comically, I attempt to move the conversation to higher ground, taking a step back, a step to the left, up the hill, hoping that in doing so I can take advantage of the difference in elevation to enter the fray. For a moment, I even consider returning to the building to get a chair on which to stand. In the end I simply leave, unnoticed.

Powerful and powerless—the kind of shapeshifting we have all experienced at different points in our lives. This chapter explores the protean nature of privilege and oppression. I consider how those of us who are academics and activists might use our personal experiences to develop greater self-awareness regarding the dynamic nature of these opposing positions. I suggest that, if those of us within the academy are to work with those facing oppression to challenge injustice, we must be able to draw upon whatever experiences of powerlessness we have had in order to develop a more humane and truly emancipatory practice. Simultaneously, we must acknowledge and be willing to wield the power granted to us by our positions of social and economic privilege in effort to achieve our shared goal of positive social change.

For nearly twenty years I have identified myself as a participatory action researcher. I was driven in this by the need to reconcile my deeply held belief in the power of democratic processes and community action with my equally valued professional and intellectual location as an academic researcher. By integrating popular education, community-based research, and an explicit commitment to social justice, participatory action research seemed to make possible the identity to which I aspired—that of the scholar/activist. But too often this practice has seemed to be grounded in the facile assumption that once we have rejected the elitism of traditional positivist research and have made public our dedication to taking part in processes of social action, our work is done. The nuanced interplay of class, gender, race, and other aspects of identity within our own ranks, as well as in the communities within which we work, have too often been overlooked. In our zeal to bring about fundamental social change, we have too often failed to address, or even to recognize, the kinds of oppression embedded in our own practice. This volume represents our attempt to address these issues in a more critical way by bringing together feminist theories and participatory action research. In feminist-informed participatory action research[1] this coming to terms with power and privilege is especially important as we attempt to negotiate the contradictions inherent in our efforts to confront injustice while at the same time occupying positions of social and economic privilege. Neither playing the victim nor taking the role of the committed but cloistered critic will suffice; we must choose to act.

SURPRISE, CHALLENGE, AND REVENGE

In recalling the scenes described in the opening of this chapter, and those that appear throughout, I have been surprised, challenged, and, if I am to be truly honest, revenged. I have been surprised at the strong emotions these memories still evoke: challenged to uncover and own instances in which I have used power shamelessly and revenged in discovering that in telling these stories I am finally able to wrest power back from those who would rob me of my own sense of autonomy and agency. I found in writing these scenes that it was relatively easy to identify and write about experiences of powerlessness. Painful, perhaps, but these moments are still vivid in my memory and the details have stayed with me. It has been much more difficult for me to recall those experiences in which I have been the one holding power over others. Perhaps this is because as a woman I have been socialized to avoid such depictions of my own behavior, perhaps such actions seem at odds with my stated belief in equality, or possibly it is difficult to see beyond my own experience of the world. Whatever the case may be, this has presented a particular challenge and I have found it harder still to imagine the effect of my use of power on others involved in those interactions—how my own good intentions might have conflicted with their needs and desires in significant, and perhaps detrimental, ways.

As an Irish-American, storytelling is a part of my own familial and cultural heritages, but as an academic, storytelling seems fraught with the dual dangers of dismissal and dispute. It seems self-indulgent, especially coming from a privileged, White academic whose story, or one very like it, is at the very heart of the dominant cultural narrative. On the other hand, if I am to encourage others to critically examine their own uses and abuses of power and privilege, it is by probing and dissecting just such experiences that I can best exemplify the process. It is only by placing this "near environment in which researchers conduct their science, learn, teach, and judge the efforts of other scientists" (Morawski, 1997, p. 677) under scrutiny that we can hope to create change in our own practice.

This use of personal narrative, once considered anathema to serious academic writing, recognizes the subjective presence and active participation of the scholar in any research endeavor. To pretend invisibility through the use of the passive voice or a bland third-person narration of events masks the multiple ways in which the researcher, scholar, author shapes any act of inquiry. As Delgado suggests, "We participate in creating what we see in the very act of describing it" (2000, p. 61).

Much of the initial impetus for this acceptance of subjectivity came from feminist scholars who searched for but did not find their own experience or that of other women reflected in the master narratives of their fields.

More recently, American feminist authors and critics have begun to weave autobiography into history and criticism, journals into analysis, and the spirit of poetry into interdisciplinary prose. This more personal writing at times even obfuscates the boundary between the author's self, the subject of the discourse, and the audience. (Tedlock, 1995, p. 276)

Thus the traditional rules of academic writing are rejected in favor of a rhetoric more consistent with the engaged, collaborative nature of feminist scholarship and participatory action research.

One scholar who has led the way in her evocative intermingling of personal narrative and ethnography is Ruth Behar (1996). At the same time that she champions this genre, luring readers and would-be writers with her open and emotionally engaging prose, she warns against it as she describes the effect her work has had on her own family.

I've adopted the strategy of silence, exile, and cunning with regard to my writing, keeping every word hidden from my father and mother, withholding from them the knowledge that I am flying around the country inscribing the story of our dissolution as a family ever more irrevocably into the academy. (1995, p. 82)

Behar's position as a Jewish Cuban immigrant to the United States reflects the emphasis on lived experience that continues to inform feminist writing from a variety of cultural perspectives, as well (for examples, see Abu-Lughod, 1995; Chen, 2000; Gonzalez, 1999).

Critical race theorists have also embraced the use of the personal narrative, or what they have called "counterstorytelling," as a means of making minority voices heard and for increasing what Delgado has called our "empathic range" (2000, p. 70). Growing out of critical legal studies, critical race theory faced the enormous challenge of making these voices heard against the dominant narratives of the legal profession (Banks, 1995; Hom, 2000; Mrsevic, 2000). As Wing notes,

Opponents have attacked this approach as nonlegal, lacking intellectual rigor, overly emotional, and subjective. This methodology, however has significant value. Many of us prize our heritages in which the oral tradition has had historical importance—where vital notions of justice and the law are communicated generation to generation through the telling of stories. Also, using stories enables us to connect to those who do not understand hypertechnical legal language, but may nonetheless seek understanding of our distinctive voices. (2000, p. 5)

Delgado goes further:

stories and counterstories can serve an equally important destructive function. They can show that what we believe is ridiculous, self-serving, or cruel. They can show us the way out of the trap of unjustified exclusion. They can help us understand when it is time to reallocate power. They are the other half—the destructive half—of the creative dialectic. (2000, p. 61)

My own mentors, Myles Horton and Paulo Freire (1991), were both immensely talented and devoted storytellers and understood the important role that storytelling can play both in giving individuals an appreciation for their own personal experience and in establishing a sense of common ground and common goals among community members. I have endeavored to follow their example by incorporating personal narrative, oral history, and other forms of storytelling into my own practice (Brydon-Miller, 2002). As these scholars and researchers suggest, storytelling can be dangerous and destructive. It can also be enlightening and affirming. In either case, stories capture the core of our experience; in telling and hearing them we acknowledge "the storied nature of human conduct" (Sarbin, 1996).

THE INSIGHTS OF IMAGINATION

Feminism has traditionally focused on gender as the location of oppressive relationships, and, as the scenes that open this chapter suggest, this is certainly where I have most commonly experienced subordination. However, feminism also has been accused of overlooking the multiple sources of power and privilege that function to create the complex webs of power relationships that, overall, have served to increase my advantages over others (Mohanty, 1997). In Wing's critique of feminism, she challenges "that movement's essentialization of all women, which subsumes the variable experiences of women of color within the experience of white middle-class women" (2000, p. 6). Writing in 1980, Audre Lorde was quite blunt in her analysis: "By and large within the women's movement today, white women focus upon their oppression as women and ignore differences of race, sexual preference, class and age" (1997, p. 375). Lorde was writing about the feminism I first encountered as a graduate student and her critique helps to explain my long-standing reluctance to identify myself as a feminist. Somehow it felt unseemly to focus on this singular location of my own disempowerment when clearly I held so many other sources of both power and prestige that in most settings seemed to vastly outweigh any disadvantages I might experience as a result of my gender.

Over the intervening 22 years, I think both feminism and I have matured and, hopefully, in the process we have both become a bit less doctrinaire and a bit more nuanced in our thinking. As a result, I now feel more comfortable and confident in identifying myself as a feminist. As Maguire notes, "Because our voices and stories cannot be extracted from our social, cultural locations in the world, the interactions of gender, multiple locations, interlocking oppressions, and voice become apparent" (2001, p. 63). Having now embraced this new identity, I ask whether I can take the lessons I've learned from feminism and from my own experiences of subordination and apply them to situations in which I am privileged. Acknowledging my own shifting positions and potential locations of continued subordination, I concurrently recognize that in most situations I do, in fact, hold considerable power. I can choose to mask this fact, allowing others to control the decision-making process, or I can choose to act, invoking my power in ways that I hope will be empowering to others.

Powerful and powerless. Frightened and fearless. From the perspective of critical race theory, Wildman and Davis (1996) describe the multiple dimensions of personal power and subordination as akin to a Koosh ball.

Picture hundreds of rubber bands, tied in the center. Mentally cut the end of each band. The wriggling, unfirm mass in your hand is a Koosh ball, still usable for throwing and catching, but changing shape as it sails through the air or as the wind blows through its rubbery limbs when it is at rest. It is a dynamic ball. (p. 23)

Rather than see ourselves and others as single points in some specified set of dichotomies, male or female, White or Black, straight or gay, scholar or activist, powerful or powerless, this image allows us to imagine ourselves as existing at the intersection of multiple identities, all of which influence one another and together shape our continually changing experience and interactions. These individual systems of power and the ways in which they intersect with those of others allow each of us to be both privileged and oppressed, with the potential to use these two aspects of our experience as counterpoints to one another, each informing our understanding of and response to the other. These tensions "can help reveal privilege, especially when we remember that the intersection is multidimensional, including intersections of both subordination and privilege" (Wildman & Davis, 1996, p. 22).

Despite these multiple positionalities, those of us who are White, American, educated, and upper middle-class, whether male or female, enjoy a level of protection from experiences of subordination that we rarely acknowledge.

When we look at privilege we see several things. First, the characteristics of the privileged group define the societal norm often benefiting those in the privileged group. Second, privileged group members can rely on their privilege and avoid objecting to oppression. And third, privilege is rarely seen by the holder of the privilege. (Wildman & Davis, 1996, p. 13)

This definition of societal norms has sometimes been referred to as master scripting. As Swartz described the dominant narratives of the American educational system,

master scripting silences multiple voices and perspectives, primarily legitimizing dominant, white, upper-class, male voicings as the "standard" knowledge students need to know. All other accounts and perspectives are omitted from the master script unless they can be disempowered through misrepresentation. (cited in Ladson-Billings, 1999, p. 21)

Scene V: I live in a city in which a young African American man was recently killed by the police. I work in another. Do I feel that the police force in my city does an effective job of protecting me? A recent public opinion survey sought to explore community attitudes toward the police. Yeah, they do a great job of protecting me, I thought. I'm a middle-aged White woman. I'm the kind of person they were hired to protect. Now if I was a 16-year old African American male, I don't think

I'd feel that way at all. There's probably not a box on the survey for that. I've been working for the past several months with a group of young Sudanese men, refugees who have survived years of war in their home country. I keep wondering what I should say to them about the police. I fear that after all that they have experienced, they will have come to this country only to be killed by a police officer who is suspicious when he sees them hanging out in a large group, mistakes their fear for threat, and fires. But, yeah, they do a great job of protecting me.

The challenge then, according to Wildman and Davis, is that "to end subordination, one must first recognize privilege" (1996, p. 20). The authors note the importance of distinguishing between perpetrators of discrimination and beneficiaries of oppression, insisting that those of us who are privileged by these systems acknowledge our complicity. Even those of us who would denounce racism still profit by racist economic and political systems. Critical race theorists would suggest that "although individual whites are 'innocent,' they do, by no personal intent benefit from dominant group membership in numerous ways" (Taylor, 1999, p. 199). And yet it can be difficult to maintain an image of ourselves as at once opposed to and the beneficiaries of systems of oppression.

One means of making the connection to another's experience of oppression or subordination may be to draw comparisons to our own experiences. As Grillo and Wildman describe, the use of analogies to try to build empathy and understanding for the experience of others can be helpful. "Starting with ourselves is important, and analogies may enable us to understand the oppression of another in a way we could not without making the comparison" (1996, p. 99).

Scene VI: I sit next to a Bosnian woman who is illiterate in her own language and struggling to write letters and to recall words in English. Her courage, determination, and good humor amaze and humble me. When another teacher comes in to discuss the schedule and exercises, I find myself speaking English rapidly and using a vocabulary unavailable to my student. The teacher and I work things out and I turn back to the woman beside me who has sat, struggling to understand what was being said, looking from one to the other as we discussed her education and her progress with the materials.

In trying to critically re-examine my interaction with this Bosnian woman, I think back to a time when I was waiting anxiously in a tent in an Italian camp site with a local doctor and a British employee of the campground who was translating for us. One of my sons had been running a high fever and the doctor was examining him and determining a treatment. I know enough French and Spanish to pick up a few words of the conversation between the two of them, but it was both frightening and humiliating to sit beside my son, unable to take part in the discussion and utterly dependent on others to determine what would happen to him. The doctor was kind and gentle and affectionate. The translator was kind and helpful and understanding. I was grateful and relieved and, yes, a bit angry.

And I remember my anger at being excluded from the debate between my two male colleagues and my inability to participate in a discussion that centered on my actions. What might they have done to make me a part of their interaction? Were they even aware of my presence standing between them? I wanted them on my level—literally. I wanted to be in a position to make eye contact with them both—to be not an object of discussion, but a participant in that discussion.

Reflecting on these experiences I can return to the classroom and my Bosnian student more aware of the frustration and feelings of infantilization, born of being talked about rather than with, and make a point of finding ways of making such conversations both inclusive and accessible to all involved.

However, despite our best efforts to uncover power relations and to engage in open dialogue, these differences of power and privilege persist in being elusive. This reflects Wildman and Davis's third point regarding privilege: that it is seldom recognized by those who hold it. How, then, am I to bring such experiences of power and privilege to light? One strategy is to try to recast experiences of powerlessness by taking on the role of the more powerful character and attempting to examine the moment from that perspective. If I take the example of the two male faculty members discussing my behavior after a meeting, I wonder if either of them was really even aware of my presence. Or the faculty colleague who said he thought I enjoyed arguing—what might have informed his perception when I experienced the moment as one of brutalizing harassment?

Perhaps such analogies are most effective when we recognize ourselves as the oppressor and not as the oppressed; taking these insights of imagination and embedding them in those moments in which we do hold power; asking questions, observing interactions, examining our own behavior in such a way that we can begin to be more alert to our own everyday abuses of power.

Mary Louise Pratt describes contact zones as "the social spaces where cultures meet, clash and grapple with each other, often in contexts of highly asymmetrical relations of power, such as colonialism, slavery, or their aftermaths as they are lived out in many parts of the world today" (1991, p. 35). Pratt's metaphor of the contact zone acknowledges the critical, and yet often unspoken, role of power in cross-cultural interactions and examines the ways in which these differences can lead to misunderstanding, frustration, and anger. It is only in recognizing my own uses and abuses of power that I can begin to engage in interactions within the contact zones that are my research sites, my classrooms, and my communities in a more genuine and reflective manner. And in so doing, perhaps I can at the same time develop a language of power and privilege that I can make available to others to enable them to participate in these negotiations in an informed and effective manner. As a participatory action researcher and as one who is both an outsider to the experiences of the communities with which I work and most often invested with greater power by dint of my race, class, education, and academic position, nothing could be more important.

THE LIMITATIONS OF IMAGINATION

Empathic imagination can give us some insight into the lives and feelings of others. However, it can also mislead us into assuming that our own experiences of oppression are equivalent to those of others, giving us the right to speak on behalf of those whose true experience we have no way of fully comprehending. In this instance, Grillo and Wildman suggest we try to "listen more carefully" (1996, p. 95). Writing from an ethnographer's perspective, Ong suggests that we must "recognize informants as active cultural producers in their own right, whose voices insist on being heard and can make a difference in the way we think about their lives" (1995, p. 354).

But "listening more carefully" implies that the voices of oppressed or subordinated persons may be heard. Spivak (1988, pp. 271–313) challenges this notion in her essay "Can the Subaltern Speak?" Using language drawn from Gramsci and the example of the British response to the practice of sati or widow sacrifice in India, Spivak problemmatizes issues of voice and representation. She offers no simple conclusions but suggests that while it is impossible for the subaltern's experience to be rendered in a truly genuine manner, it is nevertheless the responsibility of the intellectual, and especially the "female intellectual" according to Spivak, to continue to try to do so. "The subaltern cannot speak ... Representation has not withered away. The female intellectual as intellectual has a circumscribed task which she must not disown with a flourish" (p. 308). While I would agree with Spivak that intellectuals (and I would include here both male and female intellectuals) have a responsibility to represent the world as they know it, I would argue that their greater responsibility is to continue to seek means through which the subaltern can find voice and can be empowered to represent her own interests. This is the true task of the intellectual and the potential contribution of feminist participatory action research.

In a similar vein to Spivak's defense of representation, Wing claims a legitimate role for "translators," scholars whose minority status makes them a bridge between "those who have the luxury of time and capacity to read a book like this and the cultures of those who will never have the opportunity to enjoy such intellectual largesse. As translators, we therefore are assisting in demarginalizing the lives and legal concerns of women of color" (2000, p. 4). Just as I would reject the notion that as *a* woman, I can speak for *all* women, I think minority scholars are mistaken if they believe that this status alone qualifies them to speak on behalf of others, ignoring differences in class, educational attainment, and other factors that distinguish them from those they claim to represent.

I struggle with these questions of voice and representation, and I believe they will continue to confound scholars who recognize the dangerous implications of their attempts to speak on behalf of others. At the same time I feel compelled to attempt to speak out regarding important social issues and to communicate to a wider academic audience the observations and insights this work has granted me. Accepting the legitimacy of my own voice, I also believe that we must continue to seek authentic ways in which the subaltern may articulate her experience and speak on her own behalf in ways that can be heard and understood by members of the dominant culture.

Scene VII: In the spring of 2001, the city of Cincinnati saw rioting break out in Over-the-Rhine, a primarily African American inner city neighborhood, in response to the killing of a young, unarmed black man by city police, the fifteenth police killing in the community in the last six years. When sheets of plywood were put up to cover broken out windows, urban minority high school students along with university art education students, participants in a project called Art-in-the-Market, used these surfaces to create community art that reflected their reactions to the events going on around them. A cityscape in flames, a broken heart tentatively held together with a bandage, these boards provided the canvasses for murals through which they expressed their feelings about what was going on around them; how they understood the events and how they saw the city's response. (Bastos, Brown, Brydon-Miller, & Hutzel, 2003)

THE NECESSITY OF ACTION

To decry injustice and refuse to act strikes me as a cowardly stance. It is my chief criticism of many scholars who, whether they derive their critiques from feminist, postcolonial, or critical race theory, rail against injustice but only from within the protected rooms of the academy and the quiet pages of journals. There are, of course, exceptions and there are many scholars who are also passionately engaged as activists. For too many, however, these roles seem divorced from one another. Activism is an avocation, scholarship the day job, and the contradictions implied by this schism remain unspoken.

The notion that scholarship must float like a lotus of objectivity above the muddy sea of lived experience still permeates much of the academy, perhaps no more so than in my own field of psychology, in which the perennial fear of being inadequate scientists seems still to haunt us. Or perhaps it is not our fear of failure but our history as would-be social and behavioral engineers, our conviction of superior intellect and insight, that lead us to the absurd belief that we can design and impose systems of democracy, equality, and justice. Whatever its source, we continue to hide behind obtuse statistical analyses and comically complex models of social processes, leaving actual action to others.

As Mohanty so succinctly puts it, "There can, of course, be no apolitical scholarship" (1997, p. 256). Cossman echoes this sentiment when she observes, "We make no claims to neutrality in our work, but rather begin from an explicitly and unapologetically political location" (2000, p. 36). But perhaps my favorite observation on the subject comes from Gordon who says, "my impression of anthropology is that as it has come to terms with its colonial legacy, it has designated applied anthropology, advocacy, and action-oriented research as *entirely politically dirty* [italics added]" (1995, p. 384). I love the idea of being "entirely politically dirty." It sounds like fun!

Even much interpretive research, though acknowledging the legitimacy of subjective experience and the centrality of human relationships, often fails to articulate a specific agenda for taking action. The assumption seems to be that change will come about by simply giving voice to those taking part in the research, by allowing their stories to be told. But who, then, owns the stories, and who profits by their telling? Are we simply more cunning compradors, merchants in the lives of others, advancing our own careers through exposing the pain and poetry expressed to us, entrusted to us, by those participating in our research? Behar describes this process of engaging research participants only to take advantage of their trust in furthering our own careers as "commodifying" (1995, p. 80) the research participant, and she expresses her concern about her possible complicity in such a process. Newkirk calls it an "act of seduction" (1996, p. 3) and suggests that "a more disciplined response is to acknowledge the exploitative potential of qualitative research and to consider guidelines that may do what traditional consent forms clearly fail to do—protect the person being rendered" (p. 4).

Hermes refers to "the legacy of exploitation that has continued under the guise of research" (1999, p. 91) and observes that "relationships of reciprocity" (p. 95) might replace those of exploitation. Although she doesn't seem entirely clear in how the results of her research on designing a school curriculum more reflective of Ojibwe culture and the development of what she calls a "First Nations Methodology" might be applied to the issues she and her research participants identify, it is clear that she intends to continue to work within her community to effect social change and that this research is an attempt to begin that process.

It is this commitment to action that typifies participatory action research and other activist-oriented approaches. In contrast to more traditional psychological research, whether quantitative or qualitative, participatory action research is founded in the notion that action and collective reflection on that action in themselves constitute a valid form of knowledge generation and that the legitimacy of the research endeavor can be judged in part on its success in addressing community concerns (see Park, Brydon-Miller, Hall, & Jackson, 1993; Tolman & Brydon-Miller, 2001, for examples). In theory, participatory action research requires that issues of ownership and agency be openly acknowledged and negotiated with research participants who define the issues, generate and interpret the data, and determine the action to be taken as a result of the study. In too many cases, however, theory and practice diverge, often due to unacknowledged tensions and differences in perceived power and authority both between the academic researcher and members of the community in which the research is being conducted, and among community members themselves.

The challenge for participatory action researchers is in overcoming the naïve sense that we can somehow set aside differences of power and privilege that exist within our community settings, just as they exist within all aspects of our society. We have tended to overlook critical issues of representation and voice, often engaging in a kind of ventriloquism in which we pretend that we speak for the members of marginalized communities with whom we work. At the same time we have chosen to portray "the oppressed" as univocal and homogenous, failing to explore the impact of gender, class, and other differences that empower some factions within communities over others. It is at this intersection of theory and practice that participatory action researchers have the most to teach, but also the most to learn.

THE INEVITABILITY OF ERROR

I screw up. Sometimes I recognize it immediately. Sometimes it takes me months or years to realize that I have acted in such a way as to silence discussion, I have failed to recognize disagreement and resistance, or I have taken charge when others could more effectively have led. This is largely uncharted territory, and it is impossible not to make mistakes.

Scene VIII: At 24 I was a founding member and convener of the Pioneer Valley Gray Panthers—the youngest Gray Panther convener in the country. "Age and Youth in Action" is the motto of the Gray Panthers. "That means we decide what to do and you do it," my older fellow members laughingly told me when I was made convener of the local chapter. At the time we shared the experience of powerlessness, they due to their age and me to my youth, and yet through our collective action we were able to accomplish many goals. I learned a great deal about power and powerlessness from my Gray Panther friends, but at the same time I failed them. I wanted so desperately to take care of things, to be a leader, and to be in charge that I shut them out of any leadership roles themselves. Eventually, exhausted by my efforts to do it all and frustrated because no one seemed to want to assume control (how could they when I had erected such great fences around my territory), I simply quit and soon the organization folded. At the time I attributed this to a lack of leadership. Later, to my chagrin, I realized how correct I was in this assessment.

The inevitability of error is not an excuse for inaction. I learned from this mistake and have tried in more recent organizing efforts to make a point of building leadership and of acknowledging the expertise and skill of those with whom I work. Comparing myself to the groups I have worked with, I am not yet old nor disabled and I hope never to experience what the refugees I currently work with have lived through. As an outsider I have been in a position to provide resources and some degree of technical expertise, but because my experience is so different from that of the communities within which I work, the real knowledge is theirs. When I have been able to remember this, I have been able to truly learn.

At the same time, I don't believe that any of us can ever fully rid ourselves of the legacy of discrimination that shapes every aspect of our culture, nor can we truly resolve the issues of power and privilege that continue to affect our interactions with others. To assume otherwise is to fall into the trap of believing that we are done and have moved beyond, and this hubris blinds us to the new challenges we face in our attempts to confront these issues in our daily lives and in our work. We cannot transcend nor escape our cultural context and the myriad ways in which we have been socialized to respond to one another. We can only hope to remain vigilant and open to instruction.

THE TERRIFYING TRUTH (AND A MORE HOPEFUL FINAL THOUGHT)

The terrifying truth is that we have a choice. We can continue to be immobilized by the fear of making mistakes and can hide behind a veil of cynicism claiming that change is impossible, or we can choose to act, knowing that we will misjudge situations, fail to see alternatives, and be faced with the unanticipated negative consequences of our actions. It's Pandora's box. But like Pandora's box, look a bit deeper and there is hope. I have faith in people. That is at the core of my work as a participatory action researcher. I have faith in their intelligence, kind-heartedness, and basic sense of justice. Occasionally I am proven wrong. Far more often, however, I find that in approaching others with this expectation, my faith is well founded. I believe in the possibility of change and I realize that I am not responsible for bringing about that change by myself but for taking what action I can with the conviction that in the long run change is the result of shared action. And so I choose to act.

NOTE

1. Other terms have been used to describe approaches that focus to a greater or lesser extent on the active involvement of the researcher in working with communities to achieve positive social change. These include community-based research, "action research" (Greenwood & Levin, 1998), activist "feminist fieldwork" (Gordon, 1995, p. 375), "action-oriented research or advocacy research" (Gordon, 1995, p. 381), and "critical race praxis" (Wing, 2000, p. 6).

REFERENCES

Abu-Lughod, L. (1995). A tale of two pregnancies. In R. Behar & D. Gordon (Eds.), *Women writing culture* (pp. 339–349). Berkeley: University of California Press.

Banks, T. L. (1995). Two life stories: Reflections of one Black woman law professor. In K. Crenshaw, N. Gotanda, G. Peller, & K. Thomas (Eds.). *Critical race theory: The key writings that formed the movement* (pp. 329–336). New York: The New Press.

Bastos, F., Brown, L., Brydon-Miller, M., & Hutzel, K. (2003, April). *Critical race theory and participatory action research: Urban youth and university students using art to respond to their city's racial tensions*. Paper presented at the meeting of the American Educational Research Association, Chicago.

Behar, R. (1995). Writing in my father's name: A diary of Translated Woman's first year. In R. Behar & D. Gordon (Eds.), *Women writing culture* (pp. 65–82). Berkeley: University of California Press.

Behar, R. (1996). *The vulnerable observer: Anthropology that breaks your heart*. Boston: Beacon Press.

Brydon-Miller, M. (2002, August). *Understanding refugee narratives through postcolonial and critical race theory*. Paper presented at the annual convention of the American Psychological Association, Chicago.

Chen, M. (2000). Discrimination in New Zealand: A personal journey. In A. K. Wing (Ed.), *Global critical race feminism* (pp. 129–140). New York: New York University Press.

Cossman, B. (2000). Turning the gaze back on itself: Comparative law, feminist legal studies, and the postcolonial project. In A. K. Wing (Ed.), *Global critical race feminism* (pp. 27–41). New York: New York University Press.

Delgado, R. (2000). Storytelling for oppositionists and others: A plea for narrative. In R. Delgado & J. Stefancic (Eds.), *Critical race theory: The cutting edge* (pp. 60–70). Philadelphia: Temple University Press.

Gonzalez, F. E. (1999). Formations of *Mexicananess: Trenzas de identidades multiples* (Growing up Mexicana: Braids of multiple identities). In L. Parker, D, Deyhle & S. Villenas (Eds.), *Race is... race isn't: Critical race theory and qualitative studies in education* (pp. 125–154). Boulder, CO: Westview Press.

Gordon, D. (1995). Border work: Feminist ethnography and the dissemination of literacy. In R. Behar & D. Gordon (Eds.). *Women writing culture* (pp. 373–411). Berkeley: University of California Press.

Greenwood, D., & Levin, M. (1998). *Introduction to action research: Social research for social change*. Thousand Oaks, CA: SAGE Publications.

Grillo, T., & Wildman S. M. (1996). Obscuring the importance of race: The implications of making comparisons between racism and sexism (or other isms). In S. M. Wildman (Ed.), *Privilege revealed: How invisible preference undermines America* (pp. 85–102). New York: New York University Press.

Hermes, M. (1999). Research methods as a situated response: Toward a First Nations' methodology. In L. Parker, D. Deyhle, & S. Villenas (Eds.), *Race is ... race isn't: Critical race theory and qualitative studies in education* (pp. 83–100). Boulder, CO: Westview Press.

Hom, S. K. (2000). Female infanticide in China: The human rights specter and thoughts toward an(other) vision. In A. K. Wing (Ed.), *Global critical race feminism* (pp. 251–259). New York: New York University Press.

Horton, M., & Freire, P. [with Peters, J., & Gaventa, J.] (Eds.). (1991). *We make the road by walking: Conversations on education and social change.* Philadelphia: Temple University Press.

Ladson-Billings, G. (1999). Just what is critical race theory and what's it doing in a *nice* field like education? In L. Parker, D. Deyhle, & S. Villenas (Eds.), *Race is … race isn't: Critical race theory and qualitative studies in Education* (pp. 7–30). Boulder, CO: Westview Press.

Lorde, A. (1997). Age, race, class and sex: Women redefining difference. In A. McClintock, A. Mufti, & E. Shohat (Eds.). *Dangerous liaisons: Gender, nation, and postcolonial perspectives* (pp. 374–380). Minneapolis: University of Minnesota Press.

Maguire, P. (2001). Uneven Ground: Feminisms and action research. In P. Reason & H. Bradbury (Eds.), *Handbook of action research: Participative inquiry and practice* (pp. 63–69). London: SAGE Publications.

Mohanty, C. T. (1997). Under Western eyes: Feminist scholarship and colonial discourses. In A. McClintock, A. Mufti, & E. Shohat (Eds.), *Dangerous liaisons: Gender, nation, and postcolonial perspectives* (pp. 255–277). Minneapolis: University of Minnesota Press.

Morawski, J. (1997). The science behind feminist research methods. *Journal of Social Issues, 53*(4), 667–681.

Mrsevic, Z. (2000). Filthy, old and ugly: Gypsy women from Serbia. In A. K. Wing (Ed.), *Global critical race feminism* (pp. 160–175). New York: New York University Press.

Newkirk, T. (1996). Seduction and betrayal in qualitative research. In P. Mortensen & G. E. Kirsch (Eds.), *Ethics and representation in qualitative studies in literacy* (pp. 3–16). Urbana, IL: National Council of Teachers of English.

Ong, A. (1995). Women out of China: Traveling tales and traveling theories in postcolonial feminism. In R. Behar & D. Gordon (Eds.), *Women writing culture* (pp. 350–372). Berkeley: University of California Press.

Park, P., Brydon-Miller, M., Hall, B., & Jackson, T. (Eds.). (1993). *Voices of change: Participatory research in the United States and Canada.* Westport, CT: Bergin and Garvey.

Pratt, M. L. (1991). Arts of the contact zone. *Profession 91, 33*–40.

Sarbin, T. R. (Ed.). (1986). *Narrative Psychology: The storied nature of human conduct.* Westport, CT: Praeger Publishers.

Spivak, G. C. (1988). Can the subaltern speak? In C. Nelson & L. Grossberg (Eds.), *Marxism and the interpretation of culture* (pp. 271–313). Basingstoke, UK: Macmillan Education.

Taylor, E. (1999). Critical race theory and interest convergence in the desegregation of higher education. In L. Parker, D. Deyhle, & S. Villenas (Eds.), *Race is … race isn't: Critical race theory and qualitative studies in education* (pp. 181–204). Boulder, CO: Westview Press.

Tedlock, B. (1995). Works and wives: On the sexual division of textual labor. In R. Behar & D. Gordon (Eds.), *Women writing culture* (pp. 267–286). Berkeley: University of California Press.

Tolman, D. & Brydon-Miller, M. (Eds.). (2001). *From subjects to subjectivities: A handbook of interpretive and participatory methods.* New York: New York University Press.

Wildman, S. M., & Davis, A.D. (1996). Making systems of privilege visible. In S. M. Wildman (Ed.), *Privilege revealed: How invisible preference undermines America* (pp. 7–24). New York: New York University Press.

Wing, A. K. (2000). Introduction: Global critical race feminism for the twenty-first century. In A. K. Wing (Ed.), *Global critical race feminism* (pp. 1–23). New York: New York University Press.

CHAPTER 2

Understanding Muslim Women's Self-Identity and Resistance to Feminism and Participatory Action Research

Nimat Hafez Barazangi

"There is no single brain area responsible for consciousness; consciousness is not an entity but an active process that requires the participation of many components" (Restak, 2000, pp. 70–71). In this chapter, I propose that the relationship of feminism and participatory action research (PAR) is analogous to that of the brain-mind relationship. That is, together they promote an active process of individual consciousness-raising[1] and collective social action. For Muslim women scholar-activists, however, the use of gender as a central construct in this consciousness-raising process may interfere with their personal and collective transformative process. Indeed contemporary Western academic discourse that analyzes Muslim women's issues through the ethnic, race, and/or gender lens interferes with, rather than supports, their conscientization. Academic discourse, particularly feminist discourse, often dismisses Muslim women's views as "religious" and considers the prevailing Muslim males' interpretations as representative of Islamic views on gender.[2] This could explain why some of my Muslim women coresearchers resist feminist-informed PAR. I will demonstrate that the route for Muslim women to conscientization and collective action is instead through *Taqwa*. *Taqwa* (from Arabic) means the individual's conscientious balance of her autonomy with social heteronomy/hegemony and her interaction with natural and divine laws. It is also the only criterion that distinguishes individuals from one another (Qur'an, 49:13).[3] I will argue that an understanding and meaningful integration of *Taqwa* in any participatory action research process that focuses on Muslim communities can lead to the same goals as feminist-informed PAR: the creation of just behaviors and social structures for all.

As a Muslim and as an academic feminist action researcher affiliated with Cornell University's Feminist, Gender, and Sexuality Studies program, I will discuss a collaborative research project with some Muslim women scholar-activist leaders in the United States. For years my overall research concerns have grown out of my experiences as a Muslim woman scholar, activist, and feminist. Identifying primarily with the Islamic worldview helped me focus my scholarship and activism on the Qur'anic foundations of gender justice and how the prevailing Muslim male interpretations of the Qur'an resulted in gender bias. Assuming that my secondary identification with feminist-informed PAR would support rather than hinder my being a Muslim, I formulated the research question as follow: If the Qur'an, as the primary reader of Islam, is intended to dismantle hierarchies and social heteronomy/hegemony and to enact social justice, particularly gender justice, then how did contemporary discussion concerning the status of Muslim women become so polarized? Muslim women, in general, accept the Islamic worldview as a rational and just one, and yet their social realities are evidence to the contrary. True, the social realities of Muslim women, in general, are strikingly oppressive—Muslim women have the highest illiteracy rate and the highest infant mortality rate, for example. Yet, by focusing on these realities as the problem instead of understanding them as behavioral manifestations resulting partly from colonialism and mainly because of biased interpretations of the Qur'an, feminists did not support Muslim women's self-identity with Islam as a means of achieving social justice. Furthermore, by attributing these sad realities to Islam, non-Muslim or Westernized Muslim feminists caused a defensive attitude among Muslim women. Meanwhile, Muslim male elites who wrongly attribute to the Qur'an the prevention of women from public participation caused women not to be empowered with Qur'anic tools of liberation. At times, Muslim women experienced a tension in their identification with Islam because they were erroneously made to believe that males' interpretations are as binding as the Qur'anic principles themselves.

My earlier research suggests that a combination of ideological and scholarly dichotomies between the views of Western and traditional Muslim interpretations of Islam and gender justice have resulted in polarized interpretations of the status of Muslim women. There is also a discrepancy between the Muslim community's ideals and actual community practice, wherein women are idealized as mothers, daughters, and wives, but not recognized in practice as autonomous moral and rational beings as intended in the Qur'an (Barazangi, 1996). In addition, there is a confusion of identity between the Islamic worldview and ethnic identity in areas such as the Arabic culture (Barazangi, 1991a, 1991b). A Muslim needs to conscientiously and autonomously choose Islam as a primary identity in order to translate the Islamic worldview into concrete action for social justice. Meanwhile, though the Arabic language of the Qur'an and the Arabic culture in which Islam grew have considerable influence on the Islamic mindset, they are only secondary to being a Muslim.

With this in mind, I bring to the surface underlying assumptions that may reframe how a recent tension in the relationship between academic feminists and some of my coresearchers might be understood and, consequently, changed. In the process, I unravel other tensions that might lead to friction because some participatory-oriented feminist researchers focus on global "solidarity" without enough attention to worldview variation (e.g., Afkhami &Vaziri, 1996). These tensions are manifested on four levels: value claims—the ontological; knowledge claims—the epistemological; cultural or historical claims; and praxis or socialization claims, which I collectively call "worldview claims." In this chapter, I focus on the relation between the power of knowledge and social constructs.

Through feminist participatory action research, my overall research goal has been to develop a self-learning pedagogical process that will improve, through study groups, my capacities and those of my coresearchers to control our destinies as Muslim women more effectively. Effectiveness means to change life situations in the home, in the learning/teaching/research environment, and in the larger social context to support self-realization and *Taqwa*. Our intention, in addition to bridging individual consciousness and social action, is to effect a cognitive and attitudinal change on the individual level. We also seek a transformation of social structures that we hope will alleviate potential resistance to feminisms and PAR. My pedagogical assumption is that once a woman changes what is in herself, she will be able to work with others to question and change social structures (Qur'an, 13:11). While this assumption was well founded among a grassroots Muslim women's group in Damascus, Syria, with whom I collaborated, it was not confirmed in my work with my American academic Muslim women coresearchers. I believe that the latter group overlooked the power of the largely unquestioned Western approach to academic knowledge generation and dissemination processes. Specifically, this Western approach had marginalized the worldview of Muslim women by both dismissing their views as "religious" and taking, unknowingly, the prevailing Muslim male elites' views at their face value.

In the rest of the chapter, I will summarize two differing feminist PAR projects to analyze and explore what went wrong with the evolving pedagogical framework we created to assist us as Muslim women to achieve *Taqwa*. I identify the "worldview claims" that differ for Muslim women and non-Muslim academics. By understanding these differing worldviews, I identify implications for future feminist-informed participatory action research with Muslim women. In addition, I suggest a means for both Western feminists and Muslim women alike to resist uncritical academic assimilation.

THE RESEARCH PROJECTS

My action research work with Muslim women's self-identity began in 1994 with the intent that we would interpret the primary text of Islam, the Qur'an, in order to address Muslim women's human rights. Pressure to adopt a universalistic version of feminism mounted in preparation for the Beijing Conference (the Fourth World Conference on Women), which aimed to ratify the Convention on the Elimination of All Forms of Discrimination Against Women (CEDAW) document (United Nations, 1996). In response, Muslim women scholar-activists launched their own study groups to rewrite the women's human rights declaration from within the Islamic perspective of justice and human rights. Since the Qur'an defines *Taqwa* as the only difference between individuals, the groups with whom I collaborated were working with the assumption that gender, whether as a biological sex or as a social construct, could not be the unit of analysis for the new interpretation of the text, even though our goal as Muslim women scholar-activists was gender justice—similar to that of other women organizing for the Beijing Conference. Since our goal was also the Qur'anic goal, our strategy was to explain how the CEDAW items may or may not express Qur'anic intention.[4]

I worked with two groups of Muslim women on this topic, one in the United States and the other in Syria. The Syrian women were of the same ethnic and national background (Barazangi, 1997, 1999b), while the American women had different ethnic, racial, and national-origin backgrounds (Barazangi, 2000). Both groups were attempting to reclaim their primary self-identity with Islam through Islamic higher learning, but they were going through different transformation processes. The Americans were relying mainly on scholarship, while the Syrians began with grassroots activism moving toward scholarship.

In the following section I narrate two events with members from the American group to illustrate how the differing worldview claims resulted in tensions between American Muslim women and other academic feminists (Muslims and non-Muslims). Two strategic assumptions directed our American group and its later academic context. In 1995, I placed some of the American scholar-activists' work on the agenda of the Middle East Studies Association annual meeting. This interaction culminated in the book *Windows of Faith* (Webb, 2000). We assumed that (a) biological differences between the sexes do not mean different rights and responsibilities for males and females under Islam, and (b) by understanding the major historical factors that led to the prevalent Muslim male-biased interpretations of the Qur'an and their subsequent unjust practices, we might be able to change some of their present biases. Changing these biased interpretations, being mainly manifested in preventing women's public participation, especially regarding the interpretation of the Qur'an, could also mitigate other oppressive practices toward women that are not consistent with Qur'anic principles.

My work with this ethnically diverse group of Muslim women leaders in America was to develop a self-learning process of feminism within the action-oriented Islamic worldview. I hypothesized that if we remained aware of the other hindering social constructs, such as ethnicity or academic prestige and knowledge structure, just as we became aware of gender construct, we could develop *Taqwa* and be better equipped to control our destinies and improve our capacity to do so. Some results of my previous projects suggest that a learner who consciously chooses the Islamic worldview as her primary identification is actually furthering the broad sense of feminism, as the latter is rooted in the Qur'anic principle of social justice (Barazangi, 1999b). That is, a learner who self-identifies with the basic principles of the Qur'an frees herself from both the social and biological constraints of gender, race, and ethnicity. Such an individual becomes capable of exposing any discrepancies in the exclusionary interpretive process that was generated by academia and the community. This exclusionary process stems from both the academic (mainly White, non-Muslim) women's studies of the marginalization of Muslim women's worldview claims and the Middle East Studies and Middle East Women's Studies that purports a different knowledge structure that largely stems from outside the Islamic worldview. She will also be able to do so by asserting that the authority lies only in the text of the Qur'an and not in its interpretations, nor in its historical analysis. She will be able to do this by looking at the Qur'an as a collective, cohesive guide that has its own criteria for interpretations as well as a course of action for each individual to learn within its particular framework and to act on what one learns within that guidance. To the contrary, while striving to satisfy the Western "academic" demands on knowledge generation, American Muslim women may have overlooked the diverse epistemological claims among members of the group—such as whether or not to use the traditional male elites' interpretation of the Qur'an or the historical tools of academics. Muslims typically reference four "traditional" types of Islamic texts (the Qur'an, Prophet Muhammad's extrapolation of Qur'anic guidance documented in books of *Hadith,* major commentaries on the Qur'an, and major jurisprudence interpretations of Qur'an and Hadith). These sources are considered principles of all Islamic thought. What concerns us here is both the absence of women from this process of interpretation and the variations in which some Muslim male elites have combined these principles, deviating from the meaning and method of interpretation intended in the Qur'an. Meanwhile, looking at the Qur'an as mainly a historical document, as is done by most non-Muslim academics, deviates from the Qur'anic religio-moral-rational purpose. Furthermore, documenting some historical events as evidence for women's social oppression or agency may not be consistent with Qur'anic content and method for determining gender justice. Finally non-Muslim academic feminist discourse on Muslim women, mainly within the context of the Middle/Near East Studies, relies on analyzing the anthropological or sociological relationship between cultural differences, ethnicity, race, and gender.[5] These relationships as analytical tools add more variables to the existing paradigmatic tensions instead of balancing them. By doing so, academics (women and men), perhaps unknowingly, create tension between themselves and Muslim women and between these women and their communities.

THE NARRATIVES

The First Event

Shadey (a pseudonym), a community leader and an activist-scholar I have known for about 30 years, devoted herself to the founding of a national Muslim women's council—an umbrella encompassing several grassroots Muslim women's groups—to the point of sacrificing much of her personal life. The goal of the council is to educate through collective activism and through research and the production of booklets on topics that directly affect Muslim women's lives in North America (United States and Canada). As a founding member and an advisory board member of this national council, I was in close contact with Shadey. When I met with her during a professional conference, we had barely begun talking when she broke into tears, saying that no one respected her anymore or thought of her as intellectual enough.

Shadey was intellectually and professionally capable of writing. However, she often lamented that she did not know the Arabic language fluently—a necessary skill to directly access the meanings of the Qur'an. Her approach to participation in the interpretation process may have been influenced by the traditional interpretation of the Qur'an promoted by the male Muslim group with whom she had professional relationships. Her long-time association with this group and the support she received from its members for her activism—as long as it was within the parameters of their interpretations—seems to have led her to believe in and trust their terms. She often asserted that translating the work of these males from Arabic into English could become a "good" source for other women to learn about Islam. Yet, when she faced a personal problem, this same Muslim male-dominated group declined to support her own interpretation as to how to solve it. Perhaps other women in the group, as academics pressured to publish and therefore unavailable emotionally or intellectually and/or dismissive of her life experience as a valid knowledge base, have not facilitated her self-realization. This may have caused her continuous resistance to the legitimacy of her own and their "voice," and driven her to uncritically adopt the elite Muslim males' interpretation of the Qur'an as authentic. Furthermore, as long as she continued to use the traditional interpretations of the male group, the feminist-PAR voice remained, in her view, a distant rather than a supportive, active voice. Not only have academic feminists and those academics who study Islam and Muslims in general not concerned themselves with the validity of the underlying assumptions behind these predominantly male traditional interpretations (often viewing these interpretations as representing the Qur'anic view of gender justice), but non-Muslim academic feminists who investigate Muslim women have overlooked the variations in the worldview claims between the Islamic view of gender justice and that of feminist gender equality. Instead of capitalizing on the similarities between a feminist worldview and *Taqwa,* or the Islamic worldview, non-Muslim feminists did not learn from Muslim feminist scholar-activists about Qur'anic gender justice. Furthermore, academic feminists' emphasis on gender, combined with dismissing Islam as a patriarchal religion, and dismissing Muslim women's explanation of Qur'anic social justice because, in their views, it represents a "religious" worldview, have resulted in a defensive attitude concerning everything "Islamic" among Muslim women like Shadey.

The Second Event

On a different occasion, Muna (a pseudonym), a scholar-activist from the 1995 project, was telling me about some transformation in her life, views, and work. She suddenly stated, "I do not want to spend all my life searching through historical volumes to find few incidents to prove that Muslim women can be leaders or that they had a place in the public arena during the early Muslim community 14 centuries ago." Muna was referring to the historical discourse that she and some other members in the group have been using to support their arguments that a precedent in Muslim history affirms contemporary women's rights to participate in public affairs. These arguments are generally thought to further attitudinal change. On one hand, Muslim male elites would be reminded that indeed gender justice was one of the goals of the Islamic revolution. On the other hand, non-Muslim academics, particularly feminists, would realize that historical tools (i.e., analyzing the Qur'an as a historical document and dismissing Muslim women's views as "religious") do not suffice for understanding Muslim societies and gender issues. However, due to her discontent with a subgroup in her community that would not allow women to enter the community mosque, she became oblivious toward the entire process of knowledge production that she and her other Muslim women colleagues had been attempting.

This event, and the surrounding circumstances, reminded me of Middleton's (1993) description of how British and American influence dictated the sociology of education even among the feminist thinkers, and how Middleton had revolted against it because it was too condescending to the point of oppression. As a young assistant professor who was raised mainly within the U.S. educational system, Muna felt oppressed by the system and its scholarly methods. She was discontent with both the traditional male Muslim interpretation of the Qur'an and with the Western Orientalist representing the Muslim woman as either the powerful slave or the helpless, weak, secluded woman (Shirazi, 2001). So when an extremely conservative group of students took over the mosque leadership at her university, she did not have the capacity to determine her destiny when the system did not support her. That is, as neither the Western images of Muslim women nor the historical analysis of early Muslim women resulted in a change in perspectives and attitudes, including the acceptance of women's participation in the mosque as members of the collective Muslim community, she began doubting the entire discourse of her scholarly work. In addition, she could not revolt against the student group's values because they were of a similar ethnic background and belief system to hers (hooks, 1994).

It seems that Muna was bound by the Muslim community in which she associated to the point that she could not foresee herself revolting against its recent system of operation. Having grown up in a high-profile, active Muslim Arab family, she could not detach herself from those "privileges." Instead, she revolted against the knowledge discourse that she had harvested from the two systems: the academic system that she trusted for giving her the power of knowledge, and the Islamic system that was supposed to have led to change in her surroundings. Not being able to change academia—as a young assistant professor—seems to have constrained her ability to transform her community. So, not only did she continue to transform herself, but she also wanted to transform the knowledge claims—the historical findings. Just as "being white" remained invisible to White teachers in McIntyre (1997, p. 1), it seems that "Islamicity," and being academic remained invisible to Muna and to those of us who think that they "benefit from these terms." Since neither Islamicity nor academic knowledge about it was constructed by the individuals who self-identify with Islam, they did not help Muna translate her individual consciousness into concrete social action. The Islamicity that was constructed by the colonization and Orientalism projects and that which academic studies of Muslim women perpetuate and reinforce further complicated the existing tensions in Muna's mind.

The non-Muslim academic studies have stifled her efforts, and those of Muslim women in general, to proactively reframe the studies of themselves in order to free the process of knowledge creation from both the framing done by non-Muslim women and men as well as the biased interpretation of the Qur'an by traditional Muslim men.

RESEARCH DELAMINATION

Initially I wondered what might have led some of these academic Muslim women, like Shadey and Muna, to resist the continuation of a journey that they themselves had chosen. Did it have to do with their view of feminism, with their aspirations for Islamic activism, or with their lack of awareness of the worldviews that underpin their own perception?

Clark (2000) relates theory to experience, instead of relating theory and practice, arguing that one cannot remain static before such practices and, hence, one's experience becomes part of the theory. I believe that it is the uneven plane (i.e., not having the authority as interpreters of Islamic text nor as equal participants in their communities' affairs, and being perceived as Other by Western feminists) coupled with the worldviews that began to be imposed on the Muslim women by their real presence in the academy and the society at large. The increase in the number of Muslims and their institutions in Western countries has been a reality that many, particularly academics, have been trying to ignore. This uneven plane was reinforced by the academic-generated paradigm that views these women as the objects of change, as in oppressed persons who need to be researched rather than agents and subjects of their own change as they define it from within the Islamic worldview.

Secondly, I wondered, if the social composition of North America is continuously changing, why hasn't the structure of knowledge governing the different individuals in this society and its academic community also changed? Why, for example, do administrators and faculty talk about diversity in terms of student enrollment and faculty recruitment, but do not allow these diverse views in the curricular and extra-curricular choices—the life experience of students and faculty—to accommodate this diversity? (Barazangi, 2001). Unless such issues are addressed, the study of Muslim women and the relationship of these women to academic feminism and to academia will remain superficial. Women's studies curricula are not reflecting the dynamics of the historical and social forces on knowledge generation and dissemination, most likely because academic hierarchy and social constructs are still the main factors governing the politics of knowledge despite the introduction of feminist and gender theories.

In contrast, hoping to reactivate the Islamic pedagogical view as summarized in the concept of *Taqwa*, I relied on the Islamic premise that an individual may not change her surroundings unless she educates herself in Islam and approximates *Taqwa* as the goal. Academic Muslim women, including myself, were able to change ourselves, but we could not get the premise to help changing the university context or Muslim community structures and relationships in the ways we hoped. Yet, neither the aca-

demic Muslim women nor the academic researchers in general were pre-
pared to exert themselves to balance individual consciousness and social
action, as if traditional academic settings were canceling out the collective
consciousness-raising process of the academic Muslim women and their
community. That is because, in its attempt to understand the community,[6]
academic feminists rely mainly on the analytic relationship of difference (in
gender, race, and ethnicity, for instance), instead of understanding Islam. In
reality, gender, race, and ethnicity represent imposed social constructs and,
therefore, produce another kind of tension between the individual's consciousness, Muslim woman in this case, and her communal action instead
of resolving existing tensions, as evidenced in the two case studies of
Shadey and Muna. Despite my utilizing both feminist theories and the PAR
approach, the academic setting did not allow us, as Muslim women, to
reflect on and assess our own problems as stakeholders in the process.
Consequently, some of us lost our awareness of our own worldview claims.

To change our immediate surroundings, self-identification with the
Qur'an, not only gender equity, was the goal and the means for our collaboration. Being identified as a Muslim who knows the Qur'an (i.e.,
being literate in reading and interpreting the Qur'anic text) and having
the power of self-identification with the Qur'an are not the same. The self-
learning process that helped improve grassroots women's capacity to control their destinies more effectively, change their life situations, and
achieve self-realization should do the same for the academically situated
Muslim women. Self-identity, in a sense, is building simultaneously individual and social consciousness that is explicitly recognized as one, not as
a double, self (Dubois in Lemert, 1994, p. 388). As long as academics marginalize Muslim women's underlying assumptions, these women's individual consciousnesses and social action cannot be realized. Perhaps
when the academics and the Muslim community benefit from understanding how self-identified Muslim women pursue their own concerns
we will eliminate the politics of difference (Cornwall, 1998) and the politics of knowledge. We would also overcome the potential resistance of
Muslim academic women to bridging feminisms and action research and
overcome the inability of feminist action researchers to understand the
Islamic worldview of gender justice.

WORLDVIEW CLAIMS

Worldview claims determine both the understanding of the relationship
between Muslim women in general and the academic community of feminists and action researchers. These claims also determine the implications
of these relationships for research and/or educational intervention
(knowledge production and transformation) intended to promote social
justice for Muslim women and to effect a perceptual and structural transformation in the system for a sustainable change.[7]

Ontological or Value Claims

The Qur'an, the primary text of Islamic values, knowledge, and pedagogy, states that *Taqwa* is the measure by which a course of study is considered "Islamic" (Barazangi, 1998). Muslim women who work from within the Qur'anic framework rely on reason as the distinctive characteristic of human beings and as the means that enables individuals to achieve *Taqwa*. Feminists' emphasis on gender as the central concept is viewed by Muslim women scholars as replacing patriarchal power with feminist power instead of balancing individual and social relations.

Similarly, action researchers' focus on groups for social change is viewed as tipping the balance toward social solidarity without securing individual cognitive and attitudinal transformation. This transformation is seen as essential to change conventional social discourse and structure. Within this context, I analyze my understanding of the active process of individual consciousness and social action. Though I recognize racial, ethnic, gender, and religious differences, and the real material consequences of these differences, I do not invoke these differences as the criteria by which I measure social justice and individual consciousness. By theorizing about the consciousness process of my coresearchers, I am also attempting to understand and change the politics of knowledge as it relates to Muslim women in general and to my collaboration with some of them.

Epistemological or Knowledge Claims

In the Qur'an, the goal is not only to seek knowledge for its own sake or only for utilitarian benefits, rather the goal is to change the nature of the relationship of the knower (the human) with the natural law, from that of domination into a balanced creativity (Qur'an, 22:46). To realize the epistemological relationship between Muslim women and academic feminism we need to understand Western academic discourse that created, defined, and attempted to address issues related to Muslim women long before feminism. There are many theoretical arguments and much empirical evidence showing how some Orientalist inferior images and perceptions of the Muslim people and their culture had served the colonial imperial governments' and missionaries' dominating views and policies in Muslim/Arab societies (al Faruqi, 1998; Said, 1978, 1981). Yet, less known is that the discipline of Middle Eastern Studies (MES) not only formulated a large research endeavor, but also resulted in the field of Middle East Women's Studies (MEWS) without benefiting the women of the region. Muslim women either rejected the MEWS or attempted to set their own research agenda, but they found that they could not go far enough by framing the issues within their own framework. Even international development institutions' agendas were framed by this Western worldview. Kramer (2001, p. 6) argues that MES research is irrelevant to American policy in the region because it does not succumb to American government policies. I argue that most of this research is irrelevant to the people of the region. MES is an area studies discipline that is uniquely American, created during the Cold War. Within the fold of this discipline lies the study of Islam and Muslim societies. Muslim women's studies is the youngest field in this discipline, but it barely recognizes the presence of Muslim women in America. MES also operates within the premises of Orientalism in addition to those of conventional social and psychological theories, postmodernism, critical theory, and feminism. Despite their rich literary production, very few of these studies made an impact on the lives of the people there. The recent United Nations Development Programme report on Arab Human Development takes an honest look at the results, concluding that despite the significant strides in more than one area of human development in the last three decades, Arab countries (where the majority population is Muslim) still suffer from three deficits relating to freedom, empowerment of women, and knowledge (2002).

As I attempt to bridge participatory feminism and AR in the context of my collaboration with the American Muslim women, I realize why the individual consciousness and social epistemological relationship were not balanced. The tension between these women's premises and feminists' premises seemed compatible, given that they both are forging an argument for gender justice. Yet Muslim women's relationship with Western academic feminism and academia remain unchanged (Barazangi, 2001). Despite being in the same critical plane, as Sandra Harding (1987) suggests, sharing academic knowledge production among Muslim women scholars and academic feminists did not actually make a significant impact on the Muslim women scholars' life experiences nor on academic policy concerning the understanding of Islam and the Muslim community. Neither had the "new knowledge" changed the feminists' attitude. Many feminists still view their Muslim colleagues as the Other, Women of Color, or Third World women, instead of viewing them as agents of change for their own situations, as partners in the struggle for social justice, and as a living experience to learn from. In addition, Muslim women's scholarly work is viewed as applied sociology or activism. When I argued that a course on Muslim women at Cornell ought to be taught from these women's perspectives, I was accused by some of my colleagues of proselytizing and of being a fundamentalist.

Cultural or Historical Claims

Academic studies of Muslim women have created many images of these women, but instead of producing change in these women's lives, it has reinforced their status quo, adding to the negative images of the "marginal" Muslim woman.[8] Westerners valuing individual liberty over human dignity—as is the case in Arab/Islamic culture—coupled with the old philosophy of dichotomized fields of studies, have dominated Western academic cultural and historical claims about Muslim societies and "their" women. The divide between humanities and social sciences also created a gap between grassroots and academic feminisms. Placing the study of Muslim women as either under the humanities (Oriental studies) or the social sciences (area studies of the Middle East or South Asia, and more recently South East Asia) resulted in a dominant dichotomy in understanding Muslim women. A recent report by the Curriculum Committee of the Cornell College of Arts and Sciences still classifies reasoning skills into quantitative and qualitative, with an add-on of moral reasoning. Furthermore, engagement in learning is mainly still treated as a practical skill for the arts and sciences and not part of the main mission of the curriculum. How would it be possible in this context to address Muslim women's issues from the moral-cognitive rationality of the Qur'an?

The dominant dichotomy is also evident in the knowledge structure and its effect (or lack thereof) on changing the cultural and historical effectiveness of these women. The knowledge structure about Muslim women naturally followed the premises and the cultures of either of the two strands of knowledge. Oriental studies rested on philological decipherment and translation of texts; the latter also recently became prevalent in literary criticism. Meanwhile, Middle East Studies viewed strategy as having a more important role than either the culture or religion of those studied, let alone their role as subjects. Smith expounded on the "invalidity" of the disciplines whose approach was marred by "preoccupation with the techniques and methods rather than with the object of the study, and, correspondingly, with manipulation and control rather than appreciation" (1956, p. 108). As a result, the worldview claims of these women seem to have been lost both at the university level and within their particular communities. The preoccupation of academics with the promotion of "scientific" theories and interpretations of Islam, Muslims, and Muslim women has blinded many of them from realizing that they placed themselves as spokespersons for these women and their culture. Meanwhile, Muslim communities have grown defensive about these theories and/or suspicious of academicians because the latter are perceived to fulfill the strategy of the colonizing/controlling governments. Consequently, we have witnessed Muslim authoritarian elites' backlash on Muslim women who use Western methodologies as aiding the conspiracy against the Muslim social fabrics.

Praxis or Socialization Claims

Despite the fact that both academic feminists and academic Muslim women have their origin in their own suffragist movements, much of aca-

demic feminism has grown oblivious to scholarship of the Other. Most of
the rich literature resulting from feminist attempts to understand women
and gender have been made within the existing discourse of the dichotomous disciplines, and the focus on the Self or the Other as the problem did
not change either. Furthermore, university pedagogy has become so
abstract that women's studies began losing touch with the real issues facing feminist teachers and learners. As I continue to modify or change my
own course of action (praxis) to approximate the Islamic goal (*Taqwa*), I also
hoped to facilitate the same process for my coresearchers and my academic
colleagues. Being a member of a university community, my active research
collaboration with some academic Muslim women may have contributed
some ideas and case studies to feminist theories and action research ethnographies, but the claimed "objectivity" of the Western academy has
uncritically assimilated both feminism and the study of Muslim women.

If an academic institution functions as a source for understanding communities, then it needs to understand them enough to make a significant
change in its structure and paradigm in order to aid these communities to
change themselves. Social research that does not contribute to self-control
by involved subjects cannot be validated. That is because it overlooks the
inquisitive process that learners go through as they attempt to make sense
of and to act on the nature of knowledge, its origin, and its evolution, with
the goal of self-realization as citizens. In addition, academic institutions
claim to build a relationship with the surrounding community, but many
of them have not made enough change in their own structure and policy
to be credited with evidence of understanding and caring for the community's input. American Muslim women live among a loosely structured
community of feminists and action researchers like myself who are part of
academia and who claim to understand Muslim women but whose praxis
has hardly begun to be realized. How then could the academic community
realize these women's self-identity with Islam as a worldview?

By self-identity, I am assuming neither psychological ego nor the construct "identity politics." Rather, I am concerned with the Muslim
woman's ability to identify with Islam as an autonomous individual, realizing that without this ability and without reading, interpreting, and
applying Islam's guidelines as presented in the Qur'an on her own, she
may not be able to claim such an identification. This primary identification
will no doubt be affected by the secondary multiple, socially constructed
identities (gender, ethnicity, race, class, and/or academic privilege as
Mary Brydon-Miller argues in this volume) that will determine her re-
interpretation of the text. Thus, the more difficult task for the Muslim
woman is that she remains conscious of these determinants in every process of her own literacy—be it in the text or the world (Barazangi, 1999a)—
as well as her self-identification with Islam. She could remain conscious of
these determinants without making them central concepts of analyzing

her own problems and determining her own course of action to solve them. But because of the academic conformity to the dichotomous knowledge production process (between cognitive and moral development and between disciplines), such autonomous integration was not possible.

As my other work (Barazangi, 1998) suggests, though this consciousness was achieved through self-learning, using a metacognitive process that integrates the rational and the moral, some academic Muslim women have not used this process because they confused it with the processes used by either academics or people in the community. Muslim women's resistance to the academic dichotomous process has led them to resist academic feminism and PAR, instead of resisting concepts generated within the academic worldview claims. Muslim women could benefit from feminist-informed PAR by learning some consciousness-raising strategies or the tools of deconstructing hierarchies, for instance. Meanwhile, their resistance to moral hegemony has led them to resist processes of knowledge generation coming from the academy, instead of refuting only the interpretations coming from such processes.

Patricia Maguire emphasizes the need for asking feminists themselves how they have grounded action researchers' work in order to balance the "uneven ground." By the same token, she listened to some action researchers who have expressed "concern that thirty years into second wave feminism and over a decade into third wave feminism, feminist scholarship remains unfamiliar ground to many in the field" (2001, p. 59). The challenging task for Muslim women, therefore, is how to ground and balance their individual autonomy with the social hegemony of academia when each is still operating from within its own worldview claims. The challenge also is to balance their individual autonomy with the community heteronomy, when Muslim males perceive themselves as the moral guardian of women and the authority on interpreting the Qur'an.

CONCLUSION

One of the goals of bridging feminism and PAR is social justice. Another goal of bridging the two is also to create an approach to knowledge generation that includes both women and men in defining transformation for a more just, caring, participatory society respectful of individual autonomy and natural laws. For Muslim women to achieve these goals, they need direct access and conscientious knowledge of Islam and feminist-oriented PAR, and autonomous action void of the intermediary of institutionalized paradigms. Be they the paradigms of administrators who are guarding academic "values," the faculty who are guarding the old borders of the disciplines, or the institutionalized criteria of Islamicity, professionalism, and success, all must be secondary to Muslim women's self-identification.

   Feminism, instead, has focused on knowledge generation more than on those Muslim women whose issues and indigenous knowledge became hidden behind theorizing and teaching related to feminism, gender, and development. A Muslim learner who consciously chooses the feminist worldview as a reference cannot identify with feminist goals unless she reclaims her education (looking beyond the theory and the curricula). Essentially, she needs to free the curriculum from the hidden discourse(s) and worldviews of those who are writing and teaching about her before she frees herself from the social construction of gender. She needs to expose the existing ideological and scholarly dichotomies between the two views of Western and traditional Muslim interpretations of Islam and between the disciplines in the curriculum. These dichotomies exist in both the content and the form of the curriculum and in the underlying premises, as well as between the ideals and practice of the traditional liberal arts curriculum and the Muslim community. While the first emphasizes "objectivity" without appreciating the variations in worldviews, the latter emphasizes a "subjective" belief system without allowing individual autonomous rationality.

   Moving from these scholarly dichotomous paradigms, including that of academic feminism, into the paradigm of human moral and cognitive autonomy may shed new light on understanding the American Muslim woman and her education both within her own worldview and by means of the interactive rationality of Benhabib (1992). Such rationality does not in any way exclude individual human experience because one can become universal and interactive only after one is able to understand one's own particularity (Barazangi, 1993). Action research might be the approach to move this experience from the particular into the universal without imposing one's voice or paradigm, but unless it remains vigilant of the individual consciousness and its worldview claims, it will be uncritically assimilated by the institutional paradigms, just as was often the case with academic feminism.

   I suggest that non-Muslims, particularly feminists and action researchers, become more aware of Muslim women's worldview and not only look at Muslim women through the veil issues, the politics of difference, or globalization. I also suggest that Muslim women feminists unveil their conscious process in order to make their worldview claims accessible. In addition, even though academic institutions claim to affirm reason as the distinct characteristic of their operation, they are not recognizing that choice and consciousness of the learner go hand-in-hand with reason to achieve effective learning (Barazangi, 1998). Free choice and consciousness affirm reason as also essential for personal identity. Benhabib suggests that such a premise allows one to "move beyond the metaphysical assumptions of the Enlightenment universalism" (1992, pp. 5–6). Because these assumptions ignore individual worldview, they have separated reason from moral and ethical premises. Therefore, in order for the process of *Taqwa* to be completed, we need to replace human dominance of nature with creative understanding of nature. We also need to replace human dominance over other humans with a better understanding of the different worldviews.

NOTES

1. In Freire's (1973) term: individual conscientization.

2. I define Islam as an action-oriented worldview that encompasses cultural and social elements, including religion. This worldview relies on human capacity to reason, and its goal is constructive and just behavior to balance individual and social consciousness *(Taqwa)* (Qur'an, 5:93). I define feminism "as a creative theory of human relations aimed at transforming social structures that dismiss individual contributions, particularly those of females, because these contributions are perceived not to fit the 'cultural standards'" (Barazangi, 1999b, p. 2). I define action research (AR) as "a form of research that generates knowledge claims for the express purpose of taking action to promote social change and social analysis [wherein involved members may] control their destinies and improve their capacities to do so" (Greenwood & Levin, 1998, p. 6). I define ethnicity as pertaining to people of distinctive linguistic, racial, or cultural tradition.

3. The Qur'an is the Primary Text of Islam. I mainly use the original Arabic text, making my own English translation. English readers may access *The Holy Qur'an* by Abdullah Yusuf Ali (1946).

4. See, for example, the author's (2000) Muslim women's Islamic higher learning as a human right: Theory and practice. Also, Maysam al Faruqi (2000).

5. The same units of analysis are used, for instance, in both of Fernea's books despite the apparent difference of emphasis. Elizabeth Warnock Fernea and Basima Qattan Bezirgan. (Eds.). (1976). *Middle Eastern Muslim women speak*. Austin: University of Texas Press; Elizabeth Warnock Fernea, (1998).

6. See, for example, Kaye Haw's (1998) emphasis on discussing Muslim girls as being non-Whites (*Educating Muslim girls: Shifting discourses*. Buckingham: Open University Press.).

7. Though I share Sandra Harding's assessment of "some important tensions between the feminist analysis of such issues and the traditional theories of knowledge and between the feminist epistemologies themselves" (1987, p. 181), I am more concerned here with the tension between the Islamic worldview that Muslim women accept and are keen to practice its pedagogy, on the one hand, and the feminists and participant action researchers' worldviews, on the other.

8. One can detect this image easily by surveying the number of "visiting," nonpermanent academic positions that Muslim women in North America occupy vis-à-vis the number of regular academic positions and by understanding Orientalism and the study of Islam. See Maysam al Faruqi (1998) From Orientalism to Islamic studies.

REFERENCES

Afkhami, M., & Vaziri, H. (Eds.). (1996). *Claiming our rights: A manual for women's human rights education in Muslim societies.* Bethesda, MD: Sisterhood is Global Institute.

Ali, A. Y. (1946). *The holy Qur'an: Text, translation, and commentary.* Washington, DC: McGregor & Werner.

Barazangi, N. H. (1991a). Islamic education in the United States and Canada: Conception and practice of the Islamic belief system. In Y. Haddad (Ed.), *The Muslims of America* (pp. 157–174). New York: Oxford University Press.

Barazangi, N. H. (1991b). Parents and youth: Perceiving and practicing Islam in North America. In E. H. Waugh, S. M. Abu Laban, & R. B. Qureshi (Eds.), *Muslim families in North America* (pp. 132–147). Edmonton: Alberta University Press.

Barazangi, N. H. (1993). Particularism and multi-cultural education: Experience of Muslims in the United States. *Muslim Education Quarterly, 10*(4), 35–45.

Barazangi, N. H. (1996). Vicegerency and gender justice in Islam. In N. H. Barazangi, M. R. Zaman, & O. Afzal (Eds.), *Islamic identity and the struggle for justice* (pp. 77–94). Gainesville: University Press of Florida.

Barazangi. N. H. (1997). Muslim women's Islamic higher learning as a human right: The action plan. In M. Afkhami & E. Friedl (Eds.), *Muslim women and the politics of participation: Beijing Platform* (pp. 43–57). Syracuse, NY: Syracuse University Press.

Barazangi, N. H. (1998). The Equilibrium of Islamic education: Has Muslim women's education preserved the religion? *Religion and Education, 25*(1& 2), 5–19.

Barazangi, N. H. (1999a). Is language learning the object of literacy among United States female adult learners? *The Language and Literacy Spectrum, 9,* 2–16.

Barazangi, N. H. (1999b). Self-identity as a form of democratization: The Syrian experience. In J. Bystydzienski & J. Sekhon (Eds.), *Democratization and women's grassroots movements* (pp. 129–149). Bloomington: Indiana University Press.

Barazangi, N. H. (2000). Muslim women's Islamic higher learning as a human right: Theory and practice. In G. Webb (Ed.), *Windows of faith: Muslim women scholar-activists in North America* (pp. 22–47). Syracuse, NY: Syracuse University Press.

Barazangi, N. H. (2001). Future of social sciences and humanities in corporate universities: Curricula, exclusions, inclusions, and voice. *Cornell University: The Institute of European Studies Working Paper 01.1,* pp. 1–12. Also, retrieved December 26, 2002 from the World Wide Web: http://www.einaudi.cornell.edu/parfem/workingpaper.htm.

Benhabib, S. (1992). *Situating the self: Gender, community, and postmodernism in contemporary ethics.* New York: Routledge.

Clark, V. (2000). Retrofit: Gender, cultural, and class exclusions in American Studies. In The Social Justice Group at The Center for Advanced Feminist Studies, University of Minnesota, *Is Academic feminism dead? Theory in practice* (pp. 9–46). New York: New York University Press.

Cornwall, A. (1998). Gender, participation, and the politics of difference. In I. Guijt & M. Shah (Eds.), *The myth of community: Gender issues in participatory development* (pp. 46–57). London: Intermediate Technology Publications.

al Faruqi, M. (1998). From Orientalism to Islamic Studies. *Religion & Education,* 25(1&2), 20–29.

al Faruqi, M. (2000). Self identity in the Qur'an and Islamic law. In G. Webb (Ed.), *Windows of faith: Muslim women scholar-activists in North America.* Syracuse, NY: Syracuse University Press, pp. 72–101.

Fernea, E. W. (1998). *In search of Islamic feminism: One woman's global journey.* New York: Doubleday.

Fernea, E. W. & Bezirgan, B. Q. (Eds.). (1976). *Middle Eastern Muslim women speak.* Austin: University of Texas Press.

Freire, P. (1973). *Education for critical consciousness.* New York: Continuum.

Greenwood, D. & Levin, M. (1998). *Introduction to action research: Social research for social change.* Thousand Oaks, California: SAGE Publications.

Harding, S. (Ed.). (1987). *Feminism and methodology: Social science issues.* Bloomington: Indiana University Press.

Haw, K. (1998). *Educating Muslim girls: Shifting discourses.* Buckingham: Open University Press.

hooks, b. (1994). *Teaching to transgress: Education as the practice of freedom.* New York: Routledge.

Kramer, M. (2001). *Ivory towers on sand: The failure of Middle Eastern studies in America.* Washington, DC: The Washington Institute for Near East Policy.

Lemert, C. (1994). A classic from the other side of the veil: Du Bois's *The Souls of Black Folk. The Sociological Quarterly,* 35(3), 383–396.

Maguire, P. (2001). Uneven ground: Feminisms and action research. In P. Reason, & H. Bradbury, (Eds.), *Handbook of action research: Participative inquiry and practice* (pp. 59–69). London: SAGE Publications.

McIntyre, A. (1997). *Making meaning of whiteness: Exploring racial identity of white teachers.* Albany: State University of New York.

Middleton, S. (1993). *Educating feminists: Life histories and pedagogy.* New York: Teachers College Press.

Restak, R. (2000). *Mysteries of the mind.* Washington, DC: National Geographic Society.

Said, E. (1978).*Orientalism.* New York: Pantheon Books.

Said, E. (1981). *Covering Islam: How the media and the experts determine how we see the rest of the world.* New York: Pantheon Books.

Shirazi, F. (2001). *The veil unveiled: The hijab in modern culture.* Gainesville: University Press of Florida.

Smith, W. C. (1956). The Place of Oriental Studies in a Western University. *Diogenes 16,* 108.

United Nations (1996). *Covenant for the New Millennium: The Beijing Declaration & Platform for Action. From the Fourth World Conference on Women.* Santa Rosa, CA: Free Hand.

United Nations Development Programme: Arab Fund for Economic and Social Development (2002). *Foreword: Arab Human Development Report 2002: Creating opportunities for future generations.* Retrieved December 28, 2002 from http://www.undp.org/rbas/ahdr/bychapter.html.

Webb, G. (Ed.). (2000). *Windows of faith: Muslim women scholar-activists in North America.* Syracuse: Syracuse University Press.

CHAPTER 3

Testimonio: Bridging Feminist and Participatory Action Research Principles to Create New Spaces of Collectivity

Kalina Brabeck

Ethical First-World feminist and action researchers who seek to collaborate with Third-World Others must negotiate the complex issues invoked when they attempt to understand, privilege, and engage in shared dialogue with an Other (Wilkinson & Kitzinger, 1996). Embedded in the question of how to partake in a mutual, egalitarian dialogue between Self and Other is the question of how to foster a space of collectivity, meaning a site that permits fluid, back-and-forth, democratic dialogue between peoples in which there exists no center or periphery. Such a collective space must contend with the tension between, on the one hand, identifying common ground on which to stand in solidarity against oppression and, on the other hand, respecting the differences that limit the extent to which we, as engaged First-World researchers, can empathize with the reality of an Other.

Testimonio, an indigenous literary genre motivated by the narrator's goals of representing a collective experience and of resisting oppression, is offered by traditionally marginalized peoples to First-World feminist and activist researchers as a means for mediating the above tension. Testimonio shares many core principles with feminist and participatory action research (PAR). For First-World feminist and PAR practitioners, testimonio is an alternative approach for expressing and privileging the voices of Third-World Others and for creating spaces of solidarity between First- and Third-World peoples.

I first became interested in testimonio while searching for a thesis topic during my senior year of college. In my preteen years, I lived in the highlands of Guatemala for some months and have returned for six subsequent trips; I therefore searched for a topic that would take me—at least in an intellectual capacity—back to the volcanoes that encircle Lake Atitlán, back to the streets made vibrant by the colorful *traje* (indigenous dress), back among my childhood friends who taught me invaluable lessons on bracelet-weaving, *tortilla* sculpting, and social justice.

I began to follow the budding controversy surrounding David Stoll's then recent publication, *Rigoberta Menchú and the Story of All Poor Guatemalans* (1999), in which the author accuses Menchú of lying in her famous personal narrative, *I... Rigoberta Menchú* (Burgos-Debray & Menchú, 1984). Stoll charges that Menchú fabricated many of the events she claims befell her indigenous family during Guatemala's most recent civil war, and that she misrepresented her ("nonfactual") story as an "eye-witness account."

I began to wonder about the form of Menchú's text and about whether it was fair to apply the Western standards of truth and memory to a work whose content and form were clearly born out of a different tradition. Shortly after I began researching the form of Menchú's narrative, testimonio, I lost my interest in the Stoll controversy. Instead, I became absorbed in studying the characteristics of this indigenous literary form and in understanding the potential testimonio might have for communicating a Third-World experience, like that of my Mayan friends in Sololá, Guatemala, to a First-World reader, like myself.

TESTIMONIO, FEMINISMS, AND PAR

George Yúdice defines testimonio as

an *authentic* narrative, told by a *witness* who is *moved* to *narrate* by the *urgency* of a situation (e.g. war, oppression, revolution, etc.). Emphasizing *popular oral discourse,* the witness portrays his or her own *experience* as a *representative* of a *collective memory* and *identity. Truth* is summoned in the cause of denouncing a present situation of exploitation and oppression or exorcising and setting aright official history. (1985; n.p., italics in original)

Testimonio emerged in the late 1960s as part of a movement toward global reordering of the social and economic contexts of power and difference within which literature is produced and consumed. It was born in the wake of liberation theology and of consciousness-raising, grassroots, and social movements, such as the struggles of working people, ethnic and national liberation movements, the peace movement, and the women's movement of the 1960s and 1970s. People who were once the objects of anthropological and psychological study began to write and to speak for themselves, insisting on being subjects instead of objects.

However, the subject expressed in testimonio is not the individualistic, separate voice of dominant Euro-American cultures that is oftentimes expressed through autobiography. Rather, the voices that speak from the margin in testimonio offer an individual account that encompasses and expresses the reality of a whole people and can only be understood within the context of belonging to a community. For example, in Rigoberta Menchú's famous testimonio, *I... Rigoberta Menchú*, she states:

We can select what is truly relevant for our people. Our lives show us what this is. It has guaranteed our existence. Otherwise we would not have survived. We have rejected all the aims governments have tried to impose. It wasn't only me who did this, of course. I'm saying we did it together. (Burgos-Debray & Menchú, 1984, p. 170)

This statement reflects Menchú's commitment to speak about the experiences of her community, which are, by extension, the experiences of herself, rather than be spoken for by the government, Western intellectuals, and other outsiders to her community. In another example, Bolivian Domitila Barrios de Chungara emphasizes her collective stance in her testimonio, *Let Me Speak*: "That's why I don't want to tell a personal story. I want to talk about my people. I want to testify about all the experience we've acquired during so many years of struggle in Bolivia" (Barrios de Chungara & Viezzer, 1978, p. 15). Again, the narrator is committed to speak from the position of embeddedness within a particular community.

In this paper, I argue that testimonio lies at the intersection between feminist and PAR principles, its construction and characteristics encompassing core assumptions of both. While multiple branches of and approaches to feminism exist, similar commitments run throughout each. These include the resolutions to address issues of gender and power, to call attention to the ways in which patriarchy and oppression shape women's experiences and perceptions of reality, to facilitate the creation of a feminist consciousness, and to be self-reflexive (i.e., to reflect upon, examine critically, and explore analytically both the research process and one's own self) (Fonow & Cook, 1991; Worell & Johnson, 1997). The definition of feminisms that will be used in the current paper characterizes it as action-oriented in the sense of being both a political movement and a theoretical orientation that advocates social and political equality among all peoples (Sparks & Park, 2000).

Similarly, PAR is an approach to research that has roots in a variety of theoretical perspectives and encompasses a broad range of research practices and political ideologies. In this paper, I define PAR as an enterprise that engages researchers and community members as equal participants; combines popular, experiential knowledge with that of an academic, "rational" perspective; and seeks to join community members in collective action aimed at radically transforming society (Brydon-Miller, 2001; Park, 1993; Philips, 1997).

I will compare the characteristics of testimonio to the principles of feminisms and PAR, highlighting the similarities among—and thereby trying to bridge together—the three. These assumptions include the importance ascribed to subjective experience as the basis for knowledge; the resistance of imposed definitions and the reappropriation of voice; the commitment to political action; and the emphasis on collaborative work. Testimonio's unique contribution to First-World feminist and PAR practitioners is that it is born out of and expresses the speaker's experience of collective identity-through-belonging, and it invites the First-World reader to gain insight into this experience. I will briefly discuss some of the core principles of feminisms and PAR, highlighting how testimonio's characteristics and construction can become a potential bridge between feminisms and PAR.

SUBJECTIVE EXPERIENCE AS THE BASIS FOR KNOWLEDGE

Similar to testimonio, both PAR and feminist practice emphasize the importance of the subjective experience as a basis for developing knowledge. Participatory action research and feminist practitioners learn from the experiences of the participants, the researcher(s), and the shared subjectivity of the researcher-participant group that emerges through the research process.

In the process of constructing knowledge, practitioners of PAR grant primary focus to participants' knowledge (as opposed to theory-based knowledge), as well as to the knowledge that is generated by the collective researcher-participant group (McTaggart, 1991). The initial stages of problem identification in PAR begin with the participants; PAR practitioners recognize that people are aware of problems, since they, after all, are the ones who experience them. Therefore, practitioners of PAR recognize that the participants with whom they engage in the PAR process don't need an outside "expert" to identify problems for them (Park, 1993). Not only do the participants of PAR identify project problems and desired goals, they also determine realistic interventions that will be compatible with their community's lifestyle and values. Thus, the research process begins with real-life problems and ends (we hope!) with real-life changes. Such changes come about as a result of the knowledge that was co-constructed between researchers and participants through a variety of collaborative research experiences. The subjective experience of the researcher is key to the PAR process as well, for PAR demands constant self-reflexivity about the researcher's assumptions, biases, privileges, and power positionalities.

Credence granted to lived experience as a means of generating knowledge is a core commitment of feminist researchers as well (Brabeck & Ting, 2000; Lykes, Brabeck, Ferns, & Radan, 1993). People's experiences are both bases for generating problems to be researched as well as significant indicators of the "reality" against which hypotheses are tested (Harding, 1987). As opposed to viewing participants as the Other to be studied, feminists assert that the researcher must constantly consider the participants' point of view, for their realities are integral to the knowledge generation process (Baier, 1994; Fox, 1992). Important, too, is the subjectivity of practitioners who are expected to constantly engage in self-reflexivity and be critical of their own positions of power and privilege in relation to others when acting for social change:

That is, the class, race, culture, and gender assumptions, beliefs, and behaviors of the researcher her/himself must be placed within the frame of the picture that she/he attempts to paint. Thus the researcher appears to us not as an invisible, anonymous voice of authority, but as a real, historical individual with concrete, specific desires and interests. (Harding, 1987, p. 9)

Thus, individuals bring their particular set of experiences, ideas, and hopes to the research process (Brabeck & Brown, 1997). The research process itself becomes a shared experience, and "click moments" (Fonow & Cook, 1991, p. 4) for both researcher and participant are often used as sources of creative insight that are transferred into the research process.

Testimonio produces knowledge born out of the subject's experience. Because it privileges lived, experiential knowledge as the basis for knowing, testimonio disrupts what has traditionally been valued in the First World as valid bases for knowledge. Testimonio is born out of the speaker's (and not the researcher's) experiences and that individual's political agenda of resisting oppression. Testimonio produces knowledge based on subjective experience, not as empirical historical facts, but as a strategy for cultural survival and resistance. For example, Menchú states, "It's not so much that the hungrier you've been, the purer your ideas must be, but you can only have a real consciousness if you've really lived in this life" (Burgos-Debray & Menchú, 1984, p. 223). Testimonios like Menchú's, such as Barrios de Chungara's Let Me Speak (1977) and Elvia Alvarado's Don't Be Afraid, Gringo (1987) devote a great deal of text to describing various aspects of the community's life, from labor to child rearing, local religious rituals to daily food preparation. It is these daily experiences that are the basis of "knowing" about their particular communities and their cultures.

REAPPROPRIATION OF VOICE

Approaches to PAR (Lykes, 1997), feminist work (Brabeck & Ting, 2000), and testimonio (Burgos-Debray & Menchú, 1984) seek to reappropriate the traditionally silenced voice and agency of oppressed peoples, with the ultimate aim of people transforming their peripheral status and creating social change. This reappropriation of voice is an act of redefining reality from a historically marginalized point of view.

Through PAR, people move from being objects of intellectual inquiry to active subjects in their own research process. Community members develop an increasingly critical understanding of social problems, their underlying causes, and ways to overcome them. This, in turn, develops people's awareness of, belief in, and abilities to organize resources. PAR does not merely aim to alleviate or eliminate poverty while keeping people dependent and powerless, but rather it intends to help oppressed people become self-reliant, self-assertive, self-determinant, and self-sufficient (Park, 1993). This focus on people and communities, and not on problems and symptoms, stands in contrast to objective research in which the researcher has "privileged" knowledge of the project's objectives, instruments, expected results, and output. In a more traditional social science relationship there is a greater risk of exploitation and cooptation of people (McTaggart, 1991). Participants in PAR, by contrast, reappropriate the ability to define their own reality as well as the ability to change systems that oppress that reality.

Feminist researchers, too, seek to reappropriate traditionally silenced voices in order to eradicate misrepresentation, distortion, and oppression resulting from traditional, more hierarchical research relationships and from a historically male perspective (Brabeck & Ting, 2000). Feminist researchers aim to "restore women to history and to restore our history to women" (Kelly-Gadol, 1987, p. 15). It has been argued that feminist epistemology and methodology arise from a critique of traditional research's biases and distortions in the study of women (Cook, 1988). Feminist researchers have argued that traditional theories have been used in ways that make it difficult to understand women's experiences and that portray men's behaviors as "human," as opposed to gendered (Harding, 1987). In their place, feminist researchers have produced feminist versions of these traditional theories. These new feminist theories differ from traditional epistemologies that have systematically excluded the possibility that women could be "knowers" or *agents of knowledge* and have proposed alternative theories of knowledge that legitimate women as knowers (Harding, 1987). Thus, the feminist enterprise seeks to dispel gendered myths stemming from a male perspective and to redefine women's experiences from women's point of view.

The reappropriation of collective voice and the rejection of definitions imposed by others in positions of power—be they government, researchers, or landowners—are central goals of testimonio. Testimonio challenges the political and moral reality of the dominant and counteracts and denounces the official version of history: "And this confirmed my certainty that the justification for our struggle was to erase all the images imposed on us" (Burgos-Debray & Menchú, 1984, p. 169). In its unique construction, which lacks a definitive author, testimonio rejects the traditional First-World notion of the primacy of the individual's voice. While the Western writer definitely assumes the role of author, the "protagonist" of testimonio is a speaker who does not conceive of her/himself as an extraordinary individual, but as a voice for many, a representation of a people's collective memory. On the first page of her testimonio, Menchú states, "I'd like to stress that it's not only *my* life, it's also the testimony of my people" (Burgos-Debray & Menchú, 1984, p. 1). It is this collective voice that is reappropriated and expressed through testimonio.

COMMITMENT TO POLITICAL ACTION

Like testimonio, the work of PAR and many feminist practitioners is committed to a political project. Fundamentally, the individual's reality is understood within the socioeconomic/sociopolitical context and the power dynamics that exist therein. Many PAR and feminist projects, and all testimonios, are aimed at exposing and confronting injustices and oppression of peoples and at transforming society.

PAR seeks to change oppressive social structures as well as the positions of both researcher and participant—both individuals *and* the culture of the groups, institutions, and societies to which they belong (McTaggart, 1991). The community group, along with the participatory action researcher, identify existing systemic problems in the community that they wish to eliminate or change. These problems become the basis for the participatory process of change, as researchers and community members collaboratively explore the structural roots of the problem and possible avenues toward change. Facts or findings that emerge can then be used to organize and decide which community actions to take, to shape social policies, and/or to implement social change measures.

Like PAR, feminist researchers engage in action directed at achieving social justice. Feminist researchers are concerned not only with what ought to be but with how to bring what exists more in line with what ought to exist (Bell, 1993). Thus, some feminists maintain that any critique must be accompanied by a critique of all discriminatory distortions and must work to create the structural and cultural conditions for self-determination of all peoples (Brabeck & Ting, 2000). The ultimate goal of feminist practice is to enhance the human condition and to create a more caring and just world for all (Appelbaum, 1997).

Similarly, one of testimonio's main purposes is to be a cultural weapon used to transform society. John Beverly (1993) places testimonio as a genre within Third-World literature or resistance literature. George Yúdice (1985) suggests that testimonio is first and foremost an act, a tactic by means of which people engage in the process of self-constitution and sur-

vival. Thus, testimonio is intimately linked to international solidarity networks, human rights groups, revolutionary support groups, and reformist
projects. In Rigoberta Menchú's testimonio, for example, the narrator is
highly tied to the Committee for Campesino Unity, or the CUC.

A second example of the commitment to confront injustice comes from
Elvia Alvardo's testimonio *Don't Be Afraid, Gringo:*

I thought about our struggle, how we suffer hunger, persecution, abuse by the
landowners. How we fight with all the bureaucrats at the National Agrarian Institute. How we fight with the police, the army, the security forces.... But then I
decided that I couldn't pass up a chance to tell the world our story. (Alvarado,
1987, p. xiii)

Testimonio's political project is to confront oppression, and the reader is
invited to stand with the narrator and that individual's community
against injustice.

A NEW SPACE OF COLLECTIVITY AND MEANS TO
NEGOTIATE DIFFERENCE

PAR and feminist approaches both encompass a commitment to collaborative work and solidarity among peoples. As mentioned earlier, PAR
and feminist practitioners who are committed to being allies with
oppressed peoples must simultaneously acknowledge their limited ability
to truly understand and speak for the experiences of an Other. Testimonio
is a possible solution to mediating this tension between standing in solidarity and still respecting and maintaining difference, a tension that feminist researchers and practitioners of PAR know well.

The principles of shared power and collective ownership of knowledge
are crucial to the PAR process. It aims to break down barriers and to forge
alliances between grassroots community people and academia, therefore
requiring a willingness to enter another's life and allow her/him to enter
one's own (Lykes, 1997). In PAR, the researcher knows something and the
people know something, but neither party holds the definitive answer.
However, through working together, researcher-participants increase collective knowledge and learn more about how to gain and use knowledge
(Maguire, 1987; Philips, 1997).

Many feminist methodologies also require collaborative decision-
making. Grossman et al. (1997) suggest that feminists seek to create a
research process that does not exploit or oppress the participants or the
community in which they live but rather that engages people in collaboration. Like PAR, feminist methodology is always evolving and in process
as the inclusive, accessible, creative dialogue between participants develops. Feminists place more importance on the shared process of discovery,

expression, interpretation, and adjustment between people. They seek solutions that occur in collaboration rather than in competition and that affect entire communities rather than only individuals (Lykes et al., 1993).

While both PAR and feminist researchers aspire to solidarity, or locating a common ground on which to unite and stand with Others against injustice, there is simultaneously an acknowledgement of difference. Partnerships require strategies for sharing power and decision making in a context where all participants are not equal power holders in society, due to differences in skin color, gender, socioeconomic status, education, sexual orientation, and other factors that society employs to distinguish between a (powerful) "us" and a (powerless) "them" (Lykes, 1997). Therefore, within this collaborative work, feminist and/or PAR practitioners are expected to be self-reflexive and to examine the ways in which their positions in power hierarchies dominate and oppress others and shape their experience of reality (Appelbaum, 1997). In addition, they need to be aware of the ways in which, even while standing in solidarity, they may continue to be outsiders. Indeed, affirming, attending to, and authorizing the voice of the oppressed is dependent on our ability to realize our own First-World researcher roles as oppressors. This is necessary because the goal of feminist research, PAR, and, as I've argued, testimonio is not only to transform individual lives but also to transform society and to make the world a more just and caring place.

This collaboration, which embraces both commonality and difference, is eloquently described by Michelle Fine's (1994) metaphor of "working with the hyphen" of the Self-Other equation. She suggests the following steps for engaged, activist feminist researchers: Verify the validity of their representations with Others and engage them as coresearchers; listen to the dominant group's ways of constructing Others; develop opportunities for dialogue between "us" and Others; and create the conditions under which it is possible to hear the voices of Others "talking back, to 'us,' over 'us,' regardless of 'us,' to each other, or to other Others" (Wilkinson & Kitzinger, 1996, p. 17). This egalitarian, centerless dialogue presents, perhaps, the best hope for ethical First-World researchers to hear and to work with the voices of the Third World. It may further, as noted by Sampson (1993), represent our best hope for a democratic society. While the reality of such a true democracy may seem dubious given the human tendency to create strictly delineated hierarchies of power and clearly bounded categories of "us" and "them," the hope for such a truly democratic society is largely what propels the work of indigenous and "Third-World" activists, as well as that of feminist and PAR practitioners.

The very practice of creating testimonio is a collaborative endeavor produced by subject *and* interlocutor. The interlocutor, who is many times a Western intellectual, is not author but rather "activator" or "compiler" of the text. Yet despite the intellectual's presence in the text's construction, it is the subject's voice that has the ultimate control over what is said and, equally as important, what is not said—at least in theory. As feminist and PAR practitioners, as well as creators of testimonio, know well, collaboration can be a tricky issue.

In practice, the differential access to resources and power between Third-World subject and First-World interlocutor complicates the subject's complete ownership and control over the testimonio. Such differences in power lead some scholars, for example Spivak (1988), to claim that in the context of the production of knowledge, the subaltern ultimately has no voice and cannot speak.

Indeed, there exists an inherent paradox in the production of testimonio: Speakers must use the language and literature of the oppressor, which they often denounce, in order to achieve their aim of telling their story and reaching an international audience. The speaker's voice must travel first through the interlocutor and likely next through subsequent translations, leading one to question what happens to the speaker's voice through the process of mediation and translation. In the end, who speaks for whom?

There are, of course, no simple answers to such questions. Still, it can be argued that testimonio comes closest to preserving the authentic voice of the narrator in spite of transcription and translation. In the case of Rigoberta Menchú, for example, while Venezuelan anthropologist Elisabeth Burgos-Debray admits to organizing the material along themes, omitting excessive repetition, and correcting grammar, Rigoberta Menchú and the Committee for Campesino Unity (CUC) had control over *what*, if not *how* material was presented. Moreover, the story is distinctly born out of the speaker's motivation: While Menchú does little to hide her ties to political groups, her inspiration to speak clearly comes from the opportunity to share *her* (people's) story, in the hopes that their collective experience will not be forgotten by future generations. What's more, Menchú's identity is preserved in its collective form as she goes beyond the personal to pursue the truth of a community. The fact that telling her story was achieved through collaboration does not diminish her ability to speak and to take responsibility for history and truth. Moreover, we must not deny the ability of the Third-World person to appropriate our discourse and access to resources, as evident in the words of Alvarado (1987), "So here comes this *gringa* asking me to tell our story.... Even if you are a *gringa*, I thought, once you understand why we're fighting, if you have any sense of humanity, you'll have to come to our side" (Alvarado, 1987, p. xiii). Testimonio may be written in the language of the oppressor and may include collaboration with an Other (who is a First-World academic), yet it comes closer than traditional ethnography (which is more structured by the interviewer) toward authentically preserving the experiences, voice, and authority of the Third-World speaker.

What's more, testimonio produces collaborative dialogue, not only between narrator and interlocutor, but between narrator and reader as well. The reader of testimonio is called to identify—to the extent possible—with a distant reality. Beverly (1993) suggests that testimonio is meant as a means by which we (Westerners) can understand a truth of the Other's experience. Yet, this understanding has its limits, as Beverly reminds us that testimonio is only one part of a larger testimonial practice, including oral memory, storytelling, gossip, and rumor. Testimonio happens to be the part that we, as Western intellectuals, are permitted to see.

Testimonio's collaborative dialogue with the reader is achieved via the erasure of the single "I" authorial presence, which makes for a different kind of complicity between narrator and reader. Testimonio requires that a reader read metonymically, or laterally, suggesting a side-to-side movement to identity through relation. This stands in contrast to, for example, Western autobiography, which is intended to be read metaphorically, for it aspires to universal truth and identification. The danger of autobiography lies in the hero's representation as a symbol of all human condition/experience, which tempts readers to impose their own identity on top of the hero's. Autobiographies became popular during the Renaissance and Reformation, eras that celebrated and valued the self-made man. The unique individual is celebrated and the people, oftentimes, are silenced (Gugelberger & Kearny, 1991). In testimonio, there is no claim to universal representation that invites the reader to substitute one (superior) signifier for another. Testimonio seeks emancipation and survival within specific and local circumstances; thus, there is no identity imposition or appropriation.

The speaker of testimonio describes the circumstances and experiences of a particular group of which the reader is not a part but with which the reader may be an ally. Menchú, for example, does not seek to describe the experiences of all humans; she describes the particular experiences of the Maya. Through elaborate descriptions of the foods, smells, land, ceremonies, labors, joys, and pains of her community, Menchú invites the reader to see this Mayan reality. Yet, ultimately, the reader of testimonio is only permitted to see so far. Thus, the reader engages in a tenuous dance of trying to gain a deeper understanding of the speaker's experience and yet respecting and preserving difference and distance between persons.

Menchú achieves this distance from the reader in part by maintaining secrets about her community and identity (Sommer, 1991). Despite her detailed descriptions of the life of her Mayan community, Menchú states, "Nevertheless, I'm still keeping my Indian identity a secret. I'm still keeping a secret what I think no-one should know. Not even anthropologists or intellectuals, no matter how many books they have, can find out all our secrets" (Burgos-Debray & Menchú, 1984, p. 247). Thus, simultaneous with being invited to stand in solidarity, readers are held at arm's distance and reminded of the limits of their ability to empathize and to understand the reality of another. We, the readers of testimonio, the researchers with Third-World people, may be outsiders who will never "find out all the secrets" *and* yet remain allies with oppressed peoples.

This new relationship between narrator and reader creates an experience that demands both justice and caring. Collins (1990), a Black feminist and intellectual, suggests that wisdom is derived, not necessarily from having lived through an Other's experiences, but from having engaged in an empathetic, centerless dialogue with an Other in which power dynamics are fluid. To read testimonio is to gain deeper understanding and clarity, through which we align ourselves with the Other in common resistance to oppression and yet respect the cultural distances between us.

CONCLUSION

Feminist researchers and PAR practitioners are committed to projects that change individuals and society and ultimately aim to create a more just and caring world. The lives and experiences of members of oppressed groups are fundamental to these projects, as they determine the problem to be addressed, the methods most appropriate to confront the problem, and the ways in which progress is analyzed. The practitioner, too, is an important part of PAR and feminist projects, and the collaboration, dialogue, and work with participants should be ultimately transforming for her/him as well. Practitioners must, however, seek ways to mediate the tension between seeking to be a part of the researcher-participant group, yet recognizing the ways in which they continue to be outsiders (see McIntyre and Lykes, this volume).

I have argued that testimonio, born out of the speaker's experience of reality and publicized through collaboration with an Other, embodies core assumptions of feminist and PAR work such as the value ascribed to subjective experience, the commitments to reappropriate voice, to transform society, and to work in collaboration. I have further argued that testimonio is offered by oppressed peoples as a means to engage Westerners who seek to collaborate with Third-World peoples in a respectful, caring, and just way.

Testimonio has roots in Latin America; however, narrators of testimonio speak from many marginalized places. In order for First and Third World collaboration to take place through testimonio, it is necessary for First-World readers of testimonio to first understand the form's unique characteristics that create the potential for the reader to gain deeper understanding of the speaker's experience. To do so requires stepping outside of one's assumptions about narrative, truth, memory, and identity. The role of the reader, the researcher, or the practitioner in this process is to learn from the speaker and also to realize the limits of that ability to learn, thereby both coming closer and respecting the distance that remains. From such respectful understanding and learning, one hopes, will spring collaborative action to address the injustices the speaker describes.

REFERENCES

Alvarado, E. (1987). *Don't be afraid, Gringo*. (M. Benjamin, Trans.) San Francisco: Institute for Food Development Policy.

Appelbaum, B. (1997). Good liberal intentions are not enough! Racism, intentions, and moral responsibility. *Journal of Moral Education, 26*(4), 409–421.

Baier, A. (1994). *Moral prejudices: Essays on ethics*. Cambridge, MA: Harvard University Press.

Barrios de Chungara, D., & Viezzer, M. (1978). *"Si me permiten hablar ..." Testimonio de Domitila, una mujer de las minas de Bolivia*. ["If they let me speak ..." Testimonio of Domitila, a woman from the mines of Bolivia.] Mexico City: Siglo XXI.

Bell, L. (1993). *Rethinking ethics in the midst of violence: A feminist approach to freedom*. Lanham, MD: Rowman & Littlefield.

Beverly, J. (1993). *Against literature*. Minneapolis: University of Minnesota Press.

Brabeck, M. M., & Brown, L. (1997). Feminist theory and psychological practice. In J. Worell & N. Johnson (Eds.), *Shaping the future of feminist psychology: Education, research, and practice* (pp. 15–35). Washington, DC: American Psychological Association.

Brabeck, M. M., & Ting, K. (2000). Feminist ethics: Lenses for examining ethical psychological practice. In M. M. Brabeck (Ed.), *Practicing feminist ethics in psychology* (pp. 17–35). Washington, DC: American Psychological Association.

Brydon-Miller, M. (2001). Education, research, and action. In D. L. Tolman & M. Brydon-Miller (Eds.), *From subjects to subjectivities: A handbook of interpretive and participatory methods* (pp. 76–89). New York: New York University Press.

Burgos-Debray, E., & Menchú, R. (1984). *I ... Rigoberta Menchú: An Indian woman in Guatemala*. (A. Wright, Trans.). London: Verso.

Collins, P. H. (1990). *Black feminist thought: Knowledge, consciousness, and the politics of empowerment*. New York: Harper Collins.

Cook, J. A. (1988). Integrating feminist epistemology and qualitative family research. *Qualitative Family Research Network Newsletter, 2*, 3–5.

Fine, M. (1994). Working the hyphens: Reinventing self and other in qualitative research. In N. K. Denzin & Y. S. Lincoln (Eds.), *Handbook of qualitative research* (pp. 70–82). London: SAGE Publications.

Fonow, M. M., & Cook, J. A. (1991). Back to the future: A look at the second wave of feminist epistemology and methodology. In M. M. Fonow & J. A. Cook (Eds.), *Beyond methodology: Feminist scholarship as lived research* (pp. 1–15). Bloomington: Indiana University Press.

Fox, E. L. (1992). Seeing through women's eyes: The role of vision in women's moral theory. In E. B. Cole & S. Coultrap-McQuin (Eds.), *Explorations in feminist ethics: Theory and practice* (pp. 111–116). Bloomington: Indiana University Press.

Grossman, F. K., Gilbert, L. A., Genero, N. P., Hawes, S. E., Hyde, J. S., & Marecek, J. (1997). Feminist research: Practice and problems. In J. Worell & N. Johnson (Eds.), *Shaping the future of feminist psychology: Education, research, and practice* (pp. 173–202). Washington, DC: American Psychological Association.

Gugelberger, G., & Kearny, M. (1991). Voices for the voiceless: Testimonial literature in Latin America. *Latin American Perspectives, 18*(3), 3–14.

Harding, S. (1987). Introduction: Is there a feminist methodology? In S. Harding (Ed.), *Feminisms and methodology: Social science issues* (pp. 1–27). Bloomington: Indiana University Press.

Kelly-Gadol, J. (1987). Introduction to another voice: Feminist perspectives on social life and social science. In S. Harding (Ed.), *Feminisms and methodology: Social science issues* (pp. 15–28). Bloomington: Indiana University Press.

Lykes, M. B. (1997). Activist participatory action research among the Maya of Guatemala: Constructing meaning from situated knowledge. *Journal of Social Issues, 53*(4), 725–746.

Lykes, M. B., Brabeck, M. M., Ferns, T., & Radan, A. (1993). Human rights and mental health among Latin American women in situations of state-sponsored violence. *Psychology of Women Quarterly, 17*(4), 525–544.

Maguire, P. (1987). *Doing participatory research: A feminist approach.* Amherst, MA: The Center for International Education.

McTaggart, R. (1991). Principles for participatory action research. *Adult Education Quarterly, 41*(3), 168–171.

Park, P. (1993). What is participatory research? A theoretical and methodological perspective. In P. Park, M. Brydon-Miller, B. Hall, & T. Jackson (Eds.), *Voices of change: Participatory research in the United States and Canada* (pp. 1–19). Westport, CT: Bergin & Garvey.

Philips, M. A. (1997). Feminist anti-racist participatory action research: Research for social change around women's health in Brazil. *Canadian Woman Studies/Les Cahiers de la Femme, 17*(2), 100–105.

Sampson, E. (1993). *Celebrating the other: A dialogic account of human nature.* London: Harvester Wheatsheaf.

Sommer, D. (1991). Rigoberta's secrets. *Latin American Perspectives, 18*(3), 32–50.

Sparks, L., & Park, A. (2000). The integration of feminisms and multiculturalism: Ethical dilemmas at the border. In M. M. Brabeck (Ed.), *Practicing feminist ethics in psychology* (pp. 203–224). Washington, DC: American Psychological Association.

Spivak, G. (1988). Can the subaltern speak? In C. Nelson & L. Grossberg (Eds.), *Marxism and the interpretation of culture* (pp. 271–313). Urbana: University of Illinois Press.

Stoll, D. (1999). *Rigoberta Menchú and the story of all poor Guatemalans.* Boulder, CO: Westview Press.

Wilkinson, S., & Kitzinger, C. (Eds.). (1996). *Representing the other: A feminisms and psychology reader.* London: SAGE Publications.

Worrell, J., & Johnson, N. G. (Eds.). (1997). *Shaping the future of feminist psychology: Education, research, and practice.* Washington, DC: American Psychological Association.

Yúdice, G. (1985). *Central American testimonial.* Unpublished manuscript.

PART II

Issues of Status and Relationships between Communities and the Academy

CHAPTER 4

Weaving Words and Pictures in/through Feminist Participatory Action Research

Alice McIntyre and M. Brinton Lykes

> The struggle continues ever afterwards. Because afterwards is where we live.
>
> (Nicol, cited in Ross, 2001, p. 273)

As discussed in the introduction to this volume, feminist participatory action research (PAR) provides researchers and participants with opportunities to cocreate spaces where, among other things, democratic group processes, new ways of relating, and coconstructing knowledge from-the-bottom-up can contribute to just social change. As importantly, through feminist PAR, researchers from outside communities and local actors or insiders can develop relationships of trust and reciprocity through which praxis not previously envisioned by either can materialize. Much previous research has problematized tensions between these outsiders and insiders, arguing that presumed power inequities between them need to be examined, critiqued, and deconstructed (see Bartunek & Louis, 1996; Fine, 1994; Merton, 1972). These critiques, and the fieldwork described in the following text, have challenged us to stretch the boundaries of the insider-outsider dichotomy, in order to, in Michelle Fine's words, "work the hyphen" (1994, p. 71). More specifically, this chapter explores selected examples of feminist PAR in Belfast, the North of Ireland, and Chajul, Guatemala,[1] to reveal how developing relationships among researchers and participants are creative sites for knowledge construction and participatory processes of meaning-making and change. By challenging static, boundaried notions of researcher and participant, the examples elucidate the mediated nature of all knowledge and the emergence of a third voice (Lykes, TerreBlanche & Hamber, 2003) constructed through PAR and photovoice processes. This voice re-presents ways of knowing and ways of being in relationship that are frequently absent from mainstream, top-down research and theory building.

In this chapter, we explore the developing relationships and multiple positions we experienced within the North of Ireland (Alice) and rural Guatemala (Brinton). These include moments where the researcher-participant, Self-Other dichotomy disappeared and where we were able to "divine . . . the sources and currents of energy" (Wadsworth, 2001, p. 426) within ourselves, within others, and within the overall collaborative process. These moments also include tensions that we and our coparticipant researchers experienced—struggles that are normative in feminist PAR processes that involve people who inhabit multiple places and spaces, languages and cultures, social classes, and races, over time. By working through these struggles, we (Alice and Brinton) learned the significance of tolerance, acceptance, and humility in the development of reciprocal relationships. As importantly, we came to understand the subtle ways in which stories are constructed and reconstructed and how the final tale reflects an intricate weaving of people's situated knowledges, a reweaving made possible through sticking it out together, making the roads as we go.

The work in Guatemala, from which the examples here are drawn, culminated in the publication of a phototext (Women of ADMI & Lykes, 2000) and an exhibit of the women's photographs. The project participants have extended their work to women and children living in five villages surrounding Chajul. In the North of Ireland the group of women living in Belfast created a phototext exhibit documenting their everyday lives (see McIntyre, 2004). These projects reflect some of the ways in which local participants have appropriated technologies and resources that we bring from the university and our embrace of meaning-making processes among rural Maya and urban working-class Irish women.

The third voice (Lykes, Terre Blanche, & Hamber, 2003) we describe in this chapter challenges discourses of empowerment wherein outsiders are credited with giving voice to the powerless. Rather, we argue for a relational process whereby narrative is coconstructed in a relational terrain wherein indigenous meaning-making and Euro-American/Western knowledge and technologies are interlaced by coparticipants and researchers. We summarize an experience in the North of Ireland that reveals some of the bumps along a journey toward becoming coparticipants and coresearchers. Through another example, drawn from Guatemala, we demonstrate how we weaved visual, oral, and written individual and group stories into texts whose authorship transcends fixed notions of "us and them," of "self and other." We work within and across the different moments in these two research processes to elucidate the coconstruction of knowing and to further problematize traditional insider-outsider or self-other dichotomies.

GETTING FROM HERE TO THERE: OUR HOMES
AWAY FROM HOME

Our decisions to live in and with women in local communities that are not our own and engage in participatory processes of change within contexts of war and peacemaking stemmed from, among other things, our autobiographical journeys and our developing relationships with children in these contexts. My (Alice) desire to work in the North of Ireland had deep roots in my identity as a white, Irish American female who was brought up in a large, working-class Catholic family in Boston. These crisscrossing identities, coupled with my previous experiences as a feminist activist teacher and a practitioner of PAR in the United States (McIntyre, 1997, 2000), led me to explore the possibility of engaging in a participatory project in the North of Ireland in 1996. I began a project aimed at developing strategies for addressing how young children experience life and violence in a Belfast community. I later agreed to facilitate a series of workshops with a group of women with the aim of exploring issues that affect them as mothers, daughters, wives, partners, caregivers, and the primary stakeholders in community life.

I (Brinton) responded to an invitation to join a group of Mayan rural women in Chajul, Guatemala, after nearly seven years of collaboration with a rural Guatemalan health organization developing community-based, creative resources for responding to war and its psychosocial effects on children and their families, and many more years of Central American solidarity work. As the more than 36-year civil war showed signs of slowing, the women of Chajul hoped to create a better future for themselves, their children, and their community. They recognized the need for developing a process that enabled them to rethread their lives as both individual women and as neighbors with differing political, religious, linguistic, and economic perspectives and options. They realized that the divisions of war and the grief, loss, and rage, among other emotions that they were experiencing in the wake of massacres, military control, refugee experiences, and more, required a different kind of response. I agreed to join them in this journey, hoping that some of my earlier work might enable us to cocreate processes of peacemaking, rethreading, and reconstruction.

PHOTOVOICE: ARTICULATING A LIVING HISTORY
WITHIN FEMINIST PAR PROCESSES

Although much has been written about the violence in Guatemala and the North of Ireland over the last three decades, less is known about women's experiences. We know little of how women in "specific political, social, and historical contexts characterized by injustice" (Collins, 1998, p. xiv) experience, respond to, and even thrive amidst multiple forms of violence. Many women living in the North of Ireland and Guatemala, like most women in the majority of the world, have been socially excluded, economically disadvantaged, and institutionally marginalized for generations. Nonetheless, many of them remain active agents of change in their families and communities, contributing in significant ways to the making and remaking of everyday life. We slowly learned about the women's lives through conversations and work with their children (Alice) and through facilitating creative workshops (Brinton) in which women of Chajul were building a group that, over time, became an NGO with education and economic development projects (Lykes, 1994, 1999). We were guests in these communities, and the local women's hospitality contributed importantly to our developing knowledge as well as to forging relationships that enabled "us" and "them" to risk engaging in the PAR/photovoice processes described in the following text.

As outsiders with university experiences and particular skills (e.g., photovoice), we sought to respond to the women's desires to tell their stories as well as their concerns about building solidarity and stopping future wars. Photovoice is a strategy for gathering information that enables people to "reflect on photographs that mirror the everyday social and political realities that influence their lives" (Wang, Wu, Zhan, & Carovano, 1998, p. 80; see also www.photovoice.org). With photographs, people can increase their knowledge about the issues that most affect them, enrich their understandings of their lives within a particular community, have fun, and express themselves in new and imaginative ways to local, national, and/or international audiences.

We each worked closely with groups of women in the North of Ireland and Guatemala in the design of projects that emerged from and reflected local women's interests, desires, talents, and ways of telling stories through voice and picture. Women in both contexts embraced the camera as a resource to document various aspects of their lives. In Guatemala this represented a first because rural Mayan women have limited access to cameras or photography. More likely, they have been photographed either by professionals, who most typically appropriate their images for profit, or, once or twice in a lifetime, at formal occasions such as weddings and funerals, by roving photographers (see, e.g., Parker & Neal, 1982). Over time the 20 Mayan women who participated in this project not only learned to take pictures, tape interviews, and analyze data but also self-identified as photographers and researchers. In both contexts pictures and words were combined to generate stories of the past and the present as well as to reimagine the future. (For further discussions of the use of photovoice, see McIntyre, 2003; One STEP Group, McIntyre, & McKiernan, 2000; Women of ADMI & Lykes, 2000; and Wu, et al., 1995.)

For some of the women in Belfast, writing individual texts to describe particular photographs was the preferred mode of representation. For others, it was recording their thoughts about specific photographs into a tape recorder. Still other women preferred to work with other partici- pants to craft both individual and collective stories that would accom- pany their prints. In Guatemala, a group of 20 Ixil and K' iche' speaking women with widely varying levels of literacy and Spanish-language facility elected to participate in the group. The group and I (Brinton) designed an action-reflection process that took advantage of the local participants' collective skills and facilitated the sharing of indigenous and "outsider" knowledge systems through collaborative teaching and learning. In the following text, we provide several examples of story- telling within both communities that exemplify how self- and collective representations collided and then coalesced in and through participatory processes of reflection and action.

THE TELLERS OF THE STORY: SHIFTING EXPECTATIONS OF RESEARCHERS, PARTICIPANTS, AND FRIENDS

Prior to participating with the women in developing a phototext proj- ect, I (Alice) had facilitated a phototext project with a group of young peo- ple on Monument Road.[2] Many of the young people who participated in that project are sons and daughters or nieces and nephews of the women in this project. The end result of the children and youth project was a photo exhibit that was held at the local community center. Many of the women on the Road liked the youth project and decided to design a simi- lar project for themselves. Thus, nine women and I made a decision to engage in an ongoing participatory project that would include, but not be limited to, the use of photography to record and document the lives of women on Monument Road.

During one of the initial project workshops, I gave each woman two dis- posable cameras (one that used color film, the other black-and-white) and invited her to tell a visual story about her life. The instructions were broad, with the visual story described as including photographs of any- thing or anyone that the woman felt belonged in her story (e.g., children, friends at work and in the community, upcoming events, geographical locations, and holiday festivities).

I arranged to be on the Road for a second workshop five months later. During the first session of that second workshop, we reviewed the women's photographs, individually and collectively, commenting on and drawing inferences from the various people, places, and things depicted in the photographs. Each woman was invited to choose five photographs that she felt best represented her life as a woman living in a Belfast com- munity. We shared ideas about how the women might want to tell their photostories. For example, did they want to write individual texts for each photograph? Form small groups to work on particular photographs?

Speak their stories into a tape recorder? Given the women's earlier desire to create a phototext exhibit much like the young people's project, they decided to write individual stories for each of their photographs and then share those with the rest of the group.

Although the women were excited about reviewing their photographs, some of them became frustrated with what they perceived as their inability to transfer their feelings and thoughts about the photographs to paper.

Lucy: I hate to write. I know what I want to say and I can say it but I don't know how to say it in writing.

Winnie: Alice, it's like, are we doin' it right? Are we on the right track here, 'cause I think it is hard to understand what exactly we want to say about the photos. (Transcripts, March 11, 2001)

As the above discussion continued, it became clear that the women were feeling uncertain about how to engage the analysis-interpretation process. It was during that time that they looked to me for guidance—which I willingly provided. The difficulty arose when they found my guidance wanting. I preferred to ask questions that would elicit the women's thoughts and reflections on the photographs. The women preferred that I tell them exactly what their thoughts and reflections should sound like. I explained to the women that this was not about what *I* wanted, but about what *they* wanted. They agreed, stating that what they wanted was for me to tell them what to do, approve of what they wrote, and let them know if they were "doin' it right." As Nóra stated, "It's just that people are not used to writing things like this."

Nóra's reference to the women not being used to "writing things like this" is significant. Although some of the women in the group attended university after secondary school and others did not, the majority of the women are not accustomed to writing "for" others—in this case, for each other, for me, and/or for the larger community. I assured them that they could trust their own meaning-making, yet the women remained skeptical about their own abilities to articulate what they wanted to say on paper. As Patricia stated, "Ya know what you want to say but you're not the best at writin' down the words."

Although individual women experienced varying levels of discomfort and uncertainty as they engaged the writing/telling process, as a group they supported, cajoled, and encouraged one another. Some of the stories the women shared about particular photographs were met with a sense of joy, a degree of pride, and a shared feeling that the woman who was speaking was speaking for everyone. For example, Tricia chose a photograph of some of the children and youth from the Road performing at a Christmas celebration. She did so to demonstrate the community's success in securing a new neighborhood community center. Other photographs

and stories generated feelings of anger and frustration. For example, Nóra photographed a Land Rover (vehicle used by the police) parked at the top of one of the bridges that borders Monument Road to represent marching season.

This is a picture of the RUC[3] blocking the bridge into the town as an Orange march[4] makes a protest at not being allowed to march through our community. Although this was the last march of the year and it wasn't allowed down and we get a physical break from the marching during the winter, it's in the background and as the spring and summer approach it comes more and more into your thoughts and you realise that you're planning your life around expected marches. Because we don't know whether a march will be forced through the community by the RUC until the week before there's a real feeling of fear and uncertainty from this stage of the year (March/April) until the autumn (September/October).

Nóra's photograph, like many other photographs that were shown and discussed in the group sessions, facilitated the sharing of stories that had their genesis in the women's personal experiences with violence and war. These were stories that had previously been told only to small groups of friends or family members. Some of the women talked about what it felt like to be 14 years old and "have your house raided over and over again by the British army" (Jacqueline). Others discussed how they felt when the police would come to their homes and lift (arrest) their fathers and brothers. Still other women talked about their experiences of "being beaten by the police just so the Orangemen could parade down the Road" (Patricia). The sharing of stories—stories of loss, resistance, courage, and hope—provided the women with opportunities to relive events in their lives in the context of their friends who offered support, affirmation, and a deep sense of identification. In addition, the women's retelling of stories within the larger group resulted in the construction of a collective narrative that, like a mosaic, revealed the individual particularities of the women's lives at the same time that it illustrated an overall story of what life is/was like for women living in unpredictable violence and precarious peace.

After completing this first stage of generating individual and collective stories about their pictures, we discussed the similarities in the women's life experiences. Equally important, we took note of the differences in their lives and discussed how those differences could be significant factors in developing the overall visual-written story that the women hoped to create. I suggested that the women form two groups to review the five photographs that each person had chosen during the previous session and to share these photographs with the other members of their small group. As they reviewed each other's choices, I asked them to identify connections among and differences between their individual photographs and texts.

Each group developed its own strategy for clustering the photographs and identifying similarities and differences across one another's photographs. At times those strategies were unclear and led to moments of tension and frustration among and between the women and myself. This was partly due to the women's level of interest and energy on the day we chose to begin the group analysis of the photographs. (They had been out very late the evening before at a community fundraiser.) It was also due to some of the individual and collective characteristics that influence how the women in this community perceive themselves, their community, and their place in the world. A combination of self-consciousness and a hesitation to allow themselves to be—or to be seen as—vulnerable to the emotions that were generated when we discussed some of the painful events that have deeply affected the women and their community created levels of tension and frustration that were sometimes difficult to reconcile.

One of the groups easily developed a set of themes that integrated their individual photographs and texts into an overall story. They also made room for, and acknowledged, the particularities that each woman brought to the analysis. They developed four categories for their photographs:

"Family, Friends, and Neighbors"; "Physical Environment"; "Other Places" (places outside Belfast that are important to them); and "Education."

The second group understood the exercise differently. Rather than create multiple themes across the prints, the second group collapsed the 20 photographs into one group narrative with one major theme: "Women's Achievements." Yet, as Sorcha presented this group's work, it was evident by their comments that there had been disagreements.

Following, I present an excerpt from a transcribed session that reveals the extent to which different agendas, expectations, and personalities merged to directly influence the direction of PAR and how differences and disagreements between the outsider/researcher and the insider/participants affected the interpretive process and our developing relationship.

Lucy: So is [our presentation] all right, Alice? Or do you want more? Geez, you'll be drawin' blood in a minute.

Winnie: Are we representin' ourselves and our community well? And articulatin' it? Because it's very hard to describe yourself sometimes. You sort of have to get a justification from someone. D'ya know what I mean? I'm askin' you.

Deirdre: We sat around the last [workshop] and we bubbled away and we do it all day, every day. "That's our whole life and there ya go." Now, it's black and white and pink and purple and it's all sittin' on the table. It's different now …now that it's very solid and sittin' there, it's kind of …

Winnie: It becomes immortal, too, and it's completely out of your hands.

Deirdre: And is a bit like a feeling of responsibility more than chattin' the last time.… It's just a different feelin' to be representin' your life to somebody else and how you do that.

Alice: Mm mmm.

(crosstalk)

Lucy: But I'm not, I'm not sayin' that I want you to tell me or to tell us what to do. What I'm sayin' is we have never done this before. You have done it before with workin' with the kids in Bridgeport and puttin' a book and stuff together. We've never done this before. So what I'm sayin' is, ya need to be more clear, to guide us, for us to understand.

Winnie: But I know, Alice, you don't want to do that too much either because you don't want to put your mark on it 'cause it's our community; it's not your community.

Deirdre: I feel as well that somehow we put you in a position because you're Alice, and you're our friend now. And that's the way we want it to be, so we're chattin' away and tellin' you all these things and talkin' to you and whatever and then, we just switch and go like that, "Well, you're the professor. You must know."

(laughter)

Deirdre: And I know that's not very fair and I imagine you must feel it in the position you're in because you have those two roles to fill but we turn them on and off when we want.… So, yeah, it's a different dynamic I think this time around but at the same time, we want kinda guidance. Maybe we're not very nice about askin' for it. We don't do it very well....'Cause it is our story to tell, not yours, if you know what I mean. You're gonna be the teller but it's ours. (Transcripts, March 11, 2001)

After this exchange we had lengthy conversations about how we could be tellers of a collective story in ways that felt comfortable to the group. Lucy wanted more guidance from me. Winnie preferred that I review all the session transcripts and phototexts and present my thoughts on the data to the group: "I need somebody impersonal almost to come and say, 'Right, I've put all this together for ya; all that wafflin', all that crap, and there ya go. And do you agree with that?'" Others in the group felt that they had a handle on the shared responsibility they had to convey a visual and written story that effectively represented their lives.

We never fully resolved these issues. As the project moved along, we continued to grapple with different understandings of how much I needed to guide the group and how much the group needed to guide the process. In so doing, we struggled with how to question and challenged each other about project-related issues. More often than not, we responded to the challenges with sarcasm, friendly banter, and/or by simply ignoring the problem—behaviors that are not the property of the Irish but with which all of us in the group have experience and have used over our lifetimes with varying degrees of "success." These behaviors can be distancing at times. Yet they are behaviors that we forged in our relationships as women, friends, and researchers—relationships where knowledge was created, valued, and shared. It is because we are friends that we can tolerate moments of disconnection—moments that both complicate and enrich my life as a participatory researcher and the women's lives as research participants. As importantly, it is because we can tolerate moments of uncertainty and disconnection that we have become friends, that we have joined one another in creating knowledge in the context of the very humanness that characterizes our relationships.

Although I hope my Belfast friends will someday write their own accounts of our relationship as friends and researcher participants, I realize that most of them do not have the resources, the time, or the desire, to do so (Silverman, 2000). For now, I tell my version of a story—a story that has been constructed out of a creative process that is genuinely productive and purposefully collaborative.

COCONSTRUCTING CHILD LABOR: INDIVIDUAL AND COLLECTIVE STORYTELLING

The example drawn from Chajul traces a perhaps more subtle, less direct, emergence of a third voice—a dialectic wherein indigenous knowledge and academic research strategies inform knowledge construction within relationships across differences (Lykes, TerreBlanche, & Hamber, 2003). Years of previous relatedness and relationship building created a terrain in which collective storytelling emerges through creative play and contributes to the layering of local knowledge, Western psychological theories, and group-based praxis. The story or voice is not that of an individual photographer, a Western researcher, or the photovoice group. Rather, narratives are constructed at the interstices of complex community relations that mobilize and re-situate insiders and outsiders, multiple knowledge systems, and creative practices.

In Chajul 20 women took one roll of 24 pictures once a month for approximately 10 months. Given that most of these women were using a small 35 mm camera for the first time in their lives and that some women were not able to take an entire roll in a given month, the group generated between 3,500 and 4,000 usable photographs. The group identified a different theme each month and each photographer was encouraged to take pictures that reflected the chosen topic as well as of events as they emerged in the community or its neighboring villages. Bimonthly small group meetings provided opportunities for individual storytelling in pairs or small groups, whereas group analyses took place in monthly workshops. Pictures were storied and restoried in each of these contexts.

Once those analyses were completed and tape recordings transcribed, the processes of data reduction and reorganization began. The leadership of the project included Joan Williams, two local Mayan women from the group of 20, and myself (Brinton). We had increasing influence in the data reduction process, although each decision was reported back to the larger group where pros and cons were discussed and debated. In the following text I trace the creation of one of the 56 phototexts presented in the book, *Voces e imágenes: Las mujeres Maya Ixiles de Chajul/Voices and Images: Mayan Ixil women of Chajul* (Women of ADMI & Lykes, 2000). Through my reflections on this process I hope to elucidate how PAR and photovoice served as resources for developing relationships among and between the 20 Mayan women and several EuroAmericans wherein we negotiated contested meanings and generated a third voice. The phototext is neither self- nor other-speak but incontestably the storied lives of women of Chajul and their community.

Chocobanana, a Village Girl, a Child Worker

In a biweekly workshop in September of 1998, Joan Williams recorded the following story, told by Ana, while showing her photograph to the group gathered.

I took a picture of a girl who wanted a chocobanana. She lives with her mother in the village of Agro, one hour from Chajul. There they don't sell chocobananas. So, she asked her mother if when they were in Chajul she could buy a chocobanana.

Her mother did not have any money. She told her that if she wanted a chocobanana she would have to go and sell wood to have enough money. So she gathered the amount of wood that was necessary in order to make her purchase and she carried it to Chajul to sell it. She was offering to sell the wood to Ana. She was 7 or 8 years old. She had to wait to get a chocobanana here [in Chajul]. (Memoria/Group Field Notes, Williams, 1998; Translation from Spanish to English, Lykes)

Ana reported that she had selected this picture to present because she felt badly that she had not bought the child's wood and also because she felt badly for the child because she did not have shoes and was not in school. Joan reported an interest in the human dimensions of the story and its portrayal of rural children's desires.

Given the interest in this picture, it is perhaps not surprising that when we gathered in November of that year for the first of what would be a series of analysis workshops, this picture was chosen from among a large cluster of photographs about children and work. Joan, Juana, the local coordinator of PhotoVoice, and I had worked for several days before this workshop to review over 1,000 pictures (drawn from the four to six pictures that each woman had been presenting in small group discussions). Together we clustered the photographs along what seemed to us to be the salient themes that emerged from the data and were informed by the previous research processes. These included children, work, families, Chajul and its institutions (town, educational, health, religious), and the violence and war, its effects, and peace-building processes. There were between 32 and 64 photographs in each thematic cluster.

When we presented our analysis to the group, the 17 women who participated in this workshop debated our thematic clusters. Some resisted the thematic regrouping of the photographs, preferring the earlier clustering by individual photographers. Our leadership team emphasized the need to reduce mountains of data and engage together in analyzing the pictures and their stories toward generating the collective story we hoped to tell (see Memoria/Group Field Notes, Lykes, 1998). In hindsight it is clear that this debate reflected an ongoing dynamic, a point of contestation throughout our action-research process. Individual initiative and agency was central to the photo-taking process. This was nested within a shared organizational commitment that gave birth to the project, that is, to tell a community story of the violence of war in Chajul and its adjacent villages in women's voices, from their perspective. Equally important to the project was the development of group process and documentation skills that would help strengthen the wider women's organization sponsoring the project (ADMI) and thereby benefiting women and their families in Chajul and its villages beyond the time limit of the research process. Revisiting the storying process documented in my field notes, I noted other instances such as this one wherein individuals expressed personal desires that were contested by others who pressed for collective decision making.

The disagreements described in the previous text were dramatized—a process frequently used to engage creatively with group tensions. Different generations of differently aged women of differing political and religious persuasions enacted what was on the surface a conflict between giving priority to the individual photographer or to clustering the information according to themes that had evolved through the photo-taking process. The dramatization and creative multiplication of the original drama (Pavlovsky, 1990) evoked earlier tensions and created opportunities for remembering loss and rethreading a sense of shared survival, stories that would later inform the group analyses. On a more limited but practically important level, it contributed to a resorting of some photographs and to the group's eventual agreement on several clusters that were described as "working themes." Each woman then individually selected one of these thematic areas in which she wanted to work. Based on these choices we formed three groups, and each group was then asked to identify one picture from the sheets and to analyze that picture. The chocobanana picture was one of these three.

The photographer's initial story about this young barefooted girl was shared with the group. It focused on a young girl carrying wood, who desires a chocolate-covered banana, and it described her need to sell the wood on her back in order to secure money to buy herself a treat. The group generated the analysis summarized in Table 1.

The categories for analysis discussed earlier were developed through a series of workshops. They reflect issues that had emerged over several years, during which we sought to critically understand war and extreme poverty, as well as women's responses to them through dramatizations, drawing, and storytelling. In those creative workshops (see Lykes, 1994, 1999) we explored a range of emotional responses experienced in the wake of war and state-sponsored violence as well as the impact of these experiences on women's self-images. More recently, in the context of photovoice, we discussed cultural and contextual understandings of human emotions, generating lists of Ixil and Spanish words for the many emotions women experienced during the war years and in the current workshop context. I shared ideas informed by my many previous years of work in Guatemala and by psychological theories that emphasize the social embeddedness of self and family. Together we approximated ways of understanding and expressing the profound impact of intergenerational familial and community losses and of the suffering experienced by wider communities and the environment. Through creative exercises the women recovered multiple stories of these losses and explored their consequences in terms of local realities such as extreme poverty, a lack of health care, and a lack of education. Based on this work we identified these six categories (see Table 1) as well as a timeline through which we sought to story the photographs that women were taking and restory them as the community's her-story (*Memoria*/Group Field Notes, Lykes, 1998, 1999).

In contrast to Ana's story about an individual child's desire, the group-based analysis suggests that a school-age child—or school-age children more generally—are forced to sell wood to bring home cash, thereby entering a market economy. In addition, in the taped conversations that were later transcribed, the photographers described their experiences as child-workers that included gathering wood to heat their homes or to cook the family's food but not to sell to generate cash. They noted generational changes in child labor and the deepening impoverishment of their local community due to the war.

Comments about the child's torn skirt, lack of shoes, and dirty face were offered as both indices of parental neglect and of family poverty. Some members of the group were critical of the child's parents, arguing that they should be taking better care of her, interpreting her lack of shoes, torn skirt, and lack of cleanliness as a "lack of proper parental care-taking."

Table 1
A Village Girl

Context	Actors/ People	Actions	Feelings	Thoughts	Reasons/ causes/ Explanations
In our area there is corn and coffee and this girl child is in the path, and along the edge of the path there are clothes hanging on the fence surrounding a corral.	A child smiling, without shoes, *bright eyes; she does not have a mecapal for carrying wood, she is using a small, old piece of headband/ cloth on her head, to carry the wood; it is not well situated.*	She went to gather wood in the woods.	*She seems happy but also tired. We think she might be worried, and sad to not have any shoes.*	*I feel badly seeing a child carrying so much wood.*	She is working because her family does not have sufficient income to support the family. *Many children work to help gather firewood for the family but this child has to sell her wood, her labor, and so has entered into the paid labor force and a market economy. Her father uses a mecapal but perhaps he disciplined the daughter so she is using an old headband instead of a mecapal.*

Note: Italics added to indicate text developed by the group that was not in the initial story told by the photographer. (*Memoria*/Group Field Notes, Lykes, 1998)

Others rejected these attributions, suggesting that structural poverty was the primary causal factor. Women who interpreted the photograph in terms of structural poverty calculated the cost of the child's treat and the money she would get for selling the wood. They concluded that the bulk of the funds she secured would be used to enable the family to buy necessary goods for basic survival. In contrast to the photographer who had assumed that the amount of wood was equal to the value of a chocobanana, other members of the team recognized that the child had gathered wood valued at more than the cost of a chocobanana and interpreted this difference in ways that re-situated the child and her labor. Finally, some suggested that the load of wood was "overly burdensome for a small child" and that the child's labor "deprived her of access to education."

This particular phototext was reiterated in March, 1999. Ana, the original photographer, joined me and another of her colleagues from Chajul, in a U.S. tour in which we spoke of our collaborative PhotoVoice project. Among the pictures presented was the "village girl." Ana told the following story:

The town where we live is an extremely poor place. As you see here we see a small girl. She is carrying a load of wood, of 16 logs and this size [about 10–12 inches each]. And the little girl has, that is, has walked 2 hours to come to the town, as she lives in a village. She said that there were many needs in her family. She asked her mother for 25 centavos [approximately $.05 US] to buy a chocobanana. But 25 centavos is a lot for a family in Chajul and they told the little girl to gather a load of wood and sell it in the town and she could buy a chocobanana. But she told her that she could only spend 25 centavos and she needed to bring the rest of the money to her mother. So that's the story of the girl. (Lykes, Caba Mateo, & Laynez Caba, 1999)

Of note is the combined story that Ana now tells about her picture. She sustains her earlier focus on the child's desire but has added details about the cost of this treat and the surplus funds that would be generated by the sale of the wood. This information clearly came from the group discussion and analysis to which Ana was privy. The story she now tells, representing her community to a U.S. audience, is a combined tale that incorporates her original story about this child and sections of the group's analysis. The emphasis Ana has selected, for the U.S. audience, is the poverty in which children of Chajul live and the challenges they face. As we will see, the knowledge she constructs about audience and voice through this experience is threaded into the final narrative. Attributions of feelings, either those of the child or of the photographer, and hopes for the future, are notably absent in both of Ana's tellings of her story. As significantly, she does not focus on the changes or continuities in children's lives over time or generations.

The narrative or collective story that appears in the book is a combination of Ana's two stories and the group analysis:

A girl went to gather firewood in the bush. We think that she is worried and also sad since she doesn't have any shoes. She's tired from walking so much and her head hurts because she is carrying her load without a *mecapal*,[5] she uses only a rag. Her parents don't have enough money and this is the reason why she brought her wood from the village to the town to sell.

We hope that the girl can have sandals one day, that she can be neat and clean and that she not have to work like this because it's too great a burden for her. There should be work appropriate for children her age and the opportunity for this girl to go to school. (Women of ADMI & Lykes, 2000, p. 61)

The economic conditions in which children labor, both in terms of support for their families and in terms of what is considered an appropriate or inappropriate burden, is emphasized here. Although this story indicates what feelings those analyzing the picture attribute to the child, it is notable that the original desire for a chocobanana is no longer included. Nor are the attributions about parental responsibility, despite the final narrative's emphasis on personal hygiene. The phototext stories this girl-child laborer as burdened by work and as living in a desperately poor family in a community. Framed in a language of hope, it also clearly represents the group's revindications, that is, the authors' protest of overly burdensome and age-inappropriate child labor in their community and their demand for a better future for children that includes schooling and improved material well-being.

Through these multiple iterations we can trace a developing storyline. The singularity of the photographed child was the initial focus in Ana's individual story. It was appropriated by the group who gave voice to the particularities of rural Ixil childhood and poverty and universal claims for children's rights. The final narrative was further shaped by Ana's experiences in publicly presenting to a U.S. audience—an experience she shared upon her return to Chajul and one that concretized the group's understanding of audience and public presentation. The singular desire of a young child (for a chocobanana) was transformed into a collective hope for a better future for all children of this community and beyond. The individual and collective storytelling processes realized through PAR and photovoice elucidate the context in which the child labors and situates her in wider communities. The psychological knowledge constructed in previous creative workshops is threaded into the group analysis through attributions about the child's worries and hurts. Personal desire and singularity have been deconstructed and resituated in a discourse of childhood characterized by poverty, human pain, and children's rights.[6] The voice represented in the final phototext was coconstructed through negotiated relationality both in Chajul and on tour in the United States—relationships that shifted throughout the nearly three years of this project.

HUMANISTIC ENGAGEMENTS IN FEMINIST PAR

Photovoice has been a resource and a catalyst for women who have been historically sidelined in terms of reporting on, documenting, and giving testimony about their lives within communities of war and conflict to write them/ourselves into life. The lenses through which we (Alice and Brinton) access this knowledge are those we are crafting, not only as "us" in relationship to "them," but all of us in relationship to each other. We are codeveloping those relationships over time within the context of a process that enables local participants to restory their lives toward building a better, more just future for themselves and their communities. Perhaps one of the greatest ironies of this work has been the contributions of working the hyphens of insider-outsider, researcher-participant, to sustaining and developing the relationships among researchers and coparticipants described herein.

Although initially outsiders, those positions have shifted as we (Alice and Brinton) have developed as coconstructors with our coresearchers of a third voice. Yet, despite these transposed positions through which we recognize the mediated nature of all voice, the stories generated through PAR processes and photovoices described here are about their realities, not ours. As feminist PAR researchers we humbly recognize our roles as facilitators of processes whereby previously marginalized voices have generated stories within and beyond their communities. Our core-searchers in Belfast and Chajul have mediated the voices with which we speak through this text. We have thus been empowered through the mul-tiple gifts of hospitality, accompaniment, relationality, and friendship with which they have embraced us. While acknowledging their contributions to our knowing, we take full responsibility for this text and for any errors of fact or representation in our work.

Despite unpredictability, death, violence, and the fragility that mark relationships born from survival and struggle, and despite the precarious moments of peace, conflict, loss, and structural change within the com-munities in which we work, we have both maintained and sustained re-lationships that provide comfort, refuge, support, and validation for ourselves as feminists, psychologists, practitioners of feminist PAR, and invited guests in the countries in which we work. We have also accepted the fact that working in communities of struggle means living with the pangs of love, a concern for ethics, a rage at injustice, and a humility that comes from knowing that imperfections—in ourselves and in others—constitute necessary steps in feminist PAR that is constructed in a context of solidarity and a long-term commitment to building a better future.

NOTES

This chapter was equally co-authored by Alice McIntyre and M. Brinton Lykes.

1. In Guatemala, the project described here had numerous other national and international collaborators. María Caba Mateo is a long-time supporter of Aso-ciación de la Mujer Maya Ixil—Nueva Amanacer [Association of Mayan Ixil Women—New Dawn] (ADMI) and collaborated in the final stages of the project and in its publication and presentation in Guatemala. Joan W. Williams, Ph.D., lived in Chajul during one year of the project and provided invaluable technical assistance, group facilitation, and accompaniment. M. Luisa Cabrera Pérez-Armiñan, a Spanish psychologist and community educator, accompanied the data reduction phase of the work and contributed importantly to helping situate local stories within the wider countrywide story. Catherine M. Mooney, Paula Worby, and Megan Thomas contributed importantly to translating materials and Valia Garzón of Centro de Investigaciones Regionales de MesoAmerica [Center for Regional Research in MesoAmerica] (CIRMA), Guatemala, and Víctor Herrera of

MagnaTerra, Guatemala, midwifed the multiple texts and photos into the final form of the book.

2. Monument Road, the community where this project took place, is a small, Catholic working-class neighborhood with about 3,500 residents. People in the Monument Road community have suffered greatly over the past three decades from sectarian violence. Over 50 residents have been murdered and many more injured, imprisoned, or forced to leave the area.

3. Until recently, the Royal Ulster Constabulary (RUC) was the British government's predominantly Protestant police force in the North of Ireland. Under the guidelines of the Good Friday Agreement, the new Police Service of Northern Ireland came into being in November 2001. The objective for the new police force is to have equal representation of Catholics and Protestants. As of this writing, that objective has not been met.

4. Some of the 3,000 parades that occur during the summer months in the North of Ireland take place in highly contested areas—in other words, areas where Catholics protest the decision of the Parades Commission to allow Protestant Orangemen to march through their neighborhoods. Two of the most contested marches on Monument Road are scheduled each year for July 12 and August 12. July 12 is the annual Protestant celebration commemorating the victory over Catholic King James II in 1689. August 12 is another major celebration for the Apprentice Boys, an organization of Protestant men who gather to march in commemoration of the day when 13 Apprentice Boys closed the gates of Derry, keeping King James and his forces from taking over the city.

5. A *mecapal* is a tumpline or headstrap of leather or woven twine wrapped across the forehead and extending toward the back, used to distribute and balance weight of heavy loads carried on the shoulders and back.

6. I (Brinton) am grateful to Juan Jorge Michel Fariña of the University of Buenos Aires, Argentina, longtime friend and collaborator, for careful and persistent discussions about the interrelations of singularity, particularity, and universality, which I hope to have accurately employed in this discussion.

REFERENCES

Bartunek, J. M., & Louis, M. R. (1996). *Insider/outsider team research.* Thousand Oaks, CA: SAGE Publications.

Collins, P. H. (1998). *Fighting words: Black women and the search for justice.* Minneapolis: University of Minnesota Press.

Fine, M. (1994). Working the hyphens: Reinventing self and other in qualitative research. In N. K. Denzin & Y. S. Lincoln (Eds.), *Handbook of Qualitative Research* (pp. 70–82). Thousand Oaks, CA: SAGE Publications.

Lykes, M. B. (1994). Terror, silencing, and children: International multidisciplinary collaboration with Guatemalan Maya communities. *Social Science and Medicine, 38*(4), 543–552.

Lykes, M. B. (1998, August & November; 1999, June) *Memoria*/Group Field Notes. Chajul, Guatemala. Unpublished documents.

Lykes, M. B., in collaboration with Caba Mateo, A., Chávez Anay, J., Laynez Caba, I. A., Ruiz, U., & Williams, J. W. (1999). Telling stories—rethreading lives: Community education, women's development and social change among the Maya Ixil. *International Journal of Leadership in Education: Theory and Practice, 2*(3), 207–227.

Lykes, M. B., Caba Mateo, A., & Laynez Caba, I. (1999, March). Participatory action research and community photography: Cross border collaborations for a better future among Maya Ixil women. Videotaped presentation, Boston College, Boston. Trans. by Lykes.

Lykes, M. B., TerreBlanche, M., & Hamber, B. (2003). Narrating survival and change in Guatemala and South Africa: The politics of representation and a liberatory community psychology. *American Journal of Community Psychology, 31*(1/2), 79–90.

McIntyre, A. (1997). *Making meaning of whiteness: Exploring racial identity with white teachers.* Albany: State University of New York Press.

McIntyre, A. (2000). *Inner-city kids: Adolescents confront life and violence in an urban community.* New York: New York University Press.

McIntyre, A. (2003). Through the eyes of women: Photovoice and participatory research as tools for re-imagining place. *Gender, Place, and Culture: A Journal of Feminist Geography, 10*(1), 47–66.

McIntyre, A. (2004). *Women in Belfast: How violence shapes identity.* Westport, CT: Greenwood Publishing.

Merton, R. K. (1972). Insiders and outsiders: A chapter in the sociology of knowledge. *American Journal of Sociology, 78*, 9–47.

One STEP Group, McIntyre, A., & McKiernan, P. (2000). *At a split second: Visual stories of/by urban youth.* Fairfield, CT: Fairfield University.

Parker, A., & Neal, A. (1982). *Los ambulantes: The itinerant photographers of Guatemala.* Cambridge, MA: The MIT Press.

Pavlovsky, E. (1990). Psícodrama analítico: Su historia. Reflexiónes sobre los movimientos Frances y Argentino [Analytic psychodrama: Its history. Reflections on the French and Argentine Movements], *Clínica y Análisis Grupal [Clinical and Group Analysis],12*(1), 9–45.

Ross, F. C. (2001). Speech and silence: Women's testimony in the first five weeks of public hearings of the South African Truth and Reconciliation Commission. In V. Das, A. Kleinman, M. Lock, M. Ramphele, & P. Reynolds (Eds.), *Remaking a world: Violence, social suffering, and recovery* (pp. 250–279). Berkeley: University of California Press.

Silverman, C. (2000). Researcher, advocate, friend: An American fieldworker among Balkan Roma, 1980–1996. In H. G. De Soto & Dudwick (Eds.), *Fieldwork dilemmas: Anthropologists in postsocialist states* (pp. 195–217). Madison: University of Wisconsin Press.

Wadsworth, Y. (2001). The mirror, the magnifying glass, the compass and the map: Facilitating participatory action research. In P. Reason & H. Bradbury (Eds.), *Handbook of action research: Participative inquiry & practice* (pp. 420–432). Thousand Oaks, CA: SAGE Publications.

Wang, C., Wu, K., Zhan, W., & Carovano, K. (1998). Photovoice as a participatory health promotion strategy. *Health Promotion International, 13*(1), 75–86.

Williams, J.W. (1998). *Memoria*/Group Field Notes. Chajul, Guatemala. Unpublished document.

Women of ADMI & Lykes, M.B. (2000). *Voces e imágenes: Las mujeres Maya Ixiles de Chajul/Voices and images: Mayan Ixil women of Chajul.* Guatemala: Magna Terra. Copies may be purchased from EPICA, Washington, DC. Available from: epicabooks@igc.org.

Wu, K., Burris, M., Li, V., Wang, Y., Zhan, W., Xian, Y., Yang, K., & Wang, C. (Eds.). (1995). *Visual voices: 100 photographs of village China by the women of Yunnan Province.* Yunnan, China: Yunnan People's Publishing House.

CHAPTER 5

The Negotiation of Divergent Demands When Community Research Is Located in the Academy: The Mother-Adolescent Son Project

Jill Chrisp

Although an experience of incongruities in the relationship between the academy and the community is not new for researchers interested in transformative research practices, it is one that remains problematic. The social change-oriented researcher operating from within the academy is caught between opposing forces and motivations. For some this brings the research to a standstill. The researcher can never seem to "get it right." For others, seemingly necessary compromises have an impact on the integrity of the work, and for still others the endeavor for social change becomes focused on the community inside the academy—the academy itself.

The complexity of these contradictions was particularly highlighted for me over a period of six years when I worked in one tertiary institution, was enrolled in a doctoral program in another, and was engaged in research with mothers of adolescent sons. I relied on the first tertiary institution for employment and was obliged to comply with its demands in order to maintain a position within it. These obligations included meeting specified outputs that consumed large amounts of time and energy, being selective about how to spend my time, and prioritizing the formation of alliances that were internal to the institution. The second tertiary institution, within which I was enrolled for doctoral study and from which I was seeking a credential, had the ability to determine the validity of the research, its theoretical underpinnings, methods, findings, and recommendations.

Against a backdrop of these incongruities, this chapter exposes the tensions for researchers attempting to work from within the academy and for the benefit of the community. In this chapter I investigate the hierarchical differentiations that exist within the academy, between types of disciplines, between students and teachers, and between levels of credentials sought and taught. I explore the link between the institutionalized processes of gatekeeping that determine academic production and a materialist analysis of production. I make explicit the conflict between intellectual, political, and personal accountabilities for feminist academics by exploring the claims on us from inside and outside academy constituencies. I suggest that feminist participatory action research (FPAR) has a role to play in the community–academy relationship; that FPAR has the ability to ensure that research carried out from within an academic context maintains integrity to its sources; and that FPAR also has the potential to be a powerful agent for the facilitation of personal, social, institutional, and political change.

For the purposes of this work, the academy is defined as a noncompulsory, tertiary education sector that relies for its existence on the commodification, production, and trading of knowledge. Community is more difficult to define. Community *could* be that which includes all those people who are not engaged in formal academic activity. In this sense, community would be all that the academy is not. However, this definition is problematic. It presupposes that the academy itself is not a community and that the people who make up the academy do not bring with them outside-academy identities. In fact the academy is both—it creates community and is also of the community. Why then are there tensions for the social change-oriented researcher operating from within the academy? Until the dynamics between and within the academy and the community can be understood these tensions will persist.

INADEQUACY OF DUALIST THINKING

While the introduction to this chapter could imply that the sites—academy and community—are fixed and oppositional locations, it is not useful to consider them as such. The creation of a community–academy dualism does not allow the recognition of the varying identities within each location. Social change strategies based on challenging hierarchical relationships created *between* each do not take into account the multiple positionings *within* the community and *within* the academy. That is, the knowledge of a community can be determined by research that is produced by the academy, and yet the prioritizing of research attention may well be decided by specific sectors of the national and international community according to dominant political and economic persuasions.

The pluralities within the positions "community" and "academy" need to be articulated and managed before there can be a possibility of effective relationship between them. The theorizing of "woman" as a marginalized gender offers one narrative from which this discussion can be advanced.

That is, the theorizings and activities of feminists over the past 20 years exemplify the limitations that can result from searching for meaning about positions that are fixed and oppositional.

Up until the late twentieth century, feminists tended to compare the gender category "woman" with that of "man." The "sisterhood" was claimed as a powerful and shared solidarity of women against a male-dominated world. The sisterhood declared women as a homogenous group with the same issues and concerns. In reality the primary characteristics of this sisterhood of women were White, middle class, and heterosexual. Women identifying outside of that category were classed as Other. During the 1980s lesbian and Black feminist activists such as Charlotte Bunch (1987), bell hooks (1995), Audre Lorde (1992), and Adrienne Rich (1986) objected to the position of Other that had been assigned to them. In their challenge to the feminist movement, these feminist activists argued that dualistic paradigms such as male/female, heterosexual/lesbian, White/Black, and working class did not allow the varying identities *within* each position to be evident. This lack of analysis of difference within the category "woman" created the assumption, they suggested, that all women had similar access to power and resources. Clearly all women did not.

Over the last two decades feminists who have attempted to negotiate a way around and between the multiple positionings of women looked to postmodernist theories for explanation. Butler (1990), Court & Court (1998), Flax (1990), Fraser & Nicholson (1997), Lather (1991), Nicholson (1990), Scott (1993), and Wittig (1997), for example, have argued that the perception of woman as opposite to man does not enable the identification of the varieties and limitations of different women's powers and oppressions within particular societies. In their rationalization of gender as a series of social relationships, they maintain that categories are fluid social constructs incapable of constancy.

The postmodern stance has been rigorously debated by those who see activism as reliant on the need to determine fixed positions of power and powerlessness. This group, including theorists and activists such as Bell & Klein (1996), Brodribb (1992), Hartsock (1987, 1990), Humphries (1996, 1997), Stanley (1990, 1997a, 1997b, 1997c), Thompson (1996), and Waters (1996), criticizes postmodern theorists for their inability to identify and name structures of domination, thereby making these structures impossible to challenge. Alternatively, postmodernist theorists challenge those theorists who operate from notions of inequality, most commonly defined within categories of gender, race, social class, and sexual orientation, for not recognizing a multiplicity of existences and for perpetuating oppressive practices by limiting people to categories with fixed notions of opportunity.

While grappling with the either/or of this issue, Razia Aziz claims that postmodern theory does not immunize us from the responsibility to locate ourselves relative to the political movements of our time. "If a feminism of difference is to compete with reactionary forces," she argues, "it needs to incorporate both the deconstruction of subjectivity and the political necessity of asserting identity" (1992, p. 304). Bell and Klein (1996) argue similarly in *Radically Speaking: Feminism Reclaimed*, an edited compilation of works by academics, political activists, and community workers. These works highlight the inability of the postmodernist to forward the feminist cause. They advocate for the alignment of position and the determination of collaboration among specific groups in relation to that position in order to work toward a particular change. This approach assisted me to develop a framework for the research project with mothers of adolescent sons.

The mother-adolescent son research project was initiated in Aotearoa New Zealand[1] in 1995. It aimed to investigate the mother and adolescent son relationship, the interventions to the relationship, and the impact of these interventions on the mother and on the son. Statistics at the time, around the Western world, were indicating that adolescent boys were more likely than any other demographic group to be unemployed, to die from suicide or ill health, to have long-term psychological problems, and to contribute in disproportionately large numbers to crime statistics. One of the explanations for this situation that was gaining currency at the time in Aotearoa New Zealand, Australia, Canada, the UK, and the United States was that the current generation of boys was fatherless. The research sought to achieve several objectives. The first was to create a more in-depth understanding of the complexities of the mother-son relationship. The second was to deconstruct the father-absence phenomenon in order to understand its roots, agendas, and context. The third was to involve women in the research who were experiencing marginalization and disenfranchisement as mothers of adolescent sons. The project explored the situation for mothers of sons, including lesbian mothers, those parenting on their own, and those raising their sons in the context of a heterosexual relationship.

The FPAR model that was chosen to meet the methodological criteria of this project was one that combined two key concepts. It integrated the notion of "difference," as explained through feminist standpoint theory, with a participatory action research process that recognized that the participants brought with them a multiplicity of their individual life experiences into the research act. Decisions about the choice of research tools and techniques were made with the recognition that exploration of the participants' experiences was crucial to the generation of realities against which hypotheses about mothers and adolescent sons could be developed and tested. The research tools and techniques were chosen to enable the participants to describe and make sense of their own realities and to develop their own individual and collective strategies toward change. Accordingly, the research model included a feminist political agenda recognizing that a deliberate outcome of the research processes would be individual and, hopefully, collective change for mothers of adolescent sons.

Methodological considerations involved deconstructing the "participant-empowerment" agenda, examining the insider/outsider relationship of the researcher(s), and negotiating the tensions of a community and social change-based feminist research project that was also located within the academy. The project involved the recounted experiences of mothers of adolescent boys. These experiences were gathered through group sessions, journaling of a participant focus group over a period of four years, semistructured one-off interviews with individual women from throughout Aotearoa New Zealand, and interpretation of almost 400 drawings carried out by boys aged 5 to 18 years of age. The mothers in the participant focus group, while individually and collectively examining their lives and experiences during the project, were also reworking their relationships; relationships between themselves and their sons; relationships between themselves and their sons' fathers; and the myriad other interactions that made up their lives. As a mother of an adolescent son, I was part of the longitudinal focus group and therefore both researcher and research subject.

The longitudinal group came from one geographical location in Aotearoa New Zealand. The population of this provincial district is 65,000. In 1996 the percentage of single-parent families in this district was 23.7 percent of all families compared with 17.7 percent for Aotearoa New Zealand as a whole.[2] The unemployment rate was 9.6 percent compared with 7.7 percent for Aotearoa New Zealand as a whole. Income levels were similar in this district as they were for the national levels. That is, 58 percent of people aged 15 years and over had an annual income of $20,000 or less, compared with 58.6 percent for Aotearoa New Zealand as a whole; and 6.4 percent had an income of more than $50,000 compared with 7.3 percent for Aotearoa New Zealand as a whole. The percentage of people receiving a government benefit was higher than the national average, that is, 22.5 percent compared with 19.6 percent for Aotearoa New Zealand as a whole.

The members of the group ranged in age from late 20s to mid-40s. They had all been born in Aotearoa New Zealand with five identifying as Pakeha,[3] one as Maori, and one as Pakeha/Maori. During the four years of the project, all mothers in the longitudinal focus group were raising their sons as single mothers. Their sons ranged from 7 to 19 years old at the beginning of the project, and all lived with their mothers. Five of the mothers had one child and two of the mothers had three children, two of whom were males. Three of the group identified as lesbian and four as heterosexual. Although all the mothers had various partnerships during this time, only one of the lesbian mothers lived with her partner.

At the commencement of the project, four of the mothers earned an annual taxable personal income under $12,500, two between $12,500 and $35,000, and one over $35,000. Four of the group owned their own houses and three lived in rented accommodation. Four of the group owned cars over 10 years old and one over 15 years old; two relied on pushbikes and public systems for transport. The mothers of the younger boys earned the lowest incomes. The group of mothers involved in individual interviews came from various rural and urban areas throughout the North Island of Aotearoa New Zealand.

Project participants claimed the identity "mothers of adolescent sons." However, identifying ourselves as mothers of adolescent sons did not go far enough. Creating an identity comparison of either "mother of adolescent son(s)" or "other" did not allow for an acknowledgment of diversity *within* the participant group. To maintain integrity with the research process we needed to articulate and acknowledge our multiple identities as mothers of adolescent sons and multiple agendas as they related to the project (Aziz, 1992; Bell & Klein, 1996). Within the group, power relations varied according to familiarity with the project, research ability, varying experiences with sons, and the amount of time and support that enabled involvement in the project. Our identities were grouped, among other things, by ethnicity, socioeconomic status, family structure, age, and sexual orientation. We also came to the project with varying personal objectives. These objectives were clarified during the first focus group meeting. Some of the participants wanted the "outside" community to know that single mothers could effectively raise sons. Some wanted to improve the way they parented their sons. Some wanted a public voice in order that people could become aware of the realities, injustices, and strain of raising sons as single mothers. Some wanted to share issues of raising sons with other single mothers and to discuss their experiences and strategies. I wanted to use the resources and influence of the academy to create a research project that would expose and validate the mothers' experiences and objectives. I also wanted to achieve a doctoral degree. Was it possible to site community-based research within the academy in such a way that the diverging necessities could be managed and that the personal and collective objectives of the research participants could be met?

The following sections address two key challenges that, I suggest, would be shared by researchers undertaking community-based research from an academic context. These challenges were certainly experienced during the mother-adolescent son project as we attempted to maintain the integrity of the research and protect the ownership of the participants. The first of these challenges involves navigating the competing demands of academic output and those of community action. The second involves finding a way to resist the potential colonization of the research by multiple and opposing stakeholders.

ACADEMIC OUTPUT AND PRODUCTION

In my experience, the demands on the researcher who wishes to maintain a footing within the academy are numerous. There seems to be constant pressure to produce outputs that will help us ensure eligibility for promotion or ongoing funding, resist the persuasions of external agencies of control, compete for employment positions, compete for resources, and contend with the privileging of specific epistemologies and methodologies.

Liz Stanley draws parallels between materialist modes of production in Western society and "the academic mode [that] has a particular set of politics and ideology as part of the conditions of its existence" (1990, p. 4). Production and publication are required in order that academics can successfully compete within the academic market, to be promoted and to stay employable. This is definitely the case within most of the tertiary institutions in Aotearoa New Zealand where publication is measured as a job performance output. Evidence of publication is an imperative for a performance bonus, promotion, access to research resources, or in order to continue research activity. The number of publications and where they are positioned in the hierarchy of publication status also impacts the level of personal reward.

A further tension allied with the materialist analysis of production is present in the relationship between the academic and community worlds. Within the capitalist framework, on which the societal structures of modern Western societies are predominately based, commodities increase in value the more scarce they are and the more currency they earn. Competition for professional positions increases the value of postgraduate qualifications. It could be suggested that those who hold these qualifications have an investment in maintaining their scarcity. If knowledge and skill transfer were the responsibility and domain of all people, the academy would lose its ability to monopolize the ratification of specific knowledges and the favoring of those who have these knowledges. Following this argument, it could be alleged that it is not in the interest of the academy to ensure that knowledge and skill acquisition becomes a community-owned and directed benefit—an added challenge for the social change-oriented researcher.

The competition for research funding and support also leaves the academy and the researcher vulnerable to the external funding agencies. Mary Jo Deegan and Michael Hill refer to the effect of external agencies of control, such as professional organizations, collegial networks, and access to resources on academic expectations (1991). In Aotearoa New Zealand, for example, the 1999–2002 Labour Government restructured the tertiary education system. Part of this restructuring was to withdraw government-supplied research funding from all the tertiary institutions in the country where it had been previously distributed on a per capita basis. This funding was combined into a contestable fund from which five Centres of Research Expertise (COREs) were to be created. Seventy-five major applications were received, some from an amalgam of several institutions. Eleven were short-listed. Of the five applications accepted, three involved biotechnological research. I was part of an application involving a consortium of several national and international institutions and community agencies. This application, which aimed to research issues of the whanau/family, was not short-listed and, along with the other unsuccessful applications, will need to compete for private research funding if it is to continue.

It is not only the time and energy required to maintain academic production that is problematic, but also the privileging of specific media in which the work is produced. In other words, the publication source for academic accolade is not the *New Zealand Women's Weekly, The New Zealand Listener,* or even the long-standing Aotearoa New Zealand feminist magazine, *Broadsheet.* Yet it is these sources that were most accessible to the communities with which we as researchers/ participants wished to communicate. For instance, during the project it became clear to us that one of the key findings from the fieldwork was that it is the strength, confidence, and enhanced self-esteem of the mother that contributes positively to her ability to parent her adolescent son and to maintain an effective relationship with him. At the same time, national papers and magazines were covering the visit of a prolific Australian writer, Steve Biddulph, who was maintaining that the most serious problem society faces is that of inadequately raised men. He offered fatherness/father-presence as a remedy for suicide, mental illness, unemployment, drug abuse, and high crime statistics among male youths. The visit sparked a fervor of rhetoric from male liberationists who argued for the reinstatement of the father in the lives of boys. Underlying much of this text was a subtle, and not so subtle, condemnation of the mothers. We recognized the impact that this flood of opinion could have on the confidence of mothers of adolescent sons, particularly on those who were parenting on their own. We wanted to silence the voices or at least mount a media campaign to provide alternative viewpoints. We wrote several letters to the editor of the local newspaper and held interviews with local journalists, but I was focused on writing the dissertation and the other group members didn't have the time, the energy, or the resources required to do much more at that moment. We suffered through our inability to speak or be heard.

In addition to the difficulties facing the participants of the mother-adolescent son project as we attempted to negotiate and even profit from the academy, a further set of challenges faced us. These challenges involved seeking validation from the academy, not only for the awarding of a credential but also in order to gain currency for the research findings.

MULTIPLE ALLEGIANCES AND COLONIZATION OF RESEARCH

Daphne Patai discusses the ethical incongruities of the "dual allegiances" (1991, p.138) confronting feminist academics who use "other" women as subjects of research. The tensions, as she sees them, reside in the contradictions between the obligation of feminist scholars to their academic disciplines and institutions and the feminist objective of transformation politics. She challenges the emancipatory claims of empowering research designs that stem from the academy.

The problem for us academics, who are already leading privileged existences, resides in the obvious fact that our enjoyment of research and its rewards constantly compromises the ardour with which we promote social transformation. At the very least, it dilutes our energy; at the most, it negates our ability to work for change.... [It is not] possible to write about the oppressed without becoming one of the oppressors. (Patai, 1991, p.139)

As further illustration, the following extract is taken from my research journal, written during the mother-adolescent son research project,

I am experiencing the irony of being a community activist involved in academic research. In order to keep up with academic production for this dissertation I find that for much of the time I would otherwise have spent "out in my community" I am on my own reading, thinking, writing. It is difficult when people called to see me, at work or at home, and seem to stay forever. Communication with people is invariably becoming part of the "gathering of information." I seek opportunities to talk with other academics and other students working on doctoral degrees. I want to believe that all the time I am spending on this project is going to benefit mothers raising adolescent sons, the practitioners with whom they will come in contact, the boys themselves, and, in the end, the whole of society. However, as well as being grandiose, I fear this could be delusional. I am concerned that this research will make little or no difference if it is not followed up by accessible and pertinent information useful to families or those who interact with them.

As a result of their experience undertaking research with Maori from within a university environment, Hine Waitere-Ang and Maria Rahui (1998) have developed a model that articulates a three-dimensional continuum of researcher and researched positions. This multiple-position model, I believe, offers a useful framework for research engagement with the community through the academy. At one end of the continuum, Waitere-Ang and Rahui position the researcher who originates from a group as different from the researched and dominant to it. They describe this researcher position as one of *colonizer*, where "the objects of study are cast incapable of analytical understanding of their own lives and the forces that shape them" (1998, p.185). They maintain that accounts of this group undertaken by the "expert" objective researcher are deemed superior to accounts from people from within the researched group. At the other end of the continuum they locate the researcher who is a member of the researched group but who recognizes that the insider position is not homogeneous and does not claim representation. In this position, they maintain, "the knowledge of [insider] groups is more dynamic and diverse than can be encapsulated in any one person or research project" (Waitere-Ang & Rahui, 1998, p. 187). It is from this position that research can result in the development and articulation of new knowledges that are authentic to the researched. A challenge posed by the model that is useful to academics undertaking community-based research relates to the positions between those described above. A growing trend, particularly with social research, is to value the outcomes of a researcher who is an insider to the research group. This is particularly so when the position of the researcher and researched group is underrepresented within the academy. The model highlights the difficulty with the researcher who does not acknowledge the diversity within the research group or does not assert that it is inappropriate to make generalized representation from this group. It is through this process that Waitere-Ang and Rahui suggest that inaccurate accounts, endorsed by the assumptions of insider status, are generated.

Donna Matahaere-Atariki expands on this theme by highlighting the potential of the academic to perpetuate oppressive practices. "In our desire to speak on behalf of our silenced [Maori] sisters, we may be in danger of participating in their continued exclusion" (1998, p. 73). She describes experiences of being perceived by non-Maori as available to speak on, be knowledgeable about, and be representative of any issues that confront all Maori women.

I am not suggesting that we remain silent—this is an abuse of the privilege we accrue as academic women—but in our readiness to speak on behalf of Maori women we must be attentive to those mechanisms of power that allow us to speak yet also distance us further from other Maori women. (Matahaere-Atariki, 1998, p. 73)

Likewise Linda Tuhiwai Smith discusses the impact of the representation and reconceptualization of Maori images, social customs, and stories through formal academic structures. She suggests that the way she and other Maori, "re-present [them]selves to [them]selves and to others, has clear implications for notions such as authenticity and traditional tikanga or customs" (1999, p. 102).

The mother-adolescent son research project offers a further example of potential colonization. As researcher to this project I was involved in parallel activities. First, I facilitated a collaborative research process that had

development outcomes for the participants. Second, I collated and represented the information from the research in a number of public settings.
As a mother of an adolescent son researching the lives of mothers and
adolescent sons, I claimed an insider status. I was more likely to be
regarded as an ally by the participants of the project than someone who
was not a mother of an adolescent male. The participants felt confident to
connect with me as someone who had some experiences in common with
them and who could identify with issues they raised. This connection
facilitated relationships of trust and solidarity and an increase in the level
of disclosure. As I worked to enhance the level of trust the participants
had with me, I was also gathering information that was to contribute to
the dissertation written as a result of the research, a dissertation that
needed to be legitimized by the institution within which I was enrolled in
order to be awarded a doctoral degree. Although the research participants
were aware that the completion of the research and the sanctioning of it by
the academy could highlight their issues, this agenda also impacted the
data gathered. After an interview session, for example, one participant
expressed a feeling that she hadn't been "clever enough," that she hadn't
"given me" enough information to work with. "I have only told you my
story" (5), she said. Another wrote in her journal,

I was so concerned that maybe I was in the group under false pretences and that I
should withdraw. It worries me that I seemed to have gained so much (which was
completely unexpected but maybe hoped for unconsciously) but where are you
with your goal for the project. (April 1, 1997)

These participants did not initially measure the degree of their worth by
their contribution to the project as mothers of adolescent sons but rather
by what they perceived as sufficiently academic. Their statements generated further questions. If the information given to me had been filtered by
a desire to offer something the participants defined as worthwhile, what
had been left out? Were the research "findings" deficient? The comments
of these participants and their implications were discussed in the following focus group session and prompted one of the turning points of the
project.
     Australian action-researcher Robin McTaggart (1998) discusses his
attempts to negotiate the community-academy relationship. Referring to
his experience with Deakin University and the Bachelor College Teacher
Education (D-BATE) Programme Investigating Bicultural Education in
Aboriginal Schools he promotes resisting "criteria which would legitimate
research in academic eyes" and working in a way that will "make research
reporting credible and useful to participants and others" (p. 8). The
D-BATE program may have contributed to change in teaching practice
and knowledge bases among Aboriginal communities in the Northern

Territories of Australia, but it also attracted opposition from several directions. It was challenged by the university for the large amounts of time spent in the project without producing publications, by the Aboriginal teachers for the seeming self-serving motivation of academy-based researchers, and by the Northern Territories Department of Education, which dictated that the department be involved in editing Aboriginal students' work before publication.

Deegan and Hill recognize the tensions for the doctoral student when they write about "the student's search for a professional self" within the "bureaucratic and capitalist milieu" of the institution (1991, p. 325). Although in this article they are primarily discussing the development of the professional writer, Deegan and Hill also note the existence of a powerful structure of authority and legitimization within the academic world. Immunity to this process is difficult, they argue, particularly when endorsement is sought from the institution.

On a number of occasions I found myself caught between conflicting expectations. The feminist theoretical and methodological objectives that were significant to the way I wanted to work included empowering women through individual and social change, involving participants in the research processes, ensuring that participants benefit from their involvement in the project, combining research methods to enhance rigor in the research process, and emphasizing participants' realities and stories within the broader framework of the research issues. To maintain congruency with these principles, I did not want to engage in research *on* mothers of adolescent sons. Rather, I wished to research *with* mothers of adolescent sons. Accordingly, I spent much time searching for research processes and paradigms that were in compliance with the norms of academic legitimacy but would not perpetuate misleading claims of research empiricism and objectivity. The Women's Studies Department within which I was studying did not have a legacy of action research. After having made academic ground during the 1970s and 1980s, women's studies departments in Aotearoa New Zealand tertiary institutions for a variety of reasons were losing their position. In order to regain status within the academy, a number of women's studies departments withdrew from offering undergraduate programs, embraced postmodernism, and disassociated themselves with grassroots community women's concerns. Social action seemed no longer an articulated focus. When the mother-adolescent son research began, no one in Aotearoa New Zealand had completed a doctoral project using action research and only two were being undertaken.[4] Likewise, feminist scholarship was mostly invisible to the New Zealand Action Research Network. This network operated predominantly outside the academic context. Encouraged by the work of international scholars who were theorizing and practicing connections between feminisms and action research, such as Alison Bowes (1996), Beth

Humphries (1996), Shulamit Reinharz (1992), and in the later stages of the project, Patricia Maguire (2001), I was able to develop a research design for this project that I believe has successfully negotiated the conflicting expectations of the community of mothers and of the academy.

FEMINIST PARTICIPATORY ACTION RESEARCH— THE BRIDGE?

The FPAR model used for the mother-adolescent son project combined two key elements. It connected the notion of "difference," as explained through feminist standpoint theory, with a participatory action research process that recognized that the participants bring the multiplicity of their individual life experiences with them into the research act. Decisions about the choice of research tools and techniques were made with the acknowledgment that exploration of the participants' experiences was crucial to the generation of realities against which hypotheses about mothers and adolescent sons could be developed and tested. The research tools and techniques were chosen to enable the participants to describe and make sense of their own realities and to develop their own individual and collective strategies toward change. Accordingly, the research model included a feminist political agenda in the acknowledgement that a deliberate outcome of the research processes was individual and, hopefully, collective change for mothers of adolescent sons.

The findings of the project demonstrate that the mother-adolescent son relationship is disrupted by marginalizing and disenfranchising interventions and that these interventions disempower the mother. The research has shown that a major agent in the incapacitation of the mother-headed family is the lack of adequate resources available. The insufficiency of state support for the family intensifies these difficulties. The participants have also been able to demonstrate that the diversity of family and community structures *can* provide necessary and positive role models for male children. An assessment of the achievement of the participant objectives can be summarized in one of the final discussions of the participant group.

Speaker A: When [Son] does things or his mates do things I notice them a whole lot more I think, than if I wasn't involved in the project.

Speaker B: (author). I'm just wondering if there have been any changes in the decisions that we have made because we have these intimate discussions or because we've been involved in the project.

Speaker C: Not so much changing the way I do things, it's sort of validated what I've been doing, as right for me and my son.... I've been more aware...of how I've coped.

Speaker D: Coming here and talking, helps you to be more objective. I find that...everything's so hectically busy and...I'm working and I'm bringing up kids and all of that. You get smothered by it all...like being washed over by a wave all the time and I can't sort of stand back sometimes and be objective. Coming and talking like this really helps, it really does.

Speaker B: In terms of being able to have a chance to sit back and look at...

Speaker D: Yes, instead of being underneath it all the time.

Speaker A: One of the things I found really useful is that I'm not the only one?...being able to know that it's nothing wrong with me, the way my boy is reacting.... Either I can go under with it and become less of a parent in some ways, or I can try and maintain some strength to be a mother and I actually think that's made a difference to my ability...confidence in my mothering of him. Having the structure here to talk about it has been really, really good. I find myself thinking "I must discuss this with the group."

Speaker C: Yes, I think that was something else that has been good about this process, is that it's been a bit of confidence building, because I didn't feel especially confident in what I was doing after the early days of the separation and it did help me...to believe in myself in what I was doing.

One of the aims of the mother-adolescent son research proposal was that through the project, participants would gain personal and collective insight and in turn help to challenge societal prejudices about the mother-adolescent son relationship, contribute to the construction of new knowledge, and impact current social and political practices. In realizing part of these objectives, participants recognized that an academic tome was not the medium with which to publicly disseminate the research results. To this end, three members of the longitudinal focus group are currently working on an edited anthology of collected stories written by single mothers of sons. A series of newspaper advertisements has resulted in an enthusiastic response from over 30 single mothers, women who wish to be involved.

Another set of cycles in the participatory action research process has begun.

The social change-oriented researcher operating from within the academy is caught between opposing forces and motivations. For some this brings the research to a standstill; the researcher can never "get it right." My challenge is to continue knowing that I am not going to get it completely right. I am still an academic. I still rely on the academy for my living, and I am one of these mothers. My hope is that maybe I will get it more right than last time. For the sake of community participants, the risk of potentially perpetuating deficit analyses needs to be an informed one. The tensions require constant deconstructing, complexities explored and acknowledged openly, and dilemmas made transparent. Along with the search for new or uniquely reworked knowledges, there is an urgent need for a courageous search for and utilization of new research processes.

Feminist participatory action research has the ability to change that which it is investigating by the very act of the investigation. The reflection on this action offers an in-transit redefinition of the worlds in which the participants operate. The act of obtaining knowledge creates the potential for change. When participants are responsible for defining, modifying, directing, and evaluating the research they are involved in, the outcomes can become powerful and far-reaching. This research functions to ensure that specific invisible "groups" of women appear on the political, social, and economic agenda. Perhaps it can also provide a bridge for the social change-oriented researcher working from within the academy.

NOTES

1. Aotearoa New Zealand combines the Maori and English terms for the country. Key terms such as this, rangahau/research, and whanau/family are beginning to be linked in recognition that both are official languages of the country.

2. These statistics have been taken from the Aotearoa New Zealand Census 1996.

3. *Pakeha* is a term referring to White descendents of Aotearoa New Zealand.

4. These two action research doctoral projects were being carried out by Mary Melrose and Pip Bruce-Ferguson.

REFERENCES

Aziz, R. (1992). Feminism and the challenge of racism: Deviance or difference? In Crowley & Himmelweit (Eds.), *Knowing women: Feminism and knowledge.* (pp. 291–305). New York: Polity Press.

Bell, D., & Klein, R. (Eds.). (1996). *Radically speaking: Feminism reclaimed.* Melbourne, Australia: Spinifex.

Bowes, A.M. (1996). Evaluating an empowering research strategy: Reflections on action research with South Asian women. *Sociological Research Online, 1*(1). Retrieved on July 1998 from the World Wide Web: http://www.socresonline.org.uk/socresonline/1/1/1.html.

Brodribb, S. (1992). *Nothing mat(t)ers: A feminist critique of postmodernism.* Melbourne, Australia: Spinifex.

Bunch, C. (1987). *Passionate politics: Feminist theory in action.* New York: St Martin's Press.

Butler, J. (1990). *Gender trouble: Feminism and the subversion of identity.* New York & London: Routledge.

Court, H., & Court, M. (1998). Positioning, subjectivity and stories: Feminist poststructuralist research narratives. In R. Du Plessis & L. Alice (Eds.), *Feminist thought in Aotearoa New Zealand* (pp. 127–137). Auckland, New Zealand: Oxford University Press.

Deegan, M. J., & Hill, M. (1991). Doctoral dissertations as liminal journeys of the self: Betwixt and between in graduate sociology papers. In *Teaching Sociology, 19*(4), 322–332.

Flax, J. (1990). Postmodernism and gender relations in feminist theory. In L.J. Nicholson (Ed.), *Feminism/postmodernism* (pp. 39–62). New York & London: Routledge.

Fraser, N., & Nicholson, L. (1997). Social criticism without philosophy: An encounter between feminism and postmodernism. In D. Tietjens Meyers (Ed.), *Feminist social thought: A reader* (pp. 131–146). New York & London: Routledge.

Hartsock, N. (1987). The feminist standpoint: Developing the ground for a specifically feminist historical materialism. In S. Harding (Ed.), *Feminism and methodology.* (pp. 157–180). Bloomington, Indiana: Indiana University Press & Open University Press.

Hartsock, N. (1990). Foucault on power. In L. Nicholson (Ed.), *Feminism/postmodernism* (pp. 157–175). New York & London: Routledge.

hooks, b. (1995). *Killing rage: Ending racism.* New York: Henry Holt and Co.

Humphries, B. (Ed.). (1996). *Critical perspectives on empowerment.* London: Venture Press.

Humphries, B. (1997). From critical thought to emancipatory action: Contradicory research goals? *Sociological Research Online, 2*(1). Retrieved on December 1998 from the World Wide Web: http://www.socresonline.org.uk/socresonline/1/1/1.html.

Lather, P. (1991). *Getting smart: Feminist research and pedagogy with/in the postmodern.* New York: Routledge.

Lorde, A. (1992). Age, race, class and sex: Women redefining difference. In H. Crowley & S. Himmelweit (Eds.), *Knowing women: Feminism and knowledge* (pp. 47–54). Cambridge, UK: Polity Press in association with The Open University.

Maguire, P. (2001). Uneven ground: Feminisms and action research. In P. Reason & H. Bradbury (Eds.), *Handbook of action research: Participatory inquiry and practice* (pp. 59–69). London: Sage Publications.

Matahaere-Atariki, D. (1998). At the gates of the knowledge factory: Voice, authenticity and the limits of representation. In R. Du Plessis & L. Alice (Eds.), *Feminist thought in Aotearoa New Zealand* (pp. 68–75). New Zealand: Oxford University Press.

McTaggart, R. (1998, November). *Enhancing validity in participatory action research.* Keynote address presented to the New Zealand Action Research Annual Conference. Wellington Polytechnic. Wellington, New Zealand.

Nicholson, L. J. (Ed.). (1990). *Feminism/postmodernism.* New York & London: Routledge.

Patai, D. (1991). U.S. academics and Third World women: Is ethical research possible? In S. Berger Gluck & D. Patai (Eds.), *Women's words: The feminist practice of oral history* (pp. 137–154). New York & London: Routledge.

Reinharz, S. (1992). *Feminist methods in social research.* New York: Oxford University Press.

Rich, A. (1986). *Of women born: Motherhood as experience and institution.* London: Virago.

Scott, J. (1993). Deconstructing equality-versus-difference: Or, the uses of poststructuralist theory for feminism. In D. T. Meyers (Ed.) (1997), *Feminist social thought: A reader* (pp. 757–770). New York and London: Routledge.

Stanley, L. (1990). *Feminist praxis: Research, theory and epistemology in feminist sociology.* London & New York: Routledge.

Stanley, L. (Ed.). (1997a). *Knowing feminisms: Academic borders, territories and tribes.* London: SAGE Publications.

Stanley, L. (1997b). Social transformation? Exploring issues in comparison, development and change. Editorial and call for papers in *Sociological Research Online, 2*(4). Retrieved from the World Wide Web: http://www. socresonline.

Stanley, L. (1997c). Methodology matters. In V. Robinson & D. Richardson (Eds.), *Introducing women's studies* (pp. 198–219). New York: New York University Press.

Thompson, D. (1996). The self contradiction of "post-modernist" feminism. In D. Bell & R. Klein (Eds.), *Radically speaking: Feminism reclaimed* (pp. 325–338). Melbourne, Australia: Spinifex.

Tuhiwai Smith, L. (1999). *Decolonising methodologies: Research and indigenous peoples.* London & New York: Zed Books Ltd; Dunedin: University of Otago Press.

Waitere-Ang, H., & Rahui, M. (1998, November). Presentation to the 1998 Aotearoa New Zealand Women's Studies Association Conference. Palmerston North, New Zealand.

Waters, K. (1996). (Re)turning to the modern: Radical feminism and the postmodern turn. In D. Bell & R. Klein (Eds.), *Radically speaking: Feminism reclaimed* (pp. 280–296). Melbourne, Australia: Spinifex.

Wittig, M. (1997). One is not born a woman. In S. Kemp & J. Squires (Eds.), *Feminisms* (pp. 220–226). Oxford & New York: Oxford University Press.

CHAPTER 6

Doormats and Feminists: Who Is the "Community" in Action Research?

Susan E. Noffke and Marie Brennan

> I have never been able to find out precisely what feminism is: I only know that people call me a feminist whenever I express sentiments that differentiate me from a doormat.
>
> Rebecca West, 1913

In this chapter, we use our experiences in the United States and in Australia as narratives to explore four things: action research, feminism, community, and social justice. Over time, our research and activist projects both have and have not reflected feminist agendas and frameworks. Both of us have been involved for many years in school and community action research efforts with a focus on educational and social justice issues. This chapter is an opportunity for us to reflect together and separately on the resources, experiential and theoretical, that have informed our efforts and the ways in which our work at critiquing and moving beyond critique pushes us to continue to find new resources—feminist and "other"—to address the complexities we find in our various projects.

Our narratives show how our projects have and have not overtly reflected feminist agendas. Yet feminist agendas are an integral part of who we are and the work we do, regardless of whether or not we choose to use that term. In the segments of our conversations, we address the question of the construction of a community in and through action research projects. As we have struggled and continue to struggle, we have tried to find ways to hold the concrete experiences we have as forming a series of small communities, forged through shared struggle. We argue that the "who?" of our community, as well as the "what for?" of feminism and other social struggles, can form the structure of a form of action research that can assist in efforts toward greater social and economic justice. Finally, we seek to outline the kinds of experiences and theories that are needed in order to bring participatory action research (PAR) into more useful intersections with feminist and other social justice aims in each of our contexts.

WHERE AND WHAT ARE FEMINISMS IN OUR LIVES?

Our conversations over the 15 years of our relationship form the basis of this chapter. The parts included here are but a small example of the kinds of conversations that both form and sustain our work. Over time, each of us has constructed a definition in thought and practice of what feminisms mean.

Marie: I do call myself a feminist, and that sliding term has shifted my thinking and practice a lot. When working from within major public institutions, an important strategy in Australian feminism, it is too easy to go along with the dominant ways of working and to marginalize "women's issues," whose structural position is often reflected in the small, short-term-funded special projects of the overall organization. Yet as a teacher, student, supervisor of research, policy activist, senior officer in the Ministry of Education, and, now, an academic feminist, I can see that other women were significant personal and professional resources around which I have built hard thinking, strategic alliances, and collegiality. I came into the public sector at a time when Australian feminist work had already developed the strategy later called "femocrat": moving for senior positions to redefine the divide between public and private and using public resources to address issues seen as important by half the population. By the early 1980s, when I became a middle manager in the state education bureaucracy, there were many women in senior positions, often largely connected to "women's issues" in health, housing, education, and law. The equal opportunity unit of the Education Department was largely framed as working on the education of girls and kept out of mainstream decisions about curriculum or organizational change, for example. The feminist work of the 1970s and 1980s in Australia drew on a wide range of political, economic, legal, organizational, and educational theories, making space both for new theoretical work and innovations in ways of working. The emphasis on "the personal is political" came into my work life largely as making a difference in the ways of working in a bureaucracy. I found Kathy Ferguson's (1984) work on feminism and bureaucracy helpful in hindsight to make more sense of those struggles, both in terms of my own positioning and in thinking about other struggles that have gone on about control of access and expertise in authoritarian, patriarchal organizations. Whether in action research, in policy activism, or in reflecting on major world crises to teach from/with, feminist perspectives manage to provide fruitful questions, unsettling edges to work from.

Sue: I've been thinking a lot about how my work is not, at one level, "feminist" in the sense that the research topics don't reflect the "women's issues" that are part of the political sphere (day care, birth control, advertising's view of women, rape, abortion, etc.). Yet working in education and especially elementary education means that most of the collaborative projects I have been involved in have overwhelmingly involved working with women. It is then not surprising that I have for a long time sought resources from feminist theory, because these are the works that address the kinds of enigmas I have faced, and these readings have provided ways to name and work through them. I still continue to find these resources useful, especially as feminist theory has grown and changed over the 15 years I've been working with it, but it has not been enough. For me, too, it is necessary, but not sufficient. So that's why I've been working on understanding and using Black feminist theory (e.g., Collins, 1998), theories of "whiteness" (e.g., Roediger, 1999), and critical race theory (e.g., Parker, Deyhle, & Villenas, 1999) in relation to action research—because of the many gaps that feminist and other kinds of theory (e.g. neo-Marxist and "postie" things) have left in our fieldwork and in our thinking. Social class, for both of us I suspect, will always be an important category, but, like feminism, class on its own is not enough to explain what we encounter. The thoughts I hear and work through in schools cannot be subsumed under any one theory's big umbrella, especially when the practice is not lived by those writing the theory. So I'm a "doormat feminist"— it's what I get called, but mostly because it's a handy way to dismiss the ideas and the practical goals of any social justice efforts by a White woman, not because I choose to identify myself as one.

COMMUNITY AS A "PROBLEM," NOT A "GIVEN"

In the following five sections, we use conceptions of community as a focal point for thinking about action research, feminism, and social justice. We do so because that is the area in which feminism and action research seem to have most fruitful areas of overlapping traditions; also because it provides a context in which to explore the concrete meanings of social justice in particular situations. In these narrative sections, we note the kinds of theoretical resources that have informed our work and how we chose them to meet the varied meanings of community that emerged. Theory, for us, is a body of knowledge that takes us outside our current range of thought, which gives us new ways of looking at our experiences. While we do hold that theory is not the sole realm of academics, instead believing that people outside the academy also theorize their lived realities, the writings of other academics have often given us a new way to understand our experiences.

Rather than a given, or clearly defined concept, community has become for us a focal point for investigation, a problem rather than a solution. In action research efforts, collaborative work plays a major role. In feminist work, the assumption of, or building of, a community of social solidarity plays a key role. In both, issues of caring and justice have ripened in our understanding of wider social movements.

The Community of the Family as a Starting Point

Marie: As the eldest of 11 children, space and fairness were paramount considerations. At one stage, when I was about 8 and there were 7 children, one of the grumblings was about fair share of household work. Now I think of this as an early sign of "feminism." At the time it was about fairness—everyone in the family benefited from food, cleanliness, and so forth. It was "unfair" that the girls had to do the "inside work"—cooking, cleaning, washing up, tidying—while the boys got to do "outside work"—put out the milk bottles each night and the garbage once a week. Even then, we four girls usually did their work as well—or our parents did.

We girls held a march, complete with placards, songs, and a list of demands, throughout the house and refused to participate in any family work until the matter was resolved. After our parents stopped laughing, they sat down with the boys and listened and discussed the issues with us. As a result, rotation of all jobs became the norm. This early "success" within the family community perhaps led to later "optimism of the will" (to use Romain Rollard's phrase made famous by Antonio Gramsci), our hope that working together could possibly change unfair and oppressive conditions.

Multiple Communities

Sue: Memories are really hard to retrieve and very selective in what we choose to remember (Frisch, 1990), but I do sometimes think about helping to start the first annual conference at my undergraduate college to address feminist issues. A couple of years ago, I noted that the conference is still an annual event, now 30 years later. The "conference" then was really a small group thing: Some of my closest friends around a little table in the student union with a woman who was the state representative for the area. It was really great talking with this woman who spent time with a very small number of college students talking about women in the political arena. Yet even then, my feelings were ambivalent. Feminism was an issue, but my primary involvement was in our small town's version of the antiwar movement. I knew, too, that I belonged to very different communities—the university community and also the town itself as my home community—and feminism wasn't my primary concern. The young men I was dating, my large group of relatives and friends, everyone was dealing with the Vietnam War.... That was much more salient, as was the issue of working class/labor struggles. I wouldn't have talked much about Marxist theory then, but capitalism was and still is a major focal point for thought and action. Even when I intentionally didn't learn to make coffee for antiwar group meetings, it was because my then "boyfriend" made the issue of women a point to think about. Gender wasn't a category to me, despite the rhetoric of the time. It was just a part of who I was.

But even then I knew that gender was something that can't just be forgotten: It is lived most closely. Feminist issues were important; feminist politics had agendas I could share. Birth control, even birth control information, was tightly regulated by the state, and abortion was illegal. Economic freedom was curtailed by laws and business practices that made women decidedly less than equal. Most of the women in the university were middle to upper class, with issues that were not my issues. But we all had to face the same faculty and the same curriculum that left women out. I remember asking an English professor why there were no women authors in the courses. He at first replied, "Because there are none." When I mentioned Doris Lessing, he said, "She'd be too difficult for students to understand."

Membership in a community, when seen from within, is taken for granted. It's only when there is a significant change or interruption that the power lines become visible. It may be that the 1960s were such a time. Each community may have seen those revealed power lines and the boundaries they created and enforced differently. But for me, the changes emphasized how I belonged to multiple communities. Class and gender formed boundaries of communities I at least somewhat understood. Race and national identity were outside those boundaries, rendered invisible by the ways I stood inside of power and privilege. I didn't know that then, nor did I connect this idea to the ways in which doing action research necessitates asking questions from both without and within the communities we "live" in.

Community as a Process, as Constructed

Marie: One of my jobs in the Victorian Education Department gave me the opportunity to put the practices of action research into the "mainstream" by involving teachers, parents, and students as partners in school-based evaluation. The parent activist with whom I coordinated the School Improvement Unit wrote and workshopped across the state with me, working out with local school communities what might suit them and still fulfill the minimal requirements of school self-evaluation that was to replace the work of the previous central inspectors. In doing this, we had to build shared understandings and practices of what participation meant—and what an educational community might mean. Drawing on work in the parents' movement and union activity, the small head office group worked closely with departmental officers, university staff (Kemmis & McTaggart, 1982), and local committees to build our understandings of what might be appropriate practices for us that were congruent with the underlying aims of the program. The work of second-wave feminists in consciousness-raising groups and critiques mingled somewhat uneasily with our representative structure (bringing together representatives of parents, teachers, and education officers from the regions), but it brought in innovative ideas about processes and a concern for inclusion as a basic principle of working together.

In particular, we had to build shared communities of understanding that constantly questioned what our social justice agenda for education might mean and the differing ways in which various parents, teachers, students, and education officers might contribute to its development. If we wanted local participation, but also a statewide perspective, that could not come from a central vision nor by encouraging localism alone. There wasn't much around to help us think this through other than the terms that everyone used—democratic, communal, collaborative, shared, participative. Meetings got on with their tasks, with the additional role of a "critical friend" who helped build into the process a reflection on group processes and their contribution to improved schooling for those students who were most marginalized in our education system. Later, the work of Iris Marion Young (1990) seemed to echo familiar themes in our struggle not to eradicate the differences—across rural and metropolitan communities, in large and small schools, within and across different groups of participants. Each time new people came along, or a new forum brought different combinations, we had to explore what we meant by our commitment to social justice, and how our work as a "community of communities" contributed to it. The process of doing the work was part of the achievement of social justice—a process that struggled with balancing inclusiveness with product, involving as many participants as possible in widening groups with knowledge and shared understandings, even if partial.

The Community of Teachers

Sue: I've spent 30 years working with children and teachers. In my early years of teaching, I did an action research project in my classroom, although I didn't know that's what it was. It didn't have anything to do with feminist issues. I was concerned about the students in my sixth grade class who had limited proficiency in literacy, and so I developed inquiry-oriented units of study that allowed them to participate in the whole class study by adapting the materials and activities to be more accessible. Most of the practice at that time, and even now, keeps such students busy with simple tasks and worksheets instead of deeply engaging them in active study.

For that action research project, my community was very small—the students, my masters degree committee, and me. It wasn't connected to the other activities in my professional life. A lot of those centered on union activities. Some of that work and also the beginnings of my graduate study involved gender issues: Being a woman and a labor negotiator in the early 70s was a bit unusual, and I did a project for a course in which I researched the history of women in teachers' unions. My community then was an alliance of coworkers involved in the labor movement. Except for a short involvement in the unsuccessful effort to pass the Equal Rights Amendment, I have never engaged directly with feminist political action.

My teaching reflected feminist goals to a degree: I worked hard at making mathematics an area of success for girls, analyzing curriculum for gender bias, and things like that. But I had trouble understanding some of the issues that a few of the young girls had around social "cliques." Angela McRobbie's work (1978) was probably the first research I had read that was written from a feminist perspective, meshed with a class analysis. My community began to take shape as one of belonging to a profession that engages in the "gendered labor" (Apple, 1986) of teaching. But theory-reading has played a major role in my understanding of just what that profession entails.

The work of intertwining feminist and especially Marxist feminist theory with the situations I encountered as a researcher has been very fruitful. My dissertation work used feminist theory to examine action research (Noffke, 1990), and other parts of feminist theory were very useful as I tried to explore the dynamics of collaborative research work with teachers (Noffke, Mosher, & Maricle, 1994). In the latter, feminist theory was very helpful in finding a way to build relationships in which we could collaborate to examine the teachers' practice (e.g., Raymond, 1986). I found feminist theory a very useful source for analyzing how to interpret the "teacher's voice" (Noffke, 1991).

But in a later project, the "African and African American Curriculum Project" (Noffke, Clark, Palmieri-Santiago, Sadler, & Shujaa, 1994), I struggled with the dynamics of working with teachers, faculty, and administrators that brought issues of race and racism to the forefront of discussion and practice, trying to find a way to understand what was happening and what my role was in it. With the help of my colleagues in the project, I began to work at what I called "Discovering the Incredible 'Whiteness' of Being" (Noffke, 1994) and began to see curriculum as "racialized text" (Noffke & Shujaa, 1995). That gender and class had been necessary categories, pieces of who I am, but never sufficient, became increasingly clear.

I began to understand how I needed to work at understanding race as a dynamic that shapes who I am, as well as how schooling works (and doesn't). At the suggestion of a colleague, Mwalimu Shujaa, I read works by Carter G. Woodson and W. E. B. Du Bois and then moved on to read some Black feminist theory (e.g., Collins, 1990; hooks, 1990). Later, I read some of the literature on critical race theory in education (Ladson-Billings, 1998; Ladson-Billings & Tate, 1995; Parker, et al., 1999; Tate, 1997; Williams, 1997) and tried to think about how to apply them to rethinking action research (Noffke, 2000). My community became smaller in some ways: The outcomes of this effort have sometimes created distance between me and some colleagues in my university work. But it has also meant that margins have been extended by many, in person and in writing, who continue to help me learn more of who I am as a White woman (e.g., Roediger, 2002) and what it means for my practice as a scholar and activist. In many ways, teaching is my primary community: It is where and with whom I am most "at home." I sometimes wonder why I am most comfortable in this community, as opposed to others to which I belong, for instance within the academy. Is it a social class thing, or is it that elementary schools are staffed primarily by women? I am part of a geographical community, an active participant in the politics of a school and a school district. Is it that I find the shared and active struggle to better understand and improve schools and the lives of the children, teachers, and families who form those communities?

I still find myself returning to feminist theory to understand this part of my community. The community I find in schools is not wholly formed around shared tasks; it is also shared around other kinds of connections, as women, as parents, as social beings. We share food even when we do not share beliefs. The community is "serial" (Young, 1990); we derive unity through the ways in which we can pursue individual and group goals that are responses to our shared material and structural conditions. I am an outsider; I do not share their workplace in full. I do not shoulder their responsibilities. I still struggle to define what I mean by community. My experiences drive my reading of theory; theories help me to frame my experiences in new ways. My community has changed as my self-knowledge has grown. Being part of a community requires self-knowledge in relation to and in relationship with "others." Perhaps the community is part of what I am beginning to call the "public self," the site where we work out our individual identities in relation to a sense of both "public good" and group membership (Noffke, Binkley, Williams, & Kim, 2002).

Community as Temporal, Fluid, Changing

Marie: At Central Queensland University, we sponsored university-wide action research groups to tackle persistent issues facing our regional university and to build research strength. One such project focused on how to improve the appallingly high failure rates of Indigenous students. Put together jointly by the business faculty and the Aboriginal and Torres Strait Island Support Centre, this group was made up largely of inexperienced researchers. Research was problematic on two fronts. First, the Indigenous members of the group were ambivalent about "Whiteman's knowledge," having experienced generations of the colonialist "gaze" as oppressive, but still committed to building more successful participation in higher education, allowing their people's own voices to be listened to and taken seriously. Second, the White members of the group had internalized many "scientistic" assumptions about what counted as research, shared at times by their Indigenous colleagues. Yet there was knowledge there already—knowledge of pedagogy; knowledge of communities and students; knowledge of the university system and its openness to change.

After significant data had been gathered—largely statistical, with some student surveys—the framing of the analysis of the data became a source of major group disagreement. Some in the group insisted that the data told the story and that we needed to leave our "other knowledge" outside—an unknowing commitment to empirical-analytical epistemology showing lack of familiarity with recent debates about research knowledge as always interested and partial. In particular, the kind of contribution made by the Indigenous members was a source of tension. Their knowledge was not seen as "data," gathered scientifically as part of the project, so how could it be admitted into the project? How could White staff learn to listen to the community that actually had the knowledge and analysis, developed over many years of trying to support their young people in the Whiteman's university? Only by staying part of the group, by participating in analysis of data from interviews and surveys, and by showing where their existing knowledge made sense in analyzing that data, were the Indigenous members of the group able to share that knowledge. But it took a long time, and it was a time of angst and fear that history was repeating itself—there was a justifiable fear that once again they had made their community's issues visible to Whites for further intervention.

Research is easily able to become a part of a new form of colonialism, marginalizing Indigenous knowledge (Smith, 1999). There were long debates about what aspects of the group processes would be put into the final report (Anderson et al., 1996a) and what could be written about by Indigenous members in papers (Anderson et al., 1996b) and long discussions about ownership of the data and analyses (Anderson et al., 1996c; Tennent et al., 1996). That most members of the group continued to participate was a tribute to all concerned since not all the learnings were pleasant or easy.

As a latecomer to the group, invited as facilitator and research mentor, I learned much about my own prejudices and unthinking practices of research, my own White privilege, as well as about the need to invent new group processes for surfacing issues that kept the community working across our differences, rather than working towards homogeneity. The work of Iris Marion Young (1990) was a particularly timely reminder of the tendency to assume homogeneous community in our group processes and conflict resolution. Young points to the politics of difference in relation to justice, an issue that both action research and feminism have found as a "sticking point." In this project, one major difference that needed to be negotiated was the type of knowledge that was to be accepted. Academic writing is a static process. The community here is both fluid and open as well as open to change.

THE COMMUNITY AND FEMINISMS

We (Sue and Marie) are still learning. Our autobiographical fragments illustrate many aspects of community. But they also illustrate the elusiveness of feminism in our work. Outside of our own definition, people often define us as feminists. Yet feminism can't be assumed or ascribed. It is in itself not enough, without a range of politicizing theory and practice. Educational action research projects, as well, don't start with an assumed, ready-made community. And the "field" of social justice work, formed by this triangle of action research, feminism, and community, must be seen as constantly changing, even as we hold the center on human life (in these precarious times, *all* life), economic sufficiency, the freedom to think and share new thoughts, and the control over one's own body. Community is *formed* through the work.

We return to our starting points, grounding ourselves even as our lives shift around us. The communities with which we have worked began in our growing up, in our families. Our identities, both as individuals and as members of groups, are grounded in our early lives and have been continually formed and reformed in temporal contexts. The communities, too, are multiple, fluid, and constructed.

Sue: For me, the "doormat" metaphor referred to earlier represents two things. One is as a reminder that as a woman, whether I self-identify as a feminist or not, any actions out of line with the processes and purposes of power and privilege will ultimately result in someone, with however gentle or firm a tread, stepping on me. No matter what issue is behind the challenging action—class, race, or gender—it is the category of gender to which I am reduced most readily. Feminist then is a pejorative, a dismissing label. Yet the doormat is also a reminder that for others—often those feeling oppression along different dimensions—I am one of the pedestrians. As a White woman, I too often still engage in actions that, however unintentional, serve to protect my privilege.

I came to action research, not through the term itself, but through doing a study in my own classroom that allowed me, as a teacher, to let new questions enter into the improvement of my practice. It gave me a sense that what I came to "know" through the act of deliberate, self-conscious study could stand up as "knowledge" in educational debates. But these new questions were ones that fit into already existing frameworks of thought. I challenged educational practice that related to special education, to gender, and to social class, but race emerged only in relation to the few Native American, Asian American, and African American students I encountered in my classroom. I did not see my own Whiteness as part of the issue.

What seems most relevant here is that gender and social class were categories in my educational struggle, but the other categories were not addressed as analytic frames in themselves. Rather, they were spaces to look for curriculum and pedagogy for the Others. They were with me, but not a part of me. They were still doormats I walked on. Action research work became a means for me to change this. My gender and social class identity have helped me to see race and the other social categories in which I hold a privileged position. By that, I mean that gender and class help me to see what I cannot know but what I must strive to learn as my freedom is connected to and interdependent with that of Others. As a teacher, I enjoy a kind of collective identity, a safety in the shared norms of the group. But that group is also part of the system of structural inequality in society. Feminist projects, for me, are important, especially those that emphasize a broad range of identity groups' agendas. But the term is still, for me, an adjective and not a noun.

Marie: In too many projects the community is positioned as the doormat, kept outside the door, away from the action and the research. While not denying the importance of action research for teachers building their professional learning community, one of the less fortunate side effects of increased attention to teacher participation may be the exacerbation of the distinction between the professionals and the Others—the communities that provide the reason for the profession's existence. Researchers, particularly university researchers anxious to gain a project or publication, can walk all over the community in their rush to implement a pet idea or "save" a school. They do not usually do so maliciously, but by continuing to use existing relations of power, they do not make it possible to interrupt those power relations.

"Do-gooder" Whites often make similar mistakes when working across lines of racial difference. We continue to need feminist, antiracist, and anticolonialist perspectives (Moreton-Robinson, 2000; Smith, 1999) to shake up the unthinking practices of everyday research and its power relations. Feminist projects, linked with antiracist research, provide a strong set of resources that continue to disrupt business as usual in the research world, especially when I am stuck in analysis of conflict in research processes or in understanding the framing of projects.

At times, as action research facilitators and as activist educators who are women, we have been able to use our doormat status strategically. Certainly so have some communities: They know the underside of what happens, the things those outside would prefer to ignore or hide, and they keep that knowledge to themselves, sometimes over generations. While principals and teachers, even school board members, may come and go, most communities remain, with their various knowledges, rarely allowed into positions where sharing the knowledge is encouraged or expected.

"Doormat" seems to be a pejorative term: It is passively situated, and people wipe their feet on it to keep the house clean. Yet if we look from the perspective of the doormat, it acts as a gatekeeper to the house, over which people have to walk if they want entry. The doormat's position is also potentially privileged in that it gets to see all of the dirt from underneath—and it also sees that no one entering is clean. Since no one values the doormat much (except perhaps the house cleaner!), it can remain unnoticed, facilitating entry and sharing the dirt of all.

WORKING TOWARD COMMUNITY

In the many projects along our separate and shared journeys, we have noted a number of parallel agendas within some feminist and action research scholarship. What we are interested in is the overlapping and intersecting agendas when both feminist and action research scholarship look to work with and for those most marginalized. Wadsworth (1997) calls this the "critical reference group," whose interests define the criteria for whom the project would work. Feminists and action researchers usually both have a concern with unequal power relations and work to understand the politics of everyday life. Both groups, often calling on quite different resources, understand that self, institution, practices, and community are socially constructed over time, and both aim to work via collaboration and colearning in keeping with commitments to live out ethical principles in the everyday. Both also have considerable bodies of knowledge and self-consciously trace histories showing their evolution as fields over time.

Community issues are especially salient for both feminists and action researchers, both in terms of the ways in which they work and in the definitions of the object or goals of research and practice. There are multiple and diverse forms of action research (Noffke, 1997). By connecting community and action research key learnings, we can see that our preferred approaches to action research emphasize community in a number of ways. In particular, action research focuses on a social practice that has associated with it a historically defined community of practitioners. One of the reasons we prefer collaborative approaches to action research is because social practices are shared. We are usually immersed in them, making it hard to "see" ourselves and our own investments in the current form of practice. Since social practices are recognizable to others in the shared social field, it is hard to change them significantly without a group effort. What often needs to be made problematic is the very definition of the participating community: Who is included and how—and who is excluded? Thus community is both the means of conducting the action research and the object of change.

Feminisms (and here, too, the meanings are varied) also have had many intersections with the practices and concept of community. Early women's group activities in the 1960s and 1970s developed strategies to interrupt what was seen as the dominance of the patriarchal system. Women aimed to develop alternatives to the individualistic hierarchies of patriarchy, both by self-analysis and by new forms of collective organization. In the first two decades of the women's movement, the definition of community was a universal one: women. Women were to interrupt the dominant forms of patriarchy through their communal activities, the first step of which was usually "consciousness-raising"; examining language, habits, forms of interaction, and institutions to understand how patriarchy worked to oppress women. Some women's groups, such as women's health centers, shelters, and rape crisis centers, which were developed specifically to address needs not recognized as part of the public sphere, developed alternative forms of organization (Fraser, 1997). At the same time, other women were active in attempting to alter the character of existing institutions, including government, through policies of equal opportunity, affirmative action, and support for women. The works of Maria Mies (1983) and Frigga Haug (1988), for example, provide graphic evidence of the efforts to understand how oppression can be "unpacked," how identity is formed as gendered, and how institutional forms contribute to unequal power relations.

More recent feminist and action research work through communities has developed from these core efforts but with changing commitments toward a broader definition of the participants in the struggle for more equal power relations. Efforts to legitimate the knowledge of marginalized groups (e. g., McGuinness & Wadsworth, 1991, on participatory evaluation of acute mental health services) have contributed to the building of new understandings of community as well as the specific issue under investigation. Here we start to see on-the-ground work, usually ahead of theorizing, as the wellspring for change. Community activists building on a range of practice traditions in their settings draw on justifications from democratic, feminist, race/ethnic identity, participatory research, their own experience of effective community work, and political theories—

whatever works for them in the community setting. Through such inter-sections, communities build themselves in interaction with pasts, tradi-tions, and current contexts.

ON TRADITIONS AND THEIR INTERSECTIONS

Action research is a way of being in the world that is both about theory and action in and for education. We have been trying in this chapter to bring together four large bodies of knowledge and fields of practice that have often been kept separate in different disciplines: action research, feminisms, social justice, and community. In doing so, we have had to be cursory, even elliptical, in our discussions since our own experience of these fields of practice and scholarship is somewhat sprawling and impos-sible to analyze simply. Our autobiographical stories can be used to illus-trate the ways in which a particular "event" is narrated from largely within one or another field but yet is inextricably bound up with the other three. Sometimes, social justice is the actual "field" of a triangle, shaped by the other three. As each of our senses of community grew, for example, in becoming more involved in race as a category, it changed our understand-ing of social justice. Social justice can be seen as the ethical wellspring from which we derive our commitments to action research, but that, too, is not a static category.

We have each learned about nuanced changes in what counts as injus-tice, especially as they intersect in racialized, gendered, and classed experi-ences of self, of practices, and of institutions. Our experiences are also connected to our readings of, for example, feminist, Black feminist, and critical race theories. Earlier notions of participation, for example, have been altered through a mélange of analyses, including the critiques of rep-resentative democracy and rights-based approaches to justice (e.g., Fraser, 1997; Gould, 1988; Hernandez, 1997; Yeatman, 1994; Young, 1997), through efforts to understand the global in the local, as well as through reflection on experience in feminist organizations such as a women's softball team, a women's choir, or a management team of a Women's Health Center. Our reading, just as much as our participation in activities and projects, tends to be cross-disciplinary, covering at least philosophy, history, sociology, cur-riculum studies, policy analysis, and research methodologies. The older forms of disciplines do not "capture" us or provide any easy "home" for our work, which is transdisciplinary and requires both close engagement with lived experience and quite abstract debates. The "traveling compan-ions" of theory and practice emerge strongly in feminist and action research work, illuminating old debates and bringing new ones to the fore.

How our reading interacts with our practice over time is not something that is transparent to us, even though it is of great interest, especially in looking back and trying to theorize it. By this stage, through participation in separate projects, through regular communication and joint writing with one another over many years, we have not been able to trace clear lines of "causality," from reading to practice, from practice and reflection to reading, from reading to reading, or from practice to practice in action-oriented situations. Often, old reading for one project comes to the fore in trying to understand better our work in another. Or a practice undertaken in one situation reveals its power tentacles only when examined elsewhere. We have concluded that we are neither solely idealist, in the sense of being ideas-driven, nor are we solely activist, in the sense of being practice-driven. For us, one of the joys of action research has been its commitment to both the understanding of and the improvement of practice, giving both precedence rather than simple causality.

Reading and scholarship for each of us emerge from work with our students, from work with community groups, from interactions with each other, and from those "niggling" questions that continue over years. Paralleling or accidentally interrupting our "work-as-usual," participation in the scholarly communities of action research and feminisms has enabled us to raise new questions for projects and ongoing scholarship. Our consideration of community in this chapter is but the tip of the iceberg. We are both doormats and feminists, by choice and by ascription.

REFERENCES

Anderson, L., Brennan, M., Stehbens, C., Alcock, R., Field, P., Luck, J., et al. (1996a). *Whose business is business? The dilemma of participation for Aboriginal and Torres Strait Islander students enrolled in a university business course.* Paper presented to the Aboriginal and Strait Islander Literacy conference, NLLIA Expo, Brisbane, Australia.

Anderson, L., Brennan, M., Stehbens, C., Alcock, R., Field, P., Luck, J., et al. (1996b). *Coming to/going to: Aboriginal and Torres Strait Islands students transition to tertiary education.* Paper presented to the Second Pacific Rim Conference, Melbourne, Australia.

Anderson, L., Brennan, M., Stehbens, C., Alcock, R., Field, P., Luck, J., et al. (1996c). *The Business of researching: Cross-cultural perspectives.* Paper presented to the Human Research Ethics Committee's Institutional Providers Conference "Where to Now," Exploring Cultural Differences in Human Research, Adelaide, South Australia.

Apple, M. W. (1986). *Teachers and texts.* New York: Routledge and Kegan Paul.

Collins, P.H. (1990). *Black feminist thought: Knowledge, consciousness, and the politics of empowerment.* Boston: Unwin Hyman.

Collins, P.H. (1998). *Fighting words: Black women and the search for justice.* Minneapolis: University of Minnesota Press.

Ferguson, K. (1984). *The feminist case against bureaucracy.* Philadelphia: Temple University Press.

Fraser, N. (1997). *Justice interruptus: Critical reflections on the "postsocialist" condition.* New York: Routledge.

Frisch, M. (1990). *A shared authority: Essays on the craft and meaning of oral and public history.* Albany: State University of New York Press.

Gould, C. C. (1988). *Rethinking democracy: Freedom and social cooperation in politics, economy, and society.* Cambridge: Cambridge University Press.

Haug, F. (1988). *Female sexualization: A collective work of memory.* (Translated from the German by Erica Carter.) London: Verso.

Hernandez, A. (1997). *Pedagogy, democracy and feminism: Rethinking the public sphere.* Albany, NY: State University of New York Press.

hooks, b. (1990). *Yearning: Race, gender, and cultural politics.* Boston: South End Press.

Kemmis, S., & McTaggart, R. (1982). *The action research planner.* Waurn Ponds, Victoria: Deakin University.

Ladson-Billings, G. (1998). Just what is critical race theory and what's it doing in a *nice* field like education? *Qualitative Studies in Education, 11*(1), 7–24.

Ladson-Billings, G., & Tate, W. F. (1995). Toward a critical race theory of education. *Teachers College Record, 97*(1), 47–68.

McGuiness, M., & Wadsworth, Y. (1991*). Understanding, anytime: A consumer evaluation of an acute psychiatric hospital.* Thornbury, Victoria: Victorian Mental Illness Awareness Council.

McRobbie, A. (1978). Working class girls and the culture of femininity. In Centre for Contemporary Cultural Studies, *Women take issue* (pp. 96–108). London: Hutchinson.

Mies, M. (1983). Towards a methodology for feminist research. In G. Bowles & R. D. Klein (Eds.), *Theories of women's studies* (pp. 117–139). London: Routledge & Kegan Paul.

Moreton-Robinson, A. (2000). *Talkin'it up to the white woman: Indigenous women and white feminism.* St. Lucia: University of Queensland Press.

Noffke, S. E. (1990). *Action research: A multidimensional analysis.* Unpublished doctoral dissertation. University of Wisconsin, Madison.

Noffke, S. E. (1991). Hearing the "teacher's voice": Now what? *Curriculum Perspectives, 11*(4), 55–59.

Noffke, S. E. (1994, February.). *Discovering the 'Incredible whiteness of being.'* Paper presentation as part of the symposium, "Diversion and subversion: A case study in progress of collaboration between European- and African-American teachers over issues of curriculum (and pedagogical) reform," at the 15th Annual Ethnography in Educational Research Forum, Philadelphia.

Noffke, S. E. (1997). Personal, professional and political dimensions of action research. In M. W. Apple (Ed.), *Review of Research in Education, 22,* 305–343.

Noffke, S. E. (2000, September). *High class theory, working class practice: Issues of community and social justice in action research.* Keynote address, World Congress, 5th on Action Learning, Action Research and Process Management and 9th on Participatory Research. Balarrat, Australia.

Noffke, S. E., Binkley, R., Williams, D., & Kim G. (2002, November). Paper presented at the Annual Conference of the National Council for the Social Studies. Phoenix, AZ.

Noffke, S. E., Clark, B., Palmieri-Santiago, J., Sadler, J., & Shujaa, M. (1996). Conflict, learning, and change in a school university partnership. *Theory into Practice, 35*(3), 165–172.

Noffke, S. E., Mosher, L., & Maricle, C. (1994). The concept of curriculum and teacher research. In S. Hollingsworth & H. Sockett (Eds.), *Teacher research and educational reform. 93rd Yearbook of the NSSE* (pp. 166–185). Chicago: University of Chicago Press.

Noffke, S. E., & Shujaa, M. (1995, March). *Curriculum and personal transformation: Learning, the world and the child.* Presentation at the 16th annual Ethnography in Education Research Forum, Philadelphia.

Parker, L., Deyhle, D., & Villenas, S. (Eds.). (1999). *Race is ...race isn't: Critical race theory and qualitative studies in education.* Boulder, CO: Westview Press.

Raymond, J. G. (1986). *A passion for friends: Towards a philosophy of female affection.* Boston: Beacon Press.

Roediger, D. R. (1999). *The wages of whiteness: Race and the making of the American working class* (Rev. ed.). London: Verso.

Roediger, D. R. (2002). *Colored white: Transcending the racial past.* Berkeley: University of California Press.

Smith, L. T. (1999). *Decolonizing methodologies: Research and Indigenous peoples.* London: Zed Books.

Tate, W. F. (1997). Critical race theory and education: History, theory, and implications. In M. W. Apple (Ed.), *Review of Research in Education, 22,* 195–247.

Tennent, B., Luck, J., Alcock, R., Anderson, L., Brennan, M., Field, P., & Stehbens, C. (1996). Survey instruments for researching Australian Indigenous tertiary students—Action research in action. In S. Leong & D. Kirkpatrick (Eds.), *Different approaches: Theory and practice in higher education, proceedings of the 1996 annual conference of the Higher Education and Research Development Society of Australasia,* Volume 2 (pp. 880–884).

Wadsworth, Y. (1997*). Do it yourself social research* (2nd rev. ed.). St. Leonards, N.S.W.: Allen & Unwin.

West, R. (1913, November 14). *Mr. Chesterson in hysterics: A study in prejudice.* The Clarion.

Williams, P. (1997). *Seeing a color-blind future.* New York: Noonday Press.

Yeatman, A. (1994). *Postmodern revisionings of the political.* New York: Routledge.

Young, I. M. (1990). *Justice and the politics of difference.* Princeton, NJ: Princeton University Press.

Young, I. M. (1997). *Intersecting voices: Dilemmas of gender, political philosophy, and policy.* Princeton, NJ: Princeton University Press.

PART III

Ethical Dimensions and Meanings of Feminist and Participatory Action Research

Reclaiming the F-Word: Emerging Lessons from Teaching about Feminist-Informed Action Research

Patricia Maguire

To be quite honest, I really know nothing about feminists, except for the allusions that they were kind of psycho …

Lester,[1] White, male K-12 educator

I have been a feminist since I entered the world from my mother's womb.... My feminism in the early years consisted of refusing to do dishes because that was what girls were supposed to do. I hated dresses....

Jennie, part Chicana, part White, female K-12 educator

I'm drawing a blank. I really don't know. I have had very limited exposure to feminist theories in a formal setting such as the university.... I think it would be hard to live with a feminist. Why? Because you would always have issues on the table.

Drew, White, male, K-12 educator

I was for the movement when it started but I believe that it was taken too far.... I struggle with girls who want to be part of an all boys baseball league. I find it appalling that at one time they wanted to share the same locker room....

Dawn, White, female, K-12 educator

When I began teaching a newly developed action research (AR) course for educators, it became clear to me that the graduate students, who were full-time teachers, counselors, or school administrators in their own right, had a wide range of opinions about and experiences with feminism and feminists. Certainly they were entitled to their diverse views and opinions about feminism.[2] My concern was with how their opinions had been formed and how those opinions consequently shaped their action research. Many of these educators had little previous exposure to feminist theories, literature, scholarship, or even information about the most recent women's movement of the 1960s and 1970s. I began to examine how I could help the graduate students explore and expand their understandings of feminism, with its multiple perspectives and focus on activism and, in particular, gain insight into how feminism could inform their action research.

In this chapter, I describe how students' changing understandings of feminism began to influence and inform their educational action research projects. I identify emerging lessons about teaching feminist-informed action research. I share insights, developed in part with course participants, for the long-term project to build a sustainable, transformative approach to teacher action research informed by feminism. This project is a work in progress that I invite you to join.

My interest in learning more about how to teach feminist-informed action research grew out of my long-term concern with the relationship between feminism and action research. The continued and often unexamined androcentric worldview of much action research limits its transformative possibilities. Without meaningful inclusion of feminist issues, visions, and voices, there are gaps between action research's liberatory purposes and everyday practices. What would action research, uninformed by feminism, liberate us from and transform us into?

Similar to some of the other contributors to this volume, I first got involved with participatory action research through development work in U.S. and Third World settings (Maguire, 1978; Maguire, 1987). Like myself, many contributors to this volume are now university faculty members in schools of education. Through university work, I have been involved with some of the most marginalized and isolated people within U.S. public education—that is, classroom teachers and K-12 students in poor communities. This connection brought me to classroom-based, teacher action research, a traveling companion of participatory action research.

This volume is a testament to action researchers' work informed by feminism. Unfortunately, there are also many action researchers who do not come to their AR work with a grounding or interest in feminist or gender issues (for discussions of this see Brydon-Miller, Greenwood, & Maguire, 2003; Maguire, 2001). This is particularly worrisome among veteran action researchers who are situated in universities where they teach action research courses.[3] To complicate matters further, few faculty members teaching AR courses have appointments in or close relationships with women's studies departments. My own university does not have a women's studies major, courses in women's studies, or a women's studies department. University faculty members teaching action research courses work in diverse departments and are often separated from other action researchers by the artificial boundaries of academic disciplines. Examining how to promote feminist-informed action research through teaching is important to the transformative intentions of action research. As bell hooks asserts, "The classroom remains the most radical space of possibility in the academy" (1994, p. 12).

BACKGROUND AND CONTEXT

Over the past 14 years, a small group of colleagues and I have been developing an extended university graduate education center in a resource-poor but culturally rich and spiritually diverse rural area in northwest New Mexico. High on the Colorado plateau, the Gallup Graduate Studies Center (GGSC) is an off-campus component of the Western New Mexico University (WNMU) School of Education. The main campus of WNMU in Silver City is located 256 miles south, by single-lane road, from the GGSC. It is one of three small state-funded regional universities. With fewer than 3,000 students each, the three regional universities offer undergraduate and masters, but not doctoral level, programs. The northwest quadrant of the state, with high Native American and Hispanic populations, has been historically underserved by state funded higher education. No four-year university is located in northwest New Mexico.

Annually the WNMU-GGSC serves nearly 400 working educators and mental health professionals from northwest New Mexico and northeast Arizona. GGSC graduate students are primarily full-time workers engaged in part-time graduate work on nights and weekends. Some students travel over a hundred miles one way on rural roads to take classes after completing their long days as classroom teachers, school or agency counselors, or administrators. Many of our students are required by state regulations to be enrolled in a university teacher education program because they are teaching on "substandard" licenses. That is, although they have university degrees, they have not previously been trained or state certified as teachers, counselors, or administrators.

As working educators, many GGSC students are demoralized and exhausted by the threatened takeover of so-called "failing schools" by the New Mexico Department of Education or state-approved private management corporations and the subsequent implementation of school corrective action plans. They feel pressured by the state emphasis on the results of high-stakes, standardized tests. The process of identifying failing schools and developing corrective action plans is shaped in part by the Bush Administration educational initiative, *No Child Left Behind* (U.S. Department of Education, 2002). As new educators employed on substandard licenses and taking required university teacher education courses, most GGSC graduate students hope to leave each university class with practical strategies to help them survive the next day in their classrooms.

However, they also want to understand and take action to confront the larger issues of entrenched poverty and deep racism that shape their students' lives and their educational experiences. New Mexico is ranked as one of the five worst states for children in the United States. Our county, McKinley, is ranked third poorest in New Mexico for children under 18 (Annie E. Casey Foundation, 2002). As educators, GGSC graduate students work with some of the poorest children and families in North America. In addition, many work in Native American communities, racing against time to stabilize and restore their indigenous languages (Cantoni, 1996).

Three years ago, when the GGSC started a teacher education masters program for teachers working on waiver or "substandard" licenses, my colleague Julie Horwitz and I committed to a long-term project to develop and support action research as part of the program.[4] Compared to some teacher education programs, we are newcomers to the project of integrating action research into teacher education. We were inspired to do so by the work of action research advocates at the Cornell Participatory Action Research Network, the University of Illinois at Urbana-Champaign School of Education, the University of New Mexico-Albuquerque School of Education, Boston College School of Education, and other universities. We are committed to action research that is well connected to its radical roots and envision an approach to action research where teachers and students are coresearchers whose roles include the creation of knowledge and advocacy for more democratic, caring, just, and safe schools (Burnaford, Fischer, & Hobson, 2001; Noffke & Stevenson, 1995). As we began the process of developing a local critical mass of teacher action researchers and a university support system to nurture local action research efforts, we realized that we needed to start with smaller-scale, classroom-focused inquiry. We arrived at this conclusion because many of the educators enrolled in our program do not feel that they are positioned yet or have sufficient allies to initiate school-wide action research.

After teaching the action research course for two semesters, I realized that I had to teach students about both action research and feminism if I was to have any hope of promoting feminist-informed action research. The GGSC action research development project is embedded in our teacher education curriculum, through which we strive to engage students with issues of race, culture, gender, and social class, for example. With student involvement, we are working to continuously develop curriculum that helps educators meaningfully examine the dynamics of historical, structural, and individual power, privilege, and oppression and address the full range of equity challenges in public education.

I decided to include materials and activities through which students could systematically and intentionally examine and expand their understandings of the diversity of feminism and potential applications to their action research. The overall purposes of action research within educational settings include improving one's own practices, improving one's understanding of those practices, and, ultimately, improving or altering the setting in which one practices (Cochran-Smith & Lytle, 1995). The students in the AR course were all developing an action research project to reflect on and improve their practices as educators (Zeichner & Gore, 1995). It was important for me to engage in and model the very process I was asking students to carry out through the AR course. My starting point was to critically reflect on and improve my own teaching practices, curriculum, and setting—specifically to further explore how to promote feminist-informed action research through teaching.

In the next section, with students' informed consent,[5] I draw from our work and analyses to describe our journey of learning and teaching about feminist-informed action research. I have drawn emerging lessons from reflection and analysis of my journals, students' journals, students' course papers and assignments, short questionnaires, students' in-class comments, anonymous course evaluations, additional student feedback, and conversations with students and colleagues.

START WITH WHERE THEY'RE AT. WHERE ARE THEY?

If I hoped to expand students' understanding of feminism and how it might inform their action research, I had to first get some sense of what they believed, as did they. At the beginning of the semester, I asked students to share, via two different formats, what they knew and felt about feminists and feminist theories, scholarship, and issues coming into the AR course. I also asked them how they thought feminism might inform their action research.

I developed a short, four-question survey to help gauge students' prior exposure to feminism. The first question asked students whether or not they had taken women's studies, feminist studies, or gender studies courses and why or why not. The second question asked whether or not they had been exposed to feminist concepts, issues, or scholarship outside of such courses. The remaining two questions asked students to self-rate their knowledge about feminist theories, scholarship, or issues and their knowledge of how feminist theories or concepts might inform their action research projects. The class consisted of 20 students: 12 women, 8 men. Only 40 percent (8 students) reported having taken any women's studies courses. Two of those 8 students were men. Even among those 8 students, most rated their knowledge of feminist concepts and scholarship as low. Indeed on a four-point self-rating scale, 15 of the 20 students considered themselves to have little or no knowledge about feminist theories, issues, or research.

Students were also asked to write about their current views about feminists and feminist theories, research, and issues. What did they know, think, or feel about these topics? As the students' responses at the beginning of this chapter indicate, they came to the course with a variety of views and experiences.

Not surprisingly, the graduate students who had taken women's studies courses during their undergraduate work were more positive about the women's movement and feminism than those who hadn't. For example, Rose, a White female teacher who had taken two women's studies history courses, noted, "I had always thought that the women were the backbone behind all these men doing great things but I had never really thought about the fact that many women were heroes in their own right." Stephen, a White male teacher who had taken several women's studies courses, wrote, "I understand that feminism...is not a set of beliefs or action that is solely relegated to females. Males can adopt many feminist attitudes and work to correct inequities.... I can understand how feminism might intersect with action research by providing an avenue for certain previously absent voices to be vocalized." Jennie, the only student who had taken three women's studies courses, observed, "I feel the struggle of being a woman in a still overwhelmingly male-centric society.... I struggle...yet find myself keeping my mouth shut too many times...losing that voice that I have worked so hard to cultivate."

Students' views of feminism were also informed by their life experiences. Luke, a White male teacher, commented,

My wife, sister, mother, and grandmother have all felt the inequities of our male dominated culture. I have long been amazed at how blatantly women have been systematically discriminated against in the work place, home, and even in government...Why men have a phobia about competing with women and use their positions of authority (is) to assure an unequal playing field for their buddies.

Their views were also influenced by culture. Shawndene, a Diné (Navajo) woman, wrote,

As a professional woman, I find it a challenge to be a career woman and still live a life that is according to our traditional view of women. I admire Navajo women that are professionals and still can play their traditional role as a wife and mother.

Regardless of their prior exposure to feminist scholarship, which was minimal, or feelings about feminism, 16 of the 20 students indicated that they had very little to absolutely no understanding of how feminism might inform their action research projects. The action research course would have to help students develop knowledge about both action research and feminism.

SELF-REFLECTION AND EXAMINATION OF
MULTIPLE IDENTITIES

During the first two semesters that I taught the AR course, I asked students to brainstorm categories of personal identities. They were most comfortable discussing categories such as family, occupation, hobbies, or geographical location. It took some prodding to get them to consider the gendered, raced, or classed aspects of their identities. Even then, some students still had little experience examining the power, privileges, strengths, and struggles connected to their multiple identities or with examining the intersection of one's multiple identities with differing opportunities, choices, privileges, or inequities in U.S. education.

By the third semester of teaching the AR course, I approached multiple identities differently. Students needed shared language for discussing identities and a structured, safe space within which to grapple with their varied experiences of their multiple identities and implications of their identities for their work as educators and action researchers. I created a visual framework with various categories of identities already listed, including race, gender, ethnicity, culture, and class as well as space for less political identities. The diagram provided a framework for students to begin jotting down notes about their multiple identities. Students read a series of articles from *Readings on Diversity* (Adams, Blumenfeld, Castaneda, Hackman, Peters, & Zuniga, 2000) as well as Peggy McIntosh's work, "White Privilege: Unpacking the Invisible Knapsack" (1998), which provided additional ways to conceptualize one's identities. Students kept a reflection journal to promote their own process of making meaning from the readings, activities, and class discussions. They shared copies of their journals with members of small discussion groups. Reflection and conversation facilitated deeper conversations about issues of privilege and power linked to identities. Tab, a White male, noted,

This hit me very hard. I have never thought about the advantages of going to school, or watching TV shows where most of the people looked like me, most of the time.... While I may not knowingly have taken advantage of these privileges, I have nonetheless benefited from them.... It is something that white people do not want to admit or even acknowledge.

Exploring connections between multiple identities and privileges was challenging, yet most students engaged in intense conversations. In response to the readings and discussions, several of the men openly acknowledged their defensiveness at feeling "targeted" as White men. Yet many stayed engaged. Matt, a White male teacher, later wrote, "The truth is that I think about these issue rather infrequently.... Growing up in a blue-collar, working class town never felt like much of a privilege.... I have to understand the message and not get so defensive."

The articles (Adams et al., 2000) provided common language and concepts that helped shape students' written reflections and shared discourse on power and privilege of various identities. As Stephen noted, "For me, one of the most challenging aspects of trying to live as an ally comes from keeping the results of my privilege in the forefront of my thinking.... How does the challenge of redefining maleness look?" Students' journal writing and conversations also promoted the practice of self-reflection, or reflexivity, which is an integral part of both feminist practice and action research. Jennie wrote,

I think on my own experience of being ready and willing to deconstruct the society I live in, without taking into account my own place in that society and the privileges that are inherent wherein my identity and self is situated. One of the first steps in action research must be the practice of reflection.... I am moving away from the urge to blame student deficiencies for classroom failures towards an examination of the way that my own practices are either promoting or dissuading success.

Rose offered this insight:

Criticizing or reflecting upon someone else's performance is a simple matter compared to self reflection. I had not considered using this [AR] project to be critical of myself. I had depersonalized the project and targeted the system....I have become a creature of this reflection habit.

Self-reflection on the privileges and oppressions connected with multiple identities wasn't effortless. Matt, who revealed that he really hadn't previously thought much about his multiple identities—particularly Whiteness or maleness—or about feminism, noted:

I do blame myself—but I blame others as well.... Make this [feminism] meaningful to me. So do not blame me, teach me. I watch sports and I am male. I could use a little help.... I am sure that I have the privilege of ignoring gender relations because I am male....This is truly endlessly complex. To restructure my thinking is to somehow reshape the entire structure of my life up to this point.

Jennie summarized the connection between self-reflection and the students' work as educators.

Educators doing action research must be ready to incorporate constantly shifting knowledge bases and see this as positive....The classroom is not an isolated arena. Educators cannot escape the workings of sexist, racist, classist constructions. Human beings work and live in these classrooms everyday, and they carry all of things as baggage. It is not left at the door.

Through reflection activities and small group discussions, students also explored the web of oppression (Collins, 1991; hooks, 1989) and the interlocking nature of oppression, that is, the intersection of race, culture, class, spirituality, and other identities. Likewise, they explored the nature of privilege. In addition to feminist scholarship, students also read selections on critical race theory (Parker, Deyhle, & Villenas, 1999) and Diné philosophy (Benally, 1994), which helped students link issues of race, culture, gender, and class. Some students explored how sexism manifests itself in traditionally matrilineal Native societies. Some students explored the intersection of gender and class. Lydia, a White female teacher, observed, "I have been looking at how I never felt sexual discrimination. I think my class status has enabled me to do whatever I have wanted in life, thus avoiding the roadblocks that are commonly set against women."

Jennie summarized it well:

I am realizing that part of the strength of action research is that it can be a challenge to the standard ways of thinking. It is a constant re-examination.... Our identities, and our definitions of these identities, whether conscious or subconscious, affect classroom interaction and ultimately AR projects.... I am beginning to see the argument about the interconnectedness of subjugation. Really, if the social construction of gender and the dichotomized roles between male and female were truly challenged, then all structurally imposed power relationships would be re-framed as well, like dominoes.

To help students synthesize, summarize, and share their insights from the various multiple identities activities, I gave them oversized sunglasses with which to create "Multiple Identities (MI) Lenses." They were asked to create glasses that symbolized how their varied identities influenced their world views and developing action research. Their presentations were powerful visual representations.

Jennie noted,

The MI project can be a way [of] focusing on the way that power is manifested through that critical lens. Focusing on the way that power is manifested within and outside of the identities that we inhabit like comfortable old shoes. Or uncomfortable new clothes.

MEN IN THE FEMINIST STRUGGLE

Students' responses to the opening questionnaires and writing prompts indicated that they were, on the whole, more familiar with mass-media representations of radical, separatist feminist perspectives. Within the time constraints of a one-semester action research course, I wanted to introduce students to a diverse slice of feminist theories and perspectives, including Women of Color and profeminist men. I shared a selection of articles from Schacht and Ewing's (1998) *Feminism and men: Reconstructing gender relations,* including bell hooks's (1998) "Men: Comrades in struggle." Men are not the enemy according to hooks, and her invitation to men to shoulder responsibility for ending sexist oppression resonated with many students, both men and women. After reading hooks, several male students wrote about rethinking masculinity. Some explored how they unwittingly reinforced or challenged gender stereotypes and rigid social-ized roles in their classroom interactions and curriculum. Lester observed,

In my classroom I don't notice if I treat boys and girls differently. In fact I have never given it any thought.... Now that I look back, I do tend to be very domi-nant.... I suppose it is my core belief, subconsciously what a male is supposed to be.... It is typical for males to puff their chest out, use their bigger frame, and loud voice to get what they want.... I am really sending a message to both genders that is wrong. The girls may perceive that men are supposed to be strong and a women should fear them and become subordinate. Boys may perceive this is what it takes to be a man and try to be dominant and controlling. As a teacher I need to be aware of not doing these manly things of sticking out my chest and using my size to get my point across.... It works and is easy.... I can be quite intimidating to people, except other men.

He continued,

I should be using a more nurturing approach with the boys and girls.... I am quite ashamed that I didn't recognize this before. Hopefully I can be a good role model for my male students.... Make them aware of the gender biases that are occurring in my classroom and in my community.

As the course progressed, he specifically identified the need to be attentive to gender issues in his action research project.

Several of the men saw themselves as capable of change and growth, as capable of being role models for a new kind of man for their students. Some of the male students began conceiving of themselves as "advocating feminism" (hooks, 1998). Luke wrote, "If we do not accept responsibility for changing them [injustices] then we are definitely part of the problem. I want to be part of the solution."

Many of the women likewise affirmed a need for an alliance between men and women in the feminist struggle. Meg, a White teacher, wrote, "Without women, men don't have a chance of understanding feminism. Alienating yourself from them won't help." Sharee, another White teacher, observed,

Feminism should not exclude men, in fact it is writing its own death knell if it does because in order for the world to become a more balanced place, men will have to give up their power, their male superiority or privilege.... Masculinity is a practice rather than an attribute of men.

However, the women kept the pressure on, expecting their male col-leagues to act, not just talk. Maria, a White administrator, noted, "Men must prove themselves as feminist. Males must do more than advocate feminism. They must be politically active."

PRAXIS: FEMINIST THEORIES INFORMING ACTION RESEARCH

As the course progressed, students began making direct linkages among their multiple identities, feminist theories, their everyday experiences as educators, and their own developing action research projects. The process of praxis—linking theory and practice, knowing and doing, was well underway. Students began articulating how feminism was informing their action research and work as educators.

For her action research project, Maria was promoting teacher inquiry groups at her school to replace the traditional model of administrator or school district-imposed staff development. She wrote:

Many boys grow up believing feminist values are not part of the real world. As educators, we need to offer safe environments to both genders to nurture their inner selves. Often, the girls' needs are met while the boys are left to deal with things on their own. Last week I had two boys in my office crying. The male teachers suspected something was wrong so they sent the two young men to me. I suspect they did not know how to deal with things on their own.... Perhaps male teachers should go through some staff development dealing with these sensitive issues. This could be addressed in our Teacher Inquiry groups."

Meg, whose action research involved students setting their own goals for reading improvement, wrote:

I suppose I could start trying to influence this in my classroom and through my action research by picking up on those little comments that lead to bigger issues, female lack of self esteem and/or male superiority. I can also be aware in my process of grouping to make sure there isn't any combination of students that would lead to dominance...be aware of the actions of the male students who might be moving toward an attitude of superiority.... I think males acquire these attitudes from their male role models and if we try to change this we need to start with their influential relationships.

The students became deeply committed to the action component of their evolving AR projects. They wanted to make a difference in their students' lives by examining and changing their own teaching practices and school settings. Among some of the students, there was a thirst for meaningful strategies and curriculum to fight gender injustice in concrete ways in their own classrooms and AR projects (for example, Blezard, 2002). Jennie wrote, "AR is a challenge to closely examine aspects of the self and then figure out how closely those beliefs are being manifested as action within classroom walls."

Exposure to scholarship by feminists about feminism began to replace mass media sound bytes. Reflection on actual feminist scholarship began to have an impact on students' teaching and action research projects. Meg wrote,

My idea of feminism was that it was a bunch of radical, arrogant, middle class, antagonist women who burnt their bras and hated men. For the most part I'll bet that's what the majority of people think when they hear the word.

She continued,

I have been thinking about how I interact with my students and also how they interact with each other in regard to our attitudes and expectations toward gender.... When there is a mess to pick up it's hard to get the boys in the class to clean up. If I don't know who made the mess, a female student always volunteers to clean up. I'm going to make it a duty in my classroom...that the responsibility is equal. No more girls cleaning after boys.... I don't know how this informs my action research but it does inform me of necessary changes in the classroom.

Jennie, whose action research project involved increasing students' engagement by improving her own organizational skills and clarity as a teacher, wrote,

What I am watching out for as I embark on this action research is my attitude towards the males in my classroom. Since I have such tense and wounded feelings associated with gender in American society, I must be careful not to project those emotions onto the classroom. I can see myself pinpointing the boys in the class for behaviors that are forgiven in the girls. Teenage boys tormented me in my youth and I must be careful not to bring the agitation of that into my relationships with students.

Lester, whose action research project involved improving his effectiveness at teaching math, wrote:

I could see how action research could have a focus on correcting young men that use their unspoken privileges to dominate the young women in the classroom.... Take five or ten minutes and talk about these issues.... Being a white male, I need to let the girls speak and encourage them to question, respectfully, and allow their voice to be heard. I can encourage them to do well in mathematics.

Early in the semester as students began reexamining feminism based on reading actual feminists' work, Matt wrote:

I need to learn how to incorporate feminism in my AR and I am not sure how. My goal is to develop methods that are racially and sexually unbiased. I am spending a significant time processing the information and trying to make it relevant to me.... I want to use the information to develop unbiased curriculum in my language arts classroom and to eventually promote feminism.... As I form curriculum, I want to include as much of this [feminist ideals] as possible.... I have a chance to do something positive from the start.

As the semester progressed, Matt asked new questions and developed new expectations of himself. His action research project, begun as an effort to more closely align his class curriculum to district standards, evolved. He articulated an understanding of the importance of incorporating works by women and People of Color in his language arts curriculum. He asked of his curriculum, "Whose voice is heard or not? ... This alone does not limit oppressions (Harro, 2000). There still remains the problem of representation.... Whose voice is heard in school materials?" Focused on including more diverse voices in his classroom, he concluded,

This has to be the most important part of AR and feminist research. Voices have to be given to those who have not previously had one.... This can be done through reading about multiple perspectives and life experiences and most importantly translating that into giving a voice to the children in my classroom.

Lydia, a teacher whose AR was focused on improving the interpersonal skills of students through cooperative learning groups, commented,

I need to look at the way students are working together and how they are treating each other. I find a lot of my students need to learn how to treat each other, before they can work together. I think my AR project relates greatly to the ideas of feminism and the importance of the groups instead of the individual.

Lydia continued,

Prior knowledge of the gender gaps helps me better understand roles being demonstrated in cooperative learning. For example, I have collected data comparing two cooperative projects we have completed in class. There are stark differences between the roles girls play in mixed-gendered groups versus single-gendered groups. Female leaders emerged in the single-gendered groups, whereas they stayed in the periphery in the mixed-gendered groups. Without previous knowledge of this phenomenon, I may not have recognized such patterns.

Drew, whose action research project involved exploring what teaching strategies might increase student participation and improve student civility in his classroom, began to wonder,

How do traditional gender roles affect the climate of civility in my classroom? ...What can I do to become more aware of these forces acting on me and my students? ...Through my teaching, how can I create a classroom that ensures fair and equal treatment for all my students?

Even students who did not embrace feminism found that some aspects of feminism might inform their action research. For example, Dawn shared her journey: "The word feminism or feminist brings up feelings of dislike in me. I have never seen feminism from the view of these articles before. It was always in the form of trouble makers...(but) the classroom is a good place to address the equality for all people."

In response to feminist critique of assigning roles to each gender, she noted,

This ...caused me to stop and think about the validity of being assigned roles.... None of this is taught outright but through innuendo and social acceptance.... I must be careful not to assign (gender) roles and to allow my students to grow into the people they can be.

By asking students to make direct connections among feminist scholarship, their multiple identities, and their AR projects, both the men and women began to examine the gendering mechanisms at work in their everyday practices as teachers and hence their action research. Grappling with feminist language and concepts, which were new to many students, was important to this endeavor. Matt, who had written, "Exposing mechanisms is the part I need the most help with," asked in class, "Ah, exactly what *is* a mechanism?"

At the end of the semester, students made a presentation on the progress of their action research projects, including which theories grounded their work. In his presentation, Matt told the class, "If you had told me three months ago that I would be standing up here including feminism in my action research, I would have laughed...." Another student yelled out from the back, "You did laugh." At that, we all laughed in recognition of how far we had come together, exploring how feminism could inform action research. Not all the students included feminist theories in those that informed their action research. A few students left the class as suspicious of feminists as they entered. However, on a short questionnaire given at the end of the class, 16 of the 20 students indicated that, in comparison to the beginning of the course, they had a stronger understanding of how feminist theories or concepts could be used to inform their action research project. Their stronger understanding was evident in their consideration of how students' or faculty members' gender might influence the particular teaching practice or learning phenomena they were exploring. Their stronger understanding was evident in the evolution of their questions and increased inclusion of and respect for their students' voices. Their understanding was evident in their increased awareness of their own gendered, classed, and raced identities as action researchers and teachers.

EMERGING LESSONS

The lessons that emerged from our semester together seem remarkably simple. To engage in feminist-informed action research, action researchers have to have some grounding in feminist theories and scholarship written by actual feminists—not from mass media sound bytes alone. Likewise, they have to critically examine their own multiple identities and implications for their action research. Despite hundreds of women's studies programs in universities around the world, many of the graduate students in my class found it possible to complete their undergraduate university experience without any meaningful engagement with the diversity of feminist scholarship. While I cannot make any grand generalizations based on their experiences, my hunch is that this is not unusual. At the beginning of the semester, students with less previous direct exposure to feminism were more likely to emphasize the failures of feminism with little understanding of any of the ways they had personally benefited from the struggles of real feminists taking concrete collective actions. Again, mass media and university curricula that ignore or minimize feminist contributions and achievements create a view of feminism as a failed, irrelevant movement. None of this is to deny the struggles of feminism to be inclusive and diverse. As Stephen realized,

The aims of feminism should not be viewed as wholly separate and unique from other attempts to improve the quality of life. The challenge lies in viewing the action research pursuits as an extension of the same impetus for the change of the feminist movement. In my particular research focus, improving peer-peer interactions, constructing a non-competitive forum for male-female communication sits at the heart of the [AR] study.

A tenet of feminism is that people grow and develop in relationship (Miller, 1986). I saw again how important it is for teachers and students to work together as a community of learners willing to grapple with the tangled web of oppressions and privileges that make personal and structural transformation such darn hard work. I was humbled by our shared vulnerability. This is not easy work. I admire those students, educators in their own right, who were willing to examine deeply held beliefs and to try new ways of thinking about gender, sexism, and oppression and new ways of being an action researcher. For some the task was more painful and scary than for others. We questioned, we disagreed, and we pushed each other. Margaret, a White teacher, noted, "Like my students, I too must struggle to change the status quo and to become a more reflective learner, educator, and feminist. After all, the beginning of a journey begins from within." Just as "critical friends" are helpful to action researchers, they are helpful to action researchers stretching to expand their feminist understanding of experience. Stephen wrote, "I need to regularly assess my own social and political baggage. This is where working with a group of like-minded educators... would be extremely helpful in revealing personal biases and unchallenged beliefs that I might yet be aware of within myself."

There are lessons here for me as a teacher educator as well. The failure of teacher education to adequately address gender equity issues is well documented (Blackwell, 2000; Sanders, 2002). The failure of teacher education to adequately address racism as well as the meaning and privileges of Whiteness within the context of multicultural curriculum is likewise documented (McIntyre, 1997). As my colleagues and I work with our students to review and revise the teacher education curriculum, we have to scrutinize how our curriculum can be ever more inclusive and diverse to help us all confront power, privileges, and oppressions. We are traveling companions on a journey of how to do collaborative action research in service to social justice. Knowing and learning are important but not sufficient. Always, we are challenged to take action, however imperfect. When all is said and done, feminism is about action: collective politicized action. This story focuses on our semester together learning about feminism and how it can inform our action research. I initially planned the trip. After all, students didn't come to me and ask to learn about feminist-informed action research. They came to the course hoping to learn enough to engage in classroom action research required during their nine-month practice teaching. In the beginning of the course, I asked them what they wanted to learn about action research and structured those needs into the course. But I asked them for their help to learn more about teaching feminist-informed action research. They taught me that it's important to unapologetically own my feminist values and beliefs while allowing them that same space to own their values and beliefs. Journalist Paula Kamen wrote, "A natural response is to change the word feminist to a word with fewer stigmas attached. But inevitably the same thing will happen to that magical word. Part of the radical connotation of feminism is not due to the word, but to the action. The act of a woman standing up for herself is radical, whether she calls herself a feminist or not" (1991, pp. 50–51). Many times throughout the semester I wondered if it would not have been easier to quit using the term feminist and instead talk about the marginally less threatening topic of gender equity. But I was not ready to give up on reclaiming feminism. A place for that reclamation is the university classroom, my everyday context.

In conclusion, it remains impossible for action research to be a transformative approach to knowledge creation until action researchers learn more about feminism, with all its diversity, critically examine their own multiple identities and implications for their work, and open up to feminist voices and visions. The only route to feminist-informed action research is directly through feminism, the "movement to end sexism, sexist exploitation, and oppression" (hooks, 2000, p. 1).

NOTES

1. All student names are pseudonyms. The first time a student is quoted, his/her racial/ethnic and gender identities are included. For subsequent quotations, only a student's pseudonym is used.

2. I recognize the multiplicity of feminisms. However, I use feminism in the singular for smoother reading.

3. See, for example, the organizational affiliations of editorial board members and contributors to this volume, to Reason and Bradbury's (2001) *Handbook of Action Research*, and to the journal *Action Research* (2003).

4. Until fall 2001, action research was not offered as a stand-alone course at WNMU, main campus or Gallup. Instead, limited information about AR was included in other courses. For example, Libby Quattromani wedged information about action research into a curriculum course for administrators. She spearheaded the inclusion of AR in the educational leadership program. My experience teaching and training action researchers had been primarily through visiting work at other institutions. (See, for example, Maguire, 2001.) To teach an action research course at my university, I had to create it and have it institutionally approved by the university Graduate Council. In fall 2001, on an experimental basis, I offered the first explicit action research course at the university. With support from my School of Education colleagues in Gallup and Silver City, by April 2002, I was able to get a permanent AR course approved.

5. At the beginning of the semester, I explained to students that I was engaging in a classroom-based, teacher action research project in the context of the course. In addition to discussing the project, I distributed an informed consent letter in which I sought students' permission to participate in the project while taking the AR course. I wrote, "As a teacher of action research, I am interested in learning more about my own practices. Specifically, I want to explore what I can be doing to facilitate action research seminar students' deeper understanding of feminism(s) as one of the many theories that informs the field of action research." I explained the voluntary nature of the project and stressed that their agreement or disagreement to participate would in no way affect their grade or treatment in the course. Nineteen of the 20 students gave me their consent to use their class work and comments in the project. In previous classes I obtained student consent to participate in similar projects.

REFERENCES

Adams, M., Blumenfeld, W., Castaneda, R., Hackman, H., Peters, M., & Zuniga, X. (Eds.). (2000). *Readings for diversity and social justice: An anthology on racism, sexism, anti-semitism, heterosexism, classism, and ableism.* New York: Routledge.

Annie E. Casey Foundation. (2002). Kids Count 2002 Data Book On Line. Retrieved December 28, 2002, from http://www.aecf.org/cgi-in/kc2002.cgi?action=

ranking&areatype=&variable=ncr&year=1999&highlight=New1Mexico&x
=41&y=7.

Benally, H. (1994). Navajo philosophy of learning and pedagogy. *Journal of Navajo Education, 12*, 23–31.

Blackwell, P. (2000). *Education reform and teacher education: The missing discourse of gender.* Washington, DC: American Association of Colleges for Teacher Education.

Blezard, R. (2002). It takes a man. *Teaching Tolerance Magazine, 22*, 24–30.

Brydon-Miller, M., Greenwood, D., & Maguire, P. (2003). Why action research? *Action Research, 1*(1), 9–28.

Burnaford, G., Fischer, J., & Hobson, D. (Eds.). (2001). *Teachers doing research: The power of action through inquiry* (Second Edition). Mahwah, New Jersey: Lawrence Erlbaum Associates.

Cantoni, G. (Ed). (1996). Stabilizing indigenous languages. Flagstaff: Center for Excellence in Education, Northern Arizona University. Retrieved December 28, 2002, from http://www.ncela.gwu.edu/miscpubs/stabilize/intro.htm.

Cochran-Smith, M., & Lytle, S. (1995). Foreword. In S. Noffke & R. Stevenson (Eds.), *Educational action research: Becoming practically critical* (pp. vii–viii). New York: Teachers College Press.

Collins, P. H. (1991). *Black feminist thought: Knowledge, consciousness, and the politics of empowerment.* New York: Routledge.

Harro, B. (2000). The cycle of liberation. In M. Adams, W. Blumenfeld, R. Castaneda, H. Hackman, M. Peters, & X. Zuniga (Eds.), *Readings for diversity and social justice: An anthology on racism, sexism, anti-semitism, heterosexism, classism, and ableism* (pp. 463–469). New York: Routledge.

hooks, b. (1989). *Talking back: Thinking feminist, thinking black.* Boston: South End Press.

hooks, b. (1994). *Teaching to transgress: Education as the practice of freedom.* New York: Routledge.

hooks, b. (1998). Men: Comrades in struggle. In S. Schacht & D. Ewing (Eds.), *Feminism and men: Reconstructing gender relations* (pp. 265–279). New York: New York University Press.

hooks, b. (2000). *Feminism is for everybody: Passionate politics.* Cambridge, MA: South End Press.

Kamen, P. (1991). *Feminist fatale: Voices from the "Twentysomething" generation explore the future of the "Women's Movement."* New York: Donald Fine.

Maguire, P. (1978). *Evaluation of guidance & counseling services 1977–78.* Kingston, Jamaica: Ministry of Education.

Maguire, P. (1987). *Doing participatory research: A feminist approach.* Amherst: Center for International Education, University of Massachusetts.

Maguire, P. (2001). Uneven ground: Feminisms and action research. In P. Reason & H. Bradbury (Eds.), *Handbook of action research: Participative inquiry and practice* (pp. 59–69). London: SAGE Publications.

McIntosh, P. (1998). White privilege: Unpacking the invisible knapsack. In E. Lee, D. Menkart, & M. Okazawa-Rey (Eds.), *Beyond heroes and holidays* (pp. 79–82). Washington, DC: Network of Educators on the Americas.

McIntyre, A. (1997). *Making meaning of whiteness: Exploring racial identity with white teachers.* Albany: State University of New York Press.

Miller, J. B. (1986). *Toward a new psychology of women.* Boston: Beacon Press.

Noffke, S., & Stevenson, R. (Eds.). (1995). *Educational action research: Becoming practically critical.* New York: Teachers College Press.

Parker, L., Deyhle, D., & Villenas, S. (Eds). (1999). *Race is ... race isn't: Critical race theory and qualitative studies in education.* Boulder, CO: Westview Press.

Reason, P., & Bradbury, H. (Eds.). (2001). *Handbook of action research.* Thousand Oaks, CA: SAGE Publications.

Sanders, J. (2002). Something is missing from teacher education: Attention to two genders. *Phi Delta Kappan, 84*(3), 241–244.

Schacht, S., & Ewing, D. (Eds.). (1998). *Feminism and men: Reconstructing gender relations.* New York: New York University Press

U.S. Department of Education. (2002). *No child left behind.* Retrieved December 28, 2002, from U.S. Department of Education Web Site, http://www.nochildleftbehind.gov/index.html.

Zeichner, K., & Gore, J. (1995). Using action research as a vehicle for student teacher reflection. In S. Noffke & R. Stevenson (Eds.), *Educational action research: Becoming practically critical* (pp. 13–30). New York: Teachers College Press.

CHAPTER 8

An Examination of Collaborative Research in Light of the APA Code of Ethics and Feminist Ethics

Angela Shartrand and Mary M. Brabeck

This chapter explores the ethical concerns that arise within collaborative research in psychology and discusses the limitations of the American Psychological Association's Code of Ethics (2002) in resolving those tensions. We reflect on the ethics of research collaboration by drawing on two contrasting ethical perspectives: feminist ethics and traditional psychological research ethics. First, we discuss the nature of collaboration within some feminist and all participatory research and present ethical concerns unique to collaborative research. Second, we describe feminist ethical perspectives in feminist psychology and philosophy by drawing from recent work on feminist ethics in psychological practice (e.g., Brabeck, 2000) and the foundation of feminist theory and research (e.g., Worell & Johnson, 1997). Third, we examine the American Psychological Association's Code of Ethics (2002) regarding research with human participants and describe the limitations of the code regarding collaborative research. Finally, given the limitations of the APA Code, we suggest ways that a feminist ethical perspective can guide collaborative research.

THE NATURE OF COLLABORATION IN FEMINIST PSYCHOLOGY AND PARTICIPATORY RESEARCH

It has been said elsewhere (e.g., Crawford & Kimmell, 1999a, 1999b; Worell & Johnson, 1997) that feminist psychological research is characterized by multiple methods, theories, and subjects. Thus, we acknowledge that not all feminist research in psychology involves collaboration. Some feminist psychological researchers (e.g., Hyde & Linn, 1986; Lott, 1985) employ many of the methods of traditional, objective science (Harding, 1987). From a positivist perspective, traditional researchers in psychology typically direct the questions, methods, and analyses with minimal input from participants. While we recognize that there is a strong tradition of work in feminist psychological research that is not collaborative, issues related to power within the research context make it incumbent on feminist researchers to attend to the ethics of collaboration, even when they choose more traditional methods (Brabeck & Ting, 2000). As Grossman and colleagues (1997) note, all ethical feminist researchers try to develop "a research process that does not create an exploitative or oppressive relationship between researchers and study participants, for the community in which the participants live, or for the group carrying out the research" (p. 81). The groups on which feminist researchers (Crawford & Kimmel, 1999a, 1999b) tend to focus—women and children—have been at risk for exploitation because of patriarchy and sexism, or have been ignored in psychological research (Crawford & Kimmell, 1999a, 1999b; Grossman et al., 1997). This requires that feminist researchers strive to address the power inequities that give rise to such abuses in research.

Regardless of the methods they employ, feminist researchers strive in a particularly self-conscious way to minimize the potential for abuse of power. This can occur by making the "researcher/participant" relationship more egalitarian, more collaborative, or by making power inequities explicit (Brabeck & Brown, 1997). Feminist researchers who have tried to address the power inequities in the research process often have done so by collaborating with participants and communities. Such collaborations may involve participants in problem definition, question formation, method of inquiry, data collection and analysis, reporting results to various audiences, and in action research projects, taking action based on the findings.

Why Collaborate?

Collaboration in research has been promoted by participatory and feminist researchers for a variety of reasons, all of which relate to ethics. Each of these reasons for collaboration will be discussed in detail.

1. *Collaboration can address the exclusion of marginalized groups and individuals from knowledge generation.* Recognizing that women, People of Color, and other marginalized groups have historically been excluded from the process of knowledge generation (Fine, 1992; Harding & Hintikka, 1983), feminist researchers have sought alternative ways to include diverse individuals and groups in alternative forms of research. These researchers (e.g., Brabeck, 2000; Brydon-Miller, 2001; Grossman et al., 1997; Maguire, 1987) argue that research participants must participate in knowledge construction for more inclusive knowledge development. Instead of assuming that individuals and groups can be treated as the Other and

studied objectively without bias, feminist researchers assume that every person brings his/her experiences, assumptions, and expectations to the research process (Brabeck & Brown, 1997).

2. *Collaboration can ensure that research reflects the needs and concerns of the communities in which it takes place.* Feminists who do collaborative research assume that knowledge is socially constructed and socially mediated by more powerful individuals and groups (Brabeck & Brown, 1997). In other words, individuals and groups who have the power to construct knowledge create social realities that subsequently influence how all people perceive their experiences. They address this imbalance by involving participants in the planning and implementation of research projects, thereby increasing the likelihood that the knowledge developed in the process adequately reflects the realities of all stakeholders and is useful to all groups. Thus, marginalized groups must collaborate actively in identifying the problem, developing questions, and reflecting on research results so that the process of knowledge development and the knowledge itself can be complete.

3. *The process of collaboration can be mobilizing.* Collaborative researchers (both feminist and not) encourage collaboration in the research process for a number of reasons. First, one of the goals of participatory action research is to develop knowledge and to achieve social justice for individuals and communities (Fals-Borda & Rahman, 1991). To do this, the individuals and communities must be involved in the process of defining the problem, researching it, and developing strategies or interventions to address the problem. Second, the process of collaboration itself can mobilize individuals and groups that are typically excluded from such processes (see essays this volume). Thus, researchers can achieve one of the important goals of feminist and participatory research, transforming society, by empowering individuals to take control of change within their own environment.

Ethical Issues that Result from University-Based Research Collaborations

University-based research teams usually involve skilled individuals with common research tools, attitudes, and goals. Traditional research projects do not engage participants in the research, but they do involve students and researchers of varying levels of expertise and power. Such diversity (and power inequities) may lead to ethical dilemmas that include (but are not limited to) issues such as authorship on professional publications, professional development opportunities (e.g., presenting research and traveling to conferences), financial compensation for working on a project, and the types of tasks that are allocated to different members of the team (e.g., photocopying versus data analysis and report writing). When teams include students who leave a project because they graduate, a question arises about how long one must continue in the research, which may be ongoing, in order to be given credit or authorship.

Feminists who do collaborative research self-consciously examine power inequities to ensure that the processes among research team members are ethical. For example, regardless of their status in a research project, all researchers must concern themselves with their levels of competence and avoid undertaking tasks for which they are not adequately trained. This is particularly important when this poses risks to the individual research participants and community members (APA, 2002). In addition, more senior members of the research team should ensure that less experienced members have opportunities to develop such competence when it is possible. To not do so would counter feminist ethical goals aimed at achieving empowerment through the development of skills and knowledge (see following section on feminist ethics). Thus, both feminist and participatory researchers must walk the difficult line between sharing knowledge and expertise without asserting superiority or unreflexively using power against anyone who is subordinate because of status, gender, race, individual differences, and so forth.

Ethical Issues that Arise from Collaboration among Individual Research Participants

Both feminist and participatory researchers collaborate with individuals who have special expertise. For example, feminist and participatory researchers have collaborated with victims of domestic violence (e.g., Maguire, 1987), Maya women in rural Guatemala (Lykes, 1989a), and urban youth (McIntyre, 2000). Collaboration among individual participants differs from collaboration within the university-based research team, though similar issues may arise in terms of power dynamics and varying backgrounds among researchers and participants. From the university-based researcher's perspective, such differences center on association with the work, differences in research skills, and commitment to knowledge generation (often the university researcher's goal) as distinct from knowledge utilization, gaining access to resources, or problem solving (often the community-based researcher's goal) as distinct from meeting educational goals and fulfilling degree requirements (often the student researcher's goal).

From the participants' perspective, differences might involve time available for the work and financial remuneration for doing the research (it is, after all, the university-based researcher's job to conduct research). Participants may distrust both community and university members of the research team or their motives and might not perceive the relevance or usefulness of the research to their concerns and goals.

Collaborative researchers work with all stakeholders to make explicit, to the degree possible, how individuals will be involved with or engaged in shaping the questions, interpreting responses, producing the results, developing action plans designed to improve conditions, and evaluating the extent to which the outcomes and processes are successful. Collaborative researchers may find it challenging to invite participants to engage with the study without coercing or pressuring them to do so. Involvement in a research project can be empowering, draining, and in some cases, can pose risks to one's physical, economic, or psychological well-being. When marginalized groups are empowered, they can become political voices for change; their activism may lead to reactions that result in suppression, greater scrutiny by law enforcement agencies, or negative reactions from bosses, spouses, and colleagues. An ethical researcher attempts to antici-pate such potential negative outcomes of collaboration and tries to inform participants of these risks.

All psychological researchers should provide enough information to potential participants so they are aware of the anticipated effects of col-laborative research (both positive and negative) but must also make the project seem both doable and attractive. Specifying the degree of risk may be very difficult when working in war zones (Lykes, 1989a), with urban youth (McIntyre, 2000), with abused or neglected populations (Fine, 1992), or with fragile or vulnerable individuals (Fine, 1992). In fact, such effects are not often foreseeable.

In terms of benefits to individual nonuniversity-based participants, researchers should think beyond monetary compensation (though this is also important to make explicit). Both feminist and participatory re-searchers ought to consider other benefits to individuals—not only from the researchers' perspectives, but more importantly, from the participants' perspectives. That involves including them in defining the outcomes expected and desired. While it is true that developing skills and gaining experience through a project itself (e.g., developing a community newspa-per to identify what the community issues are; reducing HIV infection by implementing a community based hotline, etc.) could result in improved jobs, income, social status, or access to other important resources, this is not a guaranteed outcome of research participation.

Furthermore, it is important to note that there is no guarantee that par-ticipants will agree with researchers on the benefits and risks of their par-ticipation. While it may be empowering for individuals to participate in the research process, and enlightening to the researcher(s) who may be exposed to alternative interpretations that are more relevant to the popu-lation, when children, non-English speaking, or vulnerable groups are involved, it is challenging to be fully disclosing about possible benefits or risks, some of which may be unknown to anyone at the time.

Ethical Issues that Arise from Collaboration with Communities

The term "community" is used broadly here to encompass groups con-nected by culture, values, geography, or experience. Many of the dangers of exploitation discussed in the previous sections pertain to communities also. Risks and benefits to the communities are not always clear and often develop out of the control of the researchers or participants. In addition, researchers who undertake collaborations with a community have ethical responsibilities for the community's well-being. However, one major difficulty in community collaboration is the question of "Who speaks for the community?" While a single dominant person or group may be the most eloquent or compelling "community voice" for feminist and participatory researchers to engage, care must be taken to ensure that the full community is being represented. This is challenging for researchers who usually are not members of the community and often lack knowledge of who authentically represents the group. It is quite possible that those community voices that are most accessible to researchers are also those that hold the most power and privilege (for example, community leaders). However, collaborative researchers must strive to engage perspectives that may be more marginal and least heard.

In addition, harm to a community or exploitation of a community group is not always evident. For example, educating girls and women may destabilize marital or extended-family relationships within a community. When women come to seek and demand equality or opportunity and equity in work, relationships, and education, there are often negative responses, such as those detailed in Susan Faludi's influential book about the women's movement, *Backlash* (1992).

In sum, feminist and participatory researchers undertake collaborative research projects with university students, individuals who are participants in the research, and communities. They are conscious that collaborative research processes can be harmful and exploitative to individuals and communities. They accept the responsibility that researchers have for reducing the harm and maximizing the benefits of research to individuals and communities. They strive to develop positive relationships with research participant-collaborators, be they students, fellow researchers, individuals, or communities that respect diverse cultures, values, experiences, and knowledge. Feminist and participatory researchers deliberately seek ways to involve participants and communities in the research process to ensure that the goals and outcomes of the research reflect the concerns and realities of the communities being studied. Feminist ethics, discussed in the following section, can help the researcher negotiate these complex collaborations.

FEMINIST ETHICS

Feminist ethics developed as a subfield within philosophy and overlaps significantly with traditional ethics. That is, feminist ethicists examine the nature, consequences, and motives of action; identify and apply moral principles relevant to decision-making; and define the moral good (Brabeck, 2000). However, feminist ethics goes beyond this by also requiring individuals to act in ways that proactively create just social structures that ensure that people receive attentive and just care. In a review of the literature, Brabeck and Ting (2000) identified the following common themes of feminist ethics of psychological practice:

1. Women and their experiences are of moral significance.
2. Attentiveness to subjective knowledge can illuminate moral issues.
3. Feminist ethicists engage in analysis of the context within which individuals live and act and of the power dynamics inherent in that context.
4. Feminist critiques of male distortions must be accompanied by a critique of racist, classist, and homophobic distortions.
5. Feminist ethics requires action directed at achieving social justice (Brabeck & Ting, 2000, p. 18).

These themes are discussed briefly here, and more extensively in Brabeck (2000). The first theme of feminist ethics, that women and their experiences have moral significance, may seem obvious. However, the moral significance of women's lives has not been well understood (Shields, 1975). In the 1970s feminist psychologists (Gilligan, 1982; Miller, 1976) and philosophers (Baier, 1994; Noddings, 1984; Ruddick, 1989) examined the complexities and diversities of women and their experiences in motherhood, friendships, peacemaking, and collective and collaborative decision making.

Gilligan (1982) argued that the ethic of care is a moral orientation that can be identified by examining the voices of women and girls as they face moral dilemmas. She argued that experiences with inequality and subordination lead girls and women to develop a moral self that is grounded in human connections and concern for others. Gilligan and other relational feminists distinguish between two selves. The "feminine self," and associated values, is characterized by the "feminine voice," which is socialized to be concerned with relationships and care. In contrast, the "masculine voice" is socialized to be concerned with abstract rules of justice and individual rights.

Gilligan and other relational feminists argue that women's more subjective ways of knowing (Belenky, Clinchy, Goldberger, & Tarule, 1986) give them greater access to subjective knowledge, which is informed by affect as well as reason. This socialized and socially acceptable sensitivity leads them to value empathy, nurturance, and caring. Relational feminists characterize women's and girls' selves as interdependent and connected to, and responsible for, one another. The care moral orientation is contrasted with the justice moral orientation (Kohlberg, 1984), which values principled rational decision making, individual rights, and fairness. Relational feminists characterize men's and boys' selves as independent, separate, and autonomous.

Empirical research shows that the "woman = care, men = justice" dichotomy is both incorrect and dangerous. Empirical studies do not support the claim of gender differences in moral decision making (Brabeck, 1989; Brabeck & Ting, 2000), and by universalizing the ethic of care to all women, it fails to attend sufficiently to the diversity (class, culture, race, sexual orientation) among women (Spelman, 1988). This has led some feminists (e.g., Hare-Mustin & Marecek, 1990) to argue that rather than celebrate women's caring attributes, feminists should work to change the oppressive structures that relegate women to the private sphere and men to the public sphere. In addition, some feminists argue that both men and women should be ethically obligated to attend to relational issues and to consider the welfare of others as paramount (Tronto, 1987, 1993).

Applying the ethical theme of care and concern for others would lead the ethical feminist researcher to behave in ways that take participants' well-being into consideration. While this can become maternalistic "help," it more often means supporting participants' efforts to empower themselves. Thus, feminist ethics requires us to critically evaluate how our research contributes to the well-being of participants, students, and colleagues and how our relationships with participants are characterized by care and connection.

In placing greater emphasis on women's experiences, rather than on formal abstract principles alone, feminist ethics places great importance on grounded knowledge, the second theme of feminist ethics. This tenet urges us to examine the standpoint from which individuals construct cognitive, affective, and subjective realities (Rave & Larsen, 1995). Similarly, many participatory researchers begin with the lived experiences of participants and work together to develop their research questions and plans. Attending to the participants' subjective realities means that we must consider the participants' point of view and integrate their realities into the knowledge generation process (Baier, 1994; Fox, 1992). If the subjective experience of participants and the communities within which they reside are not considered, knowledge generation will be limited and inevitably flawed (Andolsen, Gudorf, & Pellauer, 1985). Thus we must take special care during the research process to understand the standpoint of participants and must constantly strive to learn what participants are thinking, feeling, wanting, and experiencing.

The third theme of feminist ethics obliges us to examine the context and the power dynamics inherent in that context. While the ethic of care, as described by relational theorists, enjoins us to care about the well-being of all engaged in the research, the ethic of justice requires that we attend to the power hierarchies inherent in each particular situation, even the inequities within the research relationship itself. This requires a level of self-critique and ongoing assessment regarding how greater status, knowledge, and resources may affect our relationships with our collaborators. In many cases, power inequities are inevitable; the critical ethical choice is to acknowledge the situation and its potential impact on the relationship and the work and to challenge the inequities. Ultimately, the burden of responsibility to address power inequities falls on those with more power. Thus we must consider whether "helping" actions enable and empower others, or if they render others less autonomous. For example, a researcher who takes over a project may be acting paternalistically, which may infringe on a person's autonomy.

The fourth theme of feminist ethics enjoins us to critique all stereotypical and discriminatory distortions. Feminist ethics demands that we constantly analyze the process and outcomes of knowledge construction from a gendered, sociocultural perspective. While gender discrimination has been a focus of feminist inquiry, other forms of oppression (e.g., based on ethnicity, culture, class, age, sexual orientation, ability, linguistic status) also must be considered. By identifying and working against oppression, feminist psychologists embrace human diversity as a requirement and a foundation for practice (Spelman, 1988). Those of us who work collaboratively with individuals or groups, thus, struggle to achieve the aspirational goals of respect for diversity, empowerment, and ultimately liberation (Eugene, 1989).

The final theme of feminist ethics requires us to take action directed at achieving social justice. Feminist ethics is concerned not only with what ought to be but with how we can make practices more ethical (Cole & Coultrap-McQuin, 1992). We have a mandate to use knowledge to bring about individual, familial, communal, educational, institutional, legal, and social change. When structures are not amenable to equity for all, they must be altered to be made more just. This aspect of feminist ethics also lends itself to participatory methods, particularly participatory action research. The shared process of discovery, expression, interpretation, and agenda setting can be the vehicle by which people find ways to seek solutions that affect entire communities and achieve social changes that improve the individuals' lives.

Ethical feminist researchers work to create the structural and cultural conditions for self-determination by empowerment at the individual level and transformation at the societal level. The ultimate goal of feminist ethics is to enhance the human condition and to create a more just and caring world for all (Applebaum, 1997). While these goals are in a real sense unattainable, work directed toward the goal, work that is both aspirational and inspirational, is required by feminist ethics.

In the next section, we examine the APA ethics code regarding collaborative research with human participants and discuss some of its limitations from the perspective of the feminist ethics described earlier. We conclude with recommendations for feminist and participatory researchers.

A FEMINIST CRITIQUE OF THE APA ETHICAL PRINCIPLES AND CODE OF BEHAVIOR

Typically, researchers in psychology turn to the APA Code of Ethics (APA, 2002) to guide them in carrying out ethical research with human participants. The latest version of the American Psychological Association's (APA) Ethical Principles of Psychologists and Code of Conduct, effective June 1, 2003, describes the guidelines that ought to be followed in all research conducted by psychologists. To guide decision-making, the 2002 APA Code provides five general principles that ethical psychologists should consider. These are not "standards" and do not carry obligations of conformance, but rather they are "aspirational in nature" and are meant as general guides and inspiration toward ethical ideals. These ideals are much in keeping with the tenets of feminist ethics described earlier. However, the APA Code was written with a traditional scientific model of research in mind, in which researcher and participant roles are both clearly defined and mutually exclusive. This model does not consistently reflect the reality of collaborative research in which researcher and participant roles are more complex and dynamic; nor does it adequately reflect the aspirational themes of feminist ethics described in the preceding section. In this section we offer a critique of the five ethical principles that the APA offers as guides in decision making. We apply our critique to collaborative research relationships, highlight inconsistencies between assumptions of the APA Code and collaborative research models, and suggest ways that a feminist ethical perspective can guide collaborative research practices.

Principle A, Beneficence and Nonmaleficence, requires that psychologists "strive to benefit those with whom they work and take care to do no harm. In their professional actions, psychologists seek to safeguard the welfare and rights of those with whom they interact professionally and other affected persons" (APA, 2002, p. 3). For collaborative re-searchers, concern for the welfare of others includes the affirmative mandate that we strive to discover what the community's pressing issues and concerns are and how research can contribute to the well-being of the community. However, questions arise: Who decides what contributes to a community's or participant's welfare? Who defines what constitutes harm? How can we incorporate lay people into the process of research so that communities have a voice in what information is gathered, and for what purpose? The APA Code of Ethics assumes that the professional researcher makes these judgments. While participants are "protected" from misconduct, the protection itself might reflect paternalism or maternalism (or, as

Kitchener, 2000, notes, "parentalism") if the researcher does not consider the power dynamics of the context. Feminist research ethics would require that those affected by the research have a voice in answering these questions because the welfare of participants is best ensured when they can identify such questions.

The principle of beneficence and nonmaleficence also enjoins psychologists to guard against "misuse of their influence" (APA, 2002, p. 3). This is consistent with feminist ethics, which enjoins researchers to examine critically the potential influence of power in collaborative relationship. When relationships involve status and power differences, due to education, economic resources, and/or group membership, ethical researchers acknowledge and negotiate these fissures in ways that are critical and facilitate communication. This involves a process in which researchers may deliberately "abdicate" power and participants "harness" it, flipping the status quo of power relationships. At the least, ethical researchers are required to be self-reflective and self-interrogating regarding their power status vis-à-vis those with whom they collaborate. The ethical feminist researcher further aspires to reconfigure the power relationships and create *power with*, rather than *power over*, those with whom they collaborate.

Principle B, Fidelity and Responsibility, requires that

psychologists establish relationships of trust with those with whom they work. They are aware of their professional and scientific responsibilities to society and to the specific communities in which they work. Psychologists uphold professional standards of conduct, clarify their professional roles and obligations, accept appropriate responsibility for their behavior, and seek to manage conflicts of interest that could lead to exploitation or harm. (APA, 2002, p. 3)

With the best interest and welfare of others in mind, the psychologist should consult with and collaborate with other professionals. While interprofessional sharing and professional consulting often are desirable goals, they usually exclude the nonprofessional participant, the student, community member, or parent. In contrast, feminist research ethics requires psychologists to treat participants as cocreators of knowledge, insight, and expertise. They should not be excluded or overlooked in the process of determining appropriate professional and ethical practices.

One idea that distinguishes collaborative research from more traditional models is that it re-visions the participant as researcher. Traditional psychological research tends to utilize participants as a source of data, and the meaning of that data is constructed by the researcher. In contrast, collaborative researchers assume that nonprofessionals can inform the research in ways that professionals cannot. For example, when Michelle Fine (1997) was a volunteer as a rape crisis counselor, her relationship with her client, Altamese, brought her into the complex reality of the intersection of racial and gender violence. Altamese's construction of her experience challenged Fine's professional and feminist understanding of rape, victims, and the process of conducting research. From Fine's perspective, Altamese was the "victim." But from Altamese's perspective, her attacker, an African American man, was also a victim within a racist system, a fact that complicated Altamese's construction of the crime against her. Here we see how participants' perspectives may alter the researcher's interpretation and analyses, if they are allowed consideration in the research process.

Under traditional methods, research collaborators are hierarchically related, depending on status (degree, area of expertise) and role (principal investigator, consultant, graduate, or undergraduate student). The principal investigator is "in charge" of the research project; all others are seen to be recipients of the opportunities for learning. While they may make substantive contributions to the research, they are seen as less knowledgeable, and these unequal relationships are clear and transparent. However, in collaborative research, as individuals engage in a collective process of inquiry, power differences may become more complex and dynamic. For example, Lykes (1989b) describes how class, nationality, and gender led to experiences of both "power and powerlessness" in Guatemala. Her work with Mayan women, many of whom were illiterate, revealed great wisdom, knowledge, and insight that were essential to Lykes's success in developing culturally appropriate methods of working with Mayan children who had been affected by the civil war. At the same time, Lykes, as researcher, possessed personal and material resources that were not available to the women with whom she collaborated.

Principle C, Integrity, states that ethical psychologists "seek to promote accuracy, honesty, and truthfulness in the science, teaching, and practice of psychology" (APA, 2002, p. 3). The researcher-participant relationship as it exists in traditional research methods is separate, impartial, and "objective." The APA Code is very explicit about psychologists who have more than one relationship with clients or research participants. Because of its relevance to the topic of collaboration, this section of the Code is quoted at length here.

3.05 Multiple Relationships.

(a) A multiple relationship occurs when a psychologist is in a professional role with a person and (1) at the same time is in another role with the same person, (2) at the same time is in a relationship with a person closely associated with or related to the person with whom the psychologist has the professional relationship, or (3) promises to enter into another relationship in the future with the person or a person closely associated with or related to the person.

A psychologist refrains from entering into a multiple relationship if the multiple relationship could reasonably be expected to impair the psychologist's objectivity, competence, or effectiveness in performing his or her functions as a psychologist, or otherwise risks exploitation or harm to the person with whom the professional relationship exists.

Multiple relationships that would not reasonably be expected to cause impairment or risk exploitation or harm are not unethical.

(b) If a psychologist finds that, due to unforeseen factors, a potentially harmful multiple relationship has arisen, the psychologist takes reasonable steps to resolve it with due regard for the best interests of the affected person and maximal compliance with the Ethics Code. (APA, 2002, p. 6)

In collaborative research, psychologists cultivate interpersonal relationships with individuals and communities that facilitate understanding, promote capacity building, share power, and exchange knowledge, resources, and expertise. Such relationships may extend over long periods of time and may promote long-term growth of and change within the researchers, the individual participants, and their community. However, when psychologists cultivate relationships with participants that promote open dialogue about the purpose and process of the research, multiple relationships are often inevitable. When we invite participants to contribute their insights and experiences to improve the project, and engage them in the research process to the extent that they are willing and able, friendships may develop that compromise what the APA Code characterizes as a relationship that "could reasonably be expected to impair the psychologist's objectivity" (APA, 2002, p. 6).

For example, researchers usually learn a great deal from "participants" when they receive advice or direction from those they seek to "study." Sometimes researchers are asked to deliver services (counseling, consultation) in the process of conducting the research; to withhold these services might compromise trust; to provide them involves the researcher in a dual relationship. Likewise, when university researchers work closely with students or nonuniversity community members, friendships may develop; such friendships constitute a second or dual relationship to that of researcher-participant or faculty-student and raise both research and ethical concerns (see McIntyre & Lykes, this volume).

In collaborative research projects, relationships are multifaceted and dynamic. Going beyond the formal and distant roles of researcher and participant is desirable from the perspective of feminist and participatory research. Knowledge is power and equitable relationships are necessary for the work to proceed. For this reason, open and frank relationships that are reciprocal (both parties engaged in the give and take) are important to collaborative research. In fact, failure to develop honest collaborative and reciprocal relationships can be considered harmful, paternalistic, or as maintaining the status quo of the dominant and knowledgeable researcher and the uninformed and unskilled participant.

On the other hand, collaborative researchers must be mindful of the limitations and the responsibilities inherent in developing close relationships with project members, particularly when the research ends. Collaborative researchers must strive to attain holistic connections based on mutuality and respect, yet be sensitive to the limits of their roles as researcher, collaborator, consultant, and activist. Feminist ethics also enjoins researchers to constantly interrogate themselves regarding how power in their relationships with others may influence the relationship. Of special concern is the power that researchers hold because of professional status, race, class, or dominant group status. These attributes do not disappear when a researcher engages in collaborative work and must be openly acknowledged as privileges that inevitably produce power inequities. Ethical researchers therefore understand their own and collaborators' multiple identities (influenced by race, gender, class, etc.) and how these identities affect the collaborative work (Maguire, 1987).

Principle D, Justice, entitles "all persons to access ... and benefit from the contributions of psychology and to equal quality in the processes, procedures, and services being conducted by psychologists" (APA, 2002, p. 3). Under this principle, psychologists must not assert competence beyond their training and expertise. Competence, an ethical standard related to the principle of Justice, requires that "Psychologists provide services, teach, and conduct research with populations and in areas only within the boundaries of their competence, based on their education, training, supervised experience, consultation, study, or professional experience" (APA, 2002, p. 4). In traditional research the investigator usually makes decisions without seeking advice from potential participants. Competence for collaborative researchers means that in addition to competence in the area and methods of the project, the researcher must be competent in interpersonal skills and group process techniques required for collaboration. A concern with relationships, nurturing connections, developing a sense of community, reciprocity, and rapport can provide a foundation for trust, respect, and engagement in the process. The emotional connections and sense of community that are sustained are central to the project's success. As McIntyre and Lykes note:

in the absence of affect, that is, our deep and developing caring for each other, such resources might become mere "techniques" rather than resources in the transformative meaning-making and praxis that we have described here (McIntyre & Lykes, this volume).

Thus, a collaborative researcher who does not have these skills must be willing to develop them. Competent collaborative researchers are aware of their level of skills in developing collaborative relationships with participants and other researchers and with the cultural practices and perspectives of the population with whom they are working.

Principle E is Respect for People's Rights and Dignity. All psychologists must "respect the dignity and worth of all people, and the rights of individuals to privacy, confidentiality, and self-determination" (APA, 2002, p. 4). The process of informed consent is one way that researchers have attempted to ensure that participants receive respect and that their rights are honored. Except in minimal-risk research, the investigators are responsible for establishing a clear and fair agreement with research participants prior to their project participation. The informed consent agreement clarifies the obligations and responsibilities of each party in the research project. The investigator initiates and establishes a formal agreement with the participants and has the obligation to honor all promises and commitments included in that agreement. Psychologists are required to be aware of individual differences among participants and are required to know how race, age, gender, class, culture, disability, and other factors affect the ability of a person to provide informed consent.

Collaborative researchers uphold the APA Code's principle of respect for rights and dignity and the critical role of the informed consent process in assuring those rights. However, their understanding of this principle also includes the right to define the problems, engage in development of a solution or solutions, and contribute to the research, not just as informants but as colleagues, cocreators, and critics. Furthermore, the APA Code does not address participants' rights to full access to research results or to be engaged in the process itself. While the APA Code encourages researchers to share their findings, the data themselves are not generally made available to research participants. From a collaborative research perspective, respect for people might include finding ways for participants to respond to and have access to the research methods and data, to be compensated for their time as the researchers are (including their time reviewing drafts of the research and/or the data from interviews, ethnographies, and so forth), and helping interpret results and craft recommendations for future action.

While university-based researchers often have been trained to analyze, interpret, and represent data and the results of analyses, most community-based researchers have not. Thus, an important aspect of collaborative work is to scaffold and support the development of these skills among those who need it. It is only through such training and support that community-based researchers will be able to make meaning of their experiences once the "experts" have left the field. Such teaching might in itself be a form of remuneration for their work in the project.

Finally, all psychologists are required to act in culturally competent ways. In part, this means psychologists should

try to eliminate the effect on their work of biases based on [age, gender, gender identity, race, ethnicity, culture, national origin, religion, sexual orientation, disability, language, and socioeconomic status], and ... [should] not knowingly participate in or condone activities of others based upon such prejudices. (APA, 2002, p. 4)

This is consistent with feminist ethics that requires researchers to attend to any racist, classist, homophobic attitudes or behaviors and work to reduce their occurrence (Brabeck, 2000). Collaborative researchers are further required to work toward removing structures that are discriminatory or unfair. This social justice goal is challenging, unsettling, and required if the goal of social justice is to be attained. Collaborative researchers recognize that the social system itself may be the underlying cause of the problems many marginalized participants face (e.g., poverty, discrimination, violence, etc.). The injunction from feminist ethics (Brabeck, 2000) to reshape society in more just ways is consistent but goes beyond the APA Code's (2002) preamble, which states, " Psychologists respect and protect civil and human rights" (p. 3). Collaborative researchers do more than respect and protect rights, they also actively work to make the social conditions more just so that human and civic rights are ensured.

RECOMMENDATIONS FOR COLLABORATIVE RESEARCHERS

In conclusion, collaboration is a major aspect of participatory research and much feminist research. Collaborative research extends the traditional scope of the researcher-participant relationship. In a traditional research paradigm, researcher-participant relationships are often bounded by time (the amount needed to gather data), purpose (the goal is to obtain information and perhaps share findings with the participant), and setting (the interaction is usually limited to the location in which the data is gathered). By contrast, collaborative researchers may develop relationships that go far beyond the research context. It is not unusual for collaborative researchers to develop long-term friendships with their so-called participants, and sometimes to question the extent to which they should personally assist participants with meeting their basic needs (e.g., Maguire, 1987).

Inherent in this expanded relationship are ethical concerns and challenges that are rarely faced by traditional researchers. While the APA Ethics Code offers some guidance in resolving these dilemmas, it has some significant limitations. We have suggested that collaborative researchers consider a feminist ethical perspective to supplement areas in which the more traditional APA Code of Ethics is lacking. With its attentiveness to subjective experience, power inequities, relationships, and social justice, feminist ethics can be a powerful tool in resolving the ethical challenges that collaborative research poses.

NOTE

This chapter was equally co-authored by Angela Shartrand and Mary M. Brabeck.

REFERENCES

American Psychological Association. (2002). *Ethical principles of psychologists and code of conduct.* Retrieved February 4, 2003, from http://www.apa.org/ethics/code2002.pdf.

Andolsen, B.H., Gudorf, C.E., & Pellauer, M.D. (1985). *Women's consciousness, women's conscience: A reader in feminist ethics.* Minneapolis, MN: Winston Press.

Applebaum, B. (1997). Good liberal intentions are not enough! Racism, intentions and moral responsibility. *Journal of Moral Education, 26*(4), 409–421.

Baier, A. (1994). *Moral prejudices: Essays on ethics.* Cambridge, MA: Harvard University Press.

Belenky, M.F., Clinchy, B.M., Goldberger, N., & Tarule, J.M. (1986). *Women's ways of knowing: The development of self, voice and mind.* New York: Basic Books.

Brabeck, M.M. (Ed.). (1989). *Who cares? Theory, research and educational implications of the ethic of care.* New York: Praeger.

Brabeck, M.M. (Ed.). (2000). *Practicing feminist ethics in psychology.* Washington, DC: American Psychological Association.

Brabeck, M.M., & Brown, L. (1997). Feminist theory and psychological practice. In J. Worell & N. Johnson (Eds.), *Shaping the future of feminist psychology: Education, research and practice* (pp. 15–35). Washington, DC: American Psychological Association.

Brabeck, M., & Ting, K. (2000). Feminist ethics: Lenses for examining ethical psychological practice. In M.M. Brabeck (Ed.), *Practicing feminist ethics in psychology* (pp. 17–35). Washington, DC: American Psychological Association.

Brydon-Miller, M. (2001). Education, research, and action: Theory and methods of participatory action research. In D.L. Tolman & M. Brydon-Miller (Eds.), *From subjects to subjectivities: A handbook of interpretive and participatory methods* (pp. 76–89). New York: New York University Press.

Cole, E.B., & Coultrap-McQuin, S. (Eds.). (1992). *Explorations in feminist ethics: Theory and practice.* Bloomington: Indiana University Press.

Crawford, M.C., & Kimmel, E.B. (Eds.). (1999a). Innovations in feminist research (Special Issue). *Psychology of Women Quarterly, 23*(1).

Crawford, M.C., & Kimmel, E.B. (Eds.). (1999b). Innovations in feminist research (Special Issue). *Psychology of Women Quarterly, 23*(2).

Eugene, T. (1989). Sometimes I feel like a motherless child: The call and response for a liberational ethic of care. In M.M. Brabeck (Ed.), *Who cares? Theory, research and educational implications of the ethic of care* (pp. 45–62). New York: Praeger.

Fals-Borda, O., & Rahman, M.A. (1991). *Action and knowledge: Breaking the monopoly with participatory action-research.* New York: Apex Press.

Faludi, S. (1992). *Backlash: The undeclared war against American women.* New York: Anchor Books.

Fine, M. (1992). *Disruptive voices: The possibilities of feminist research.* Ann Arbor: University of Michigan Press.

Fine, M. (1997). Coping with rape: Critical perspectives on consciousness. In M. Crawford and R. Unger (Eds.), *In our own words: Readings on the psychology of women and gender* (pp. 152–164). New York: McGraw Hill.

Fox, E. L. (1992). Seeing through women's eyes: The role of vision in women's moral theory. In E. B. Cole & S. Coultrap-McQuin (Eds.), *Explorations in feminist ethics: Theory and practice* (pp. 111–116). Bloomington: Indiana University Press.

Gilligan, C. (1982). *In a different voice: Psychological theory and women's development.* Cambridge, MA: Harvard University Press.

Grossman, F. K., Gilbert, L. A., Genero, N. P., Hawes, S. E., Hyde, J. S., & Marecek, J. (1997). Feminist research: Practice and problems. In J. Worell & N. Johnson (Eds.), *Shaping the future of feminist psychology: Education, research and practice* (pp. 73–91). Washington, DC: American Psychological Association.

Harding, S. (1987). *Feminism and methodology.* Bloomington: Indiana University Press.

Harding, S., & Hintikka, M. B. (Eds.). (1983). *Discovering reality: Feminist perspectives on epistemology, metaphysics, methodology and philosophy of science.* Boston: D. Reidel.

Hare-Mustin, R. T., & Marecek, J. (Eds.). (1990). *Making a difference.* New Haven, CT: Yale University Press.

Hyde, J. S., & Linn, M. C. (Eds.). (1986). *The psychology of gender: Advances through meta-analysis.* Baltimore, MD: Johns Hopkins University Press.

Kitchener, K. (2000). *Foundations of ethical practice, research and teaching in psychology.* Mahway, NJ: Lawrence Erlbaum.

Kohlberg, L. (1984). *The psychology of moral development: The nature and validity of moral stages.* San Francisco: Harper and Row.

Lott, B. (1985). The potential enrichment of social/personality psychology through feminist research and vice versa. *American Psychologist, 40*(2), 155–164.

Lykes, M. B. (1989a). Dialogue with Guatemalan Indian women: Critical perspectives on constructing collaborative research. In R. K. Unger (Ed.), *Representations: Social constructions of gender* (pp. 167–185). Amityville, NY: Baywood.

Lykes, M. B. (1989b). The caring self: Social experiences of power and powerlessness. In M. Brabeck (Ed.), *Who cares? Theory, research, and educational implications of the ethic of care* (pp. 164–179). New York: Praeger.

Maguire, P. (1987). *Doing participatory research: A feminist approach.* Amherst, MA: The Center for International Education, University of Massachusetts.

McIntyre, A. (2000). *Inner-city kids: Adolescents confront life and violence in an urban community.* New York: New York University Press.

McIntyre, A., & Lykes, M. B. (this volume). Weaving words and pictures in/through feminist participatory action research. *Traveling companions: Feminism, teaching, and action research.* New York: Praeger.

Miller, J. B. (1976). *Toward a new psychology of women.* Boston: Beacon Press.

Noddings, N. (1984). *Caring: A feminine approach to ethics and moral education.* Berkeley, CA: University of California Press.

Rave, E. J., & Larsen, C. (1995). *Ethical decision making therapy: Feminist perspectives.* New York: Guilford.

Ruddick, S. (1989). *Maternal thinking: Toward a politics of peace.* Boston: Beacon Press.

Shields, S. (1975). Functionalism, Darwinism, and the psychology of women: A study in social myth. *American Psychologist, 30*(7), 739–754.

Spelman, E. (1988). *Inessential woman: Problems of exclusion in feminist thought.* Boston: Beacon Press.

Tronto, J. (1987). Beyond gender difference to a theory of care. *Signs, 12,* 644–661.

Tronto, J. (1993). *Moral boundaries: A political argument from ethic of care.* New York and London: Routledge.

Worell, J., & Johnson, N. G. (Eds.). (1997). *Shaping the future of feminist psychology: Education, research, and practice.* Washington, DC: American Psychological Association.

CHAPTER 9

Feminism and Action Research: Is "Resistance" Possible and, If So, Why Is It Necessary?

Davydd J. Greenwood

The relationship between feminism and action research is deep and complex. These approaches are closely interlinked, and I believe their fates are intertwined. Feminism and action research (AR) actually are wound together, but their interdependency has not been discussed sufficiently. As a result, both approaches tend to proceed quite independently of each other. Given the evident rightward turn of most of the globalizing economic system and of the academy, this kind of separation among critical social scientists and activist groups is risky, and so I believe something important is at stake in building an arena for feminist/AR dialogue. I also believe that AR owes an important debt to feminists and that this debt should promote greater solidarity.

Making this argument in a brief chapter risks homogenizing both feminism and AR.[1] For convenience I use these cover terms, but both feminism and AR are deeply plural notions and this rhetorical convenience has a cost. There are many varieties of feminism, based on generational differences in the movement, different epistemological stances, politics, and concrete situations. There is plenty of room for disagreement within this umbrella. The same is true of AR, which is anything but a homogeneous field; the differences between participatory research, collaborative inquiry, action science, action learning, transformational learning, participatory action research, participatory learning analysis, and many others being significant methodologically, epistemologically, and politically. So, this chapter operates at a very abstract level, and relations among the various groups within these two broad umbrellas can be dramatically different. My justification for doing this is to open up an arena for dialogue, not to give what is said a final shape.

My specific argument is that AR owes its recent resurgence to the feminist movement in a very direct way. At the same time, I think that the feminist movement, especially in the academy, has fallen on hard times. I assert that AR should take seriously a combined intellectual/moral obligation to support feminist voices that continue to struggle against ongoing and worsening injustice worldwide for its own sake, in recognition of the contributions feminists have made to goals that AR has long advocated.

The vantage point of this chapter is that both feminism and AR are elements in a modest but academically important Polanyi "counter-movement" (Polanyi, 1944). Briefly, in Karl Polanyi's view, capitalist commodification of labor and land necessarily ignite a variety of efforts at social self-protection because of the impossibility of converting human beings and natural resources into true commodities. These movements for social self-protection insist on justice, fairness, and local social coherence, and they oppose the complicity of the conventional social sciences in the promotion of worldwide social inequality and the marketization of human relationships. Well guided, these Polanyi counter-movements can result in significant social reforms, as in the case of the European social democracies. Misguided, they can result in authoritarianism in the form of fascist regimes, terrorist attacks, and other forms of destructive action. Just what the future holds for the United States is anything but clear, but the signs are not promising.

Action research and feminism are mutually implicated because action research involves collaboration among all the legitimate stakeholders, the valuation of all knowledge, and the enhancement of fairness, justice, healthfulness, and sustainability—all values that underlie feminism. AR provides important methodological and epistemological tools for feminists and vice versa. Feminists, examining one of the world's central gradients of inequality, developing epistemological and methodological critiques of conventional social science and humanistic research, and carrying forward a broad critique of inegalitarian bias and business as usual, have taken their struggles right into the heart of the humanities and the social sciences. They have also been active in the courts, social service agencies, and the NGO world. Predictably, these efforts have generated turmoil, and enormous forces are arrayed to co-opt feminist critiques and continue business as usual.

REFORMIST SOCIAL SCIENCE: A THUMBNAIL HISTORY

After a flurry of development of social research between 1880 and 1920 as socially conscious and reformist activities with a university and national resource base, the social sciences became quickly institutionalized as separate professional disciplines extracted from their engagement with social reform. This is too long and complex a story to tell here, and there are excellent treatments of some dimensions of this history (Furner, 1975; Lengermann & Niebrugge-Brantley, 1998; Ross, 1991). A brief rendering of some examples will serve my purpose here.

It appears, at least in the United States, that the justificatory rationales for the development of the social sciences as professions originally centered on their contribution to solving social problems and to providing insights into the design of good public policies. There is an ambiguity in this mission because being a reformer and advising reformers and politicians can lead to very different visions of the mission of the social sciences. However, in the early days of all the current social science disciplines, both reformers and academic analysts coexisted in the same professional associations. By the time of the consolidation of the professional powers of these associations, the reformers had generally been ejected and the academic social scientists were fully in charge (Furner, 1975; Krause, 1996; Ross, 1991).

Just why this happened in case after case is a matter that usually ends up being explained by the philosophy of history of the observer. In my case, I see it as the result of pressures from industrial and political groups to silence academic analysts who called public attention to the antidemocratic dimensions of their doings. Others might bring forward a more internalist view of the changes (e.g., the consolidation of power in the hands of one group of professionals, one set of universities, etc., at the expense of others). I have no doubt that some of these internal forces and competitions also played a role.

However, perhaps more important on a longer time scale are the purges of socially critical social scientists. Dorothy Ross's *The Origin of American Social Science* (1991) recounts incident after incident of purges of social scientists for articulating ideas not in the interest of the ruling class, even in the pre-McCarthy era. Indeed, the purging of senior social scientists for their socially critical views was a routine feature of American academic life. The founding of the American Association of University Professors (in 1915) and the development of the tenure system were the social sciences' responses to this ideological coercion. Ross's evidence destroys the comfortable illusion that McCarthyism was a historical fluke, a single bad moment in a generally positive relationship, and opens us up to the consideration of other forms of coercive control. In this context, it probably seems rather clear why action researchers would have gotten in trouble and would have disappeared from the professional social science scene; the pressure to keep the academics in the academy talking to each other about things of little moment beyond the ivy walls and in a language that would be confusing enough not to cause public concern.

The story of feminist issues is more complex, and we are indebted to the scholarship of Pat Lengermann and Jill Niebrugge-Brantley for beginning to tell this story, in this case, for sociology. If what Dorothy Ross describes might be called "hard purges," an equally coercive and, in some ways, more insidious form of purge might be called the "soft purges." What Lengermann and Niebrugge-Brantley assiduously document, as an example from one social science discipline, is the great prominence of women in the founding days of sociology, including many great reformers like Jane Addams. In the early configuration of sociology, these reformers, many of them women, were core members of the American Sociological Association, widely published, and widely recognized. Yet, within a generation, not only had these reformers been removed from the American Sociological Association, but all memory of their existence and references to their scholarship had been eliminated from the history of the profession as well (Lengermann and Niebrugge-Brantley, 1998). The documentation these authors developed on this process makes their argument undeniable. It is a shame and a challenge to the rest of us that similar work has not been done for the rest of the social sciences. For my home discipline of anthropology, for example, the role of women founders is certainly widely noted (Margaret Mead, Ruth Benedict, Elsie Clews Parsons, etc.) but any look at the history of anthropological theory and of the profession will show you that their contributions are rarely included and that the history of anthropological theory came to be dominated by a "masculinized" view of the profession as well.

Once these pressures had done their work, only a few social scientists, among them Kurt Lewin, persisted in their belief that all good social science had to be developed and tested in action and that the purpose of social science was to improve society, not merely to improve the socioeconomic well-being and social class position of the social scientists. Despite Lewin's high profile in the United States during World War II and his creation of a major research unit at M.I.T., he too was quickly eclipsed. This might be attributed to the fact that he died suddenly in 1947, but the death of a single individual that stops a whole social movement suggests that the social movement is not very well rooted. Not long after his death, Lewin's books went out of print and he became as forgotten as the women Lengermann and Niebrugge-Brantley refer to. In this history, the McCarthy hearings, in which the academy was purged of "communists," were just a kind of late clean-up action after most of the battle had been won by the positivists.

Just in case it is tempting to tell this story in terms of the politics of "left" and "right," it is worth noting that one of the later and most effective purges of social science activists came in the left critique of the "Camelot" project and the irresponsible spreading of stories of putative involvement of many scholars in counter-insurgency efforts around the world

(Horowitz, 1967). Most of these accusations were later withdrawn with public apologies, but the chilling effect remained when everyone realized that they could be attacked from both the right and the left. I certainly am not excusing counterinsurgency any more than I would pardon Elton Mayo's union-busting research at Hawthorne Electric (Gillespie, 1991) in the early twentieth century, but I think it is worth remembering that both the right and the left have collaborated and continue to collaborate in making sure that most social science stays quietly in the library on university campuses. And, even now, what is called "political correctness" (as if we needed a new term for ideological coercion) is clearly a force on all campuses, with a wide variety of ideological watchdog groups making sure that we behave ourselves in a properly irrelevant way.

In the end, reform-oriented social research subsisted in the United States only in schools of social work, education, and other academically peripheral locations (i.e., out of harm's way). It also persisted in a few renegade institutions like the Tavistock Institute of Human Relations in the United Kingdom and in the Scandinavian social democracies where the "social partners" insisted that social research be done on issues of national importance and in terms that could be relevant for improving the application of social policies.

The picture of the social sciences in the 1970s, when I began my academic career, was truly depressing. Positivism reigned supreme and departments and disciplines became the hegemonic organizational matrix for social inquiry. In a parody of Taylor's scientific management, they made futile attempts to understand the complexities of the turbulent, interconnected social world by cutting it up into discrete bits. This was a patriarchal, peer-enforced intellectual panopticon in which social critique unaccompanied by a "literature review" within a subdiscipline, a hypothesis, and a dependent, independent, and intervening variable was ruled out of bounds. Nothing like AR could possibly gain a foothold in this world, and most action researchers abandoned the academy completely or simply worked independently of it (e.g., Budd Hall, Orlando Fals Borda, Paulo Freire, Myles Horton). Yet now, AR is possible in academic settings once again and the reason for this, in my view, is the advent of feminism in the 1960s.

The emergence of academically based feminism, building on and contributing to the ferment around the Vietnam War and ongoing civil rights and ethnic struggles, was one of the most powerful changes I have witnessed in the academy in my now over three decades as a university professor. I remember us going from a male-dominated and gender-intolerant kind of positivistic notion of academic professions and professionalism to a world in which gender came to mind at every step and in which the very canon we had struggled to learn began to look like worn-out cheesecloth. I remember the sense of defensiveness and loss of the moral high ground that occurred and a growing desire to be identified as anything but a male chauvinist.

The professional and social effects of this transformation were considerable. Even if the world is hardly perfect, it has changed more than I would ever have thought possible when I was 21 years old. But I think academic feminism did more than just include women and shake the canon; academic feminism blew gaping holes in the positivist framework by showing that positivism was just another ideological mask, hiding power, hiding oppression, and profiting from a passive role in the face of the injustices that it documented without confronting them politically. From this point, there has been no going back. While the positivists still abound and control lots of resources, their intellectual legitimacy is easily questioned. Indeed, between feminism and the expansions into constructivism, deconstruction, and postmodernism, there is not a tenet of positivism that has not been undermined, including the claim that it is scientific in any sense.

While this was bad news for the positivists and the power structures that rely on their work, it was wonderful news for AR. By shaking the foundations of the very framework that had driven out social reformist, collaborative, and democratizing social science and revealing the conventional social sciences' complicity with power, the feminists recreated the intellectual and academic space that the action researchers had long since lost. The loss of the ability to claim impartiality and objectivity as their foundation left the positivists as just another group of self-interested social actors and with the distinct look of "damaged goods."

The feminists did not just open up space for AR. They also created the institutional space and theoretical justifications for a broader identity politics that has come to include ethnic studies and gender studies more generally. The face of most institutions has been transformed by these actions. After feminism, it has not been enough to describe something as a "contribution to the literature"; it has to be a contribution to something more than narrow professional interests.

But the story does not end there. Were this the current state of affairs, this would be a happy tale. It is not.

NEOLIBERALISM AND SOCIAL "DE-FORM"[2]

Unfortunately for all of us, the space opened up by the feminists that so altered the structure of knowledge in the period between 1970 and the present is no longer nearly as open as it was. The frontal attack on power and privilege by a small group of academics eventually resulted in a significant conservative reaction. Though it took the forces in favor of the status quo a while to regroup, they did regroup very effectively and they had a good deal of help from their conservative allies.

What Immanuel Wallerstein and others call the "conservative restoration" took full flight beginning generally with the administration of Ronald Reagan. Threats to close the U.S. Department of Education completely, to roll back OSHA regulations, to relax environmental pollution standards, to hold the minimum wage at below subsistence, to undermine Social Security's financial stability, to turn agriculture over to speculative industrial capitalists, to put more people in prison than are employed in agriculture, and to break up the remaining strong labor unions all took their toll. All of this, combined with revisions of the tax code to provide tax cuts to the wealthy, resulted in the greatest growth of economic inequality in U.S. history, a trend that has continued unabated since (Harrison and Bluestone, 1990).

Coupled with this was a vicious counterattack on the reformist-minded social scientists and humanists who had shaken the "canon" to its foundations. The likes of Alan Bloom (1987), Diane Ravitch (2000), Dinesh D'Souza (1991), Richard Herrnstein and Charles Murray (1994) and a host of others inflamed themselves and each other with absurd claims that the still astonishingly conservative universities of the United States were hotbeds of "liberal" (now an insult) ideologies, that the accomplishments of the past were being undermined, and that a chaotic *lumpenproletariat* of People of Color and of "unconventional" sexual orientations were perverting the minds and bodies of America's youth, taking them away from Americanism, godliness, and goodness. Soon the National Endowment for the Humanities and the National Endowment for the Arts were embroiled in attacks launched almost daily from the right.

On campuses, this took a variety of forms. There was a resurgence of rightwing political clubs, the use of the concept of "political correctness" as a neutron bomb against freedom of speech, and the elaboration of a series of speech and behavior codes on campus that enforced a middle-of-the-road conformity on students and faculty alike (Kors and Silverglate, 1998). But, in many respects, it seems to me that these were the trivial, superficial dimensions of the changes taking place. The deeper changes were taking place at an institutional level.

The counterattack on feminism seems to me to have proceeded along two dimensions. First, there was a full-scale effort to impose the U.S. distributive justice model on women's studies. As Iris Marion Young has pointed out, the key tenet of this model is the notion that justice is a "good" that can be distributed. So, if you have suffered an injustice, your remedy is to be given some more goods than your own immediate social power could command (Young, 1990). If you accept this mode of proceeding, what happens thereafter is simply a negotiation about the price of your allegiance. How many faculty lines do you have to have? How many Third-World Women of Color should there be in the entering class? How many women should there be in the central administration?

In this regard, the women's movement ended up being treated much as the civil rights movement had been. The diversity/affirmative action system turns on negotiating quotas with the affected parties and asking constantly "How many is enough to quiet you down?" Broader issues of social justice are crushed. The fact that the majority of the poor and dispossessed here in the United States are White and that the greatest inequality in our society is produced by economic differences, not race and gender differences, matters little. Instead, what matters is coming to agreements with the producers of conflict about the resources they require to quiet down. The larger issues of solidarity among the working class, among the poor of the planet, and so forth, are thereby made moot. Faced with this, most feminist programs came up with a world picture that included a resource package that could secure their collaboration. And as this divide-and-conquer approach to social protest proceeded, those who remained outside the tent found themselves increasingly alone and likely to be dismissed as trivial or simply fired.

At the organizational level, there was also a conservative restoration going on. Feminism, constructivism, postmodernism, and deconstruction had all arisen in a complex and dynamic multidisciplinary environment. The unmasking of power and authority required multidisciplinary perspectives and often involved partnerships both across campuses and between campuses and the communities beyond them. The Women's Studies program at Cornell University is a case in point. When initially structured, this program included people from the sciences, social sciences, and humanities. The appointment, tenure, and promotion procedures included not only people from diverse disciplines but also people from the nonacademic part of the community who were considered to be equal stakeholders in the future of the program. Since those days, the program split into the Women's Studies, Women in Development (later Gender and Global Change), and Lesbian, Bi-sexual, and Gay Studies programs. And recently, the Women's Studies program has changed its name to Feminist, Gender, and Sexuality Studies.

One of the most significant changes is that people who are not tenured members of the Cornell faculty cannot participate in tenure and promotion decisions in the program anymore. From being a program built on a cross-disciplinary, university-community linkage, Women's Studies, by whatever name, has become basically one more college department, following all the business-as-usual rules that apply to other departments and excluding the voices of a great many from their decisions. While one can understand the reasons why the program accepted these outcomes, it is also clear that these programs paid a price in political power for these changes. Divide and conquer, follow the same rules as everyone else, how many articles in peer-reviewed journals rather than "how much good did you do" are all familiar co-optations from the history of the social sciences in general. So, in effect, feminism might be viewed as the most recently co-opted of the social science-based social reform efforts.

I have little hesitation in interpreting these processes. It seems to me that feminism arose as one of the most recent and potentially explosive social reform movements, especially within the university. After all, feminists were dealing with the lives of half the population and their implications for the other half, while the race/ethnic movements were all dealing with smaller segments of our society. At the same time, women have joined the workforce in unprecedented numbers, and universities, without female students, would be in very dire straits. So feminists were more of a threat than most of the other movements afoot at the time.

However, the feminists also missed their opportunities. Some opted for a "female only" view of feminism and lost the chance for broader support. Others were so deeply engaged in identity politics that subdividing women into different interest groups seemed to be absolutely necessary, despite the power this gave to the forces favoring the status quo. Some were just terribly anxious to "make it" and be respected by their disciplinary peers and found themselves tired of defending the unconventionality of feminist work and being dismissed by the core members of their fields. So what began as a direct confrontation with gender bias, hierarchy, and authoritarianism has evolved, in most institutions, into quasi-departments that generally operate in accordance with business-as-usual procedures.

Universities have not been inert during this period. In addition to finding ways to comply with affirmative action and gender-sensitive mandates, universities have become far more "corporate" than they were in the 1970s. Research is much more of an economically entrepreneurial activity that universities "invest" in, as they invest their endowments in the stock market. Universities try to guess at research areas and the costs of getting the research done in order to make decisions that both minimize their costs and optimize their chances for patent income and major grants with significant overhead to help defray the cost of doing the work. Thus, universities are strongly tempted to see their scientists and social scientists as revenue generators.

By contrast, social science as reformist social criticism is not very profitable. While it is not identical, the kind of co-optation experienced by feminism is similar to the way the social sciences were desocialized and institutionalized in earlier generations. The difference is that now the neo-liberal forces and the process of globalization create even more potent force fields for socially critical social science to negotiate. Many women's studies programs have now themselves become part of the "system" and engage in practices and announce standards that are increasingly academy centered. To be sure, there are discrepant voices, but these voices do not face an easy struggle.

IF FEMINISM'S CRITIQUE IS BLUNTED, CAN
ACTION RESEARCH SURVIVE?

The argument of this chapter is that action research, as an avowedly social reform activity based on democratic values of respect for the knowledge of all people and their rights to autonomy and self-direction in their lives, very quickly disappeared from the academy in all but the smallest corners. The subsistence of action researchers in programs of adult education, in extension work, and here and there dotted over the university landscape was possible, but their collective voice and the strength of their critique of "social science" and university-society relationships was effectively muted. It was only with the feminist on-slaught that AR and ethnic studies both were able to find some footing in the academy and add their voices to the critique of business-as-usual.

But while feminists did manage to found formal programs, majors, and, occasionally, departments, as did people in ethnic studies, action re-searchers have not. Action researchers continue to be spread around the university, one or two in various departments, held together by joint activ-ities, networks, seminars, and projects. This organizationally diffuse char-acter makes AR even more vulnerable to pressure than feminist and ethnic studies programs.

Individual faculty members always face a majority of colleagues in their home departments who reject the epistemology, methodology, and prac-tices of AR. Attempts to hire new faculty are influenced usually by major-ity rule and often by the more senior members of the departments. Getting an action researcher to surface on a short list in an academic search is far from easy. Graduate students who work with action researchers often find themselves at odds with their home fields or going outside of their depart-ment (or even university) to get advice and support on the AR dimensions of their work.

This is not a sustainable situation for action researchers. It is patently difficult for feminists and ethnic studies faculty to survive even with departmental and program structures built around them. Thus, it seems to me that the most reasonable response to these ongoing problems is to form alliances among feminists, action researchers, and others concerned with social change and democratization for the purposes of mutual sup-port. United by the values of social criticism, democratization, and respect for the differences and common ground among people, these modalities of social research really could gain from being mutually supportive. At this point, there is no peace movement, no major women's movement, and no democracy movement, but there is massive inequality, decreasing unionism, and decreasing social support. Unless we can learn to count on each other, we have no allies at all.

ARE THERE REASONS, OTHER THAN POLITICAL/ETHICAL, TO COLLABORATE?

It could appear from the foregoing that the only reasons for action researchers and feminists to collaborate are political. While that might be a sufficient justification, it would miss the significant intellectual values involved in this collaboration. There are theoretical, methodological, and ethical connections between AR and feminism that can really make a substantial difference in the quality of social research overall.

Action research offers feminists lengthy and diverse experiences in collaborative research with stakeholders, including a considerable variety of alternative ways of managing group processes, pooling knowledge, and "speaking the truth to power." The AR emphasis on the inherent value and power of local knowledge, the vision of theory and knowledge as embodied practices, and both the social psychological traditions and human relations traditions that feed into AR are all relevant to the concerns and conundrums faced by feminists.

From feminism, AR stands to gain greatly in the depth of epistemological critique, in the tough-minded defense of alternative methods and framings of social research, in the connection to a vital and assertive democratic politics and set of value commitments both inside and beyond the academy, and most especially in activism within the academy, something that AR has been far too passive about.

Both traditions also reinforce each other's commitments to multidisciplinarity, setting research directions around extra-academic stakeholders' issues, multi-method approaches, and a serious reevaluation of issues of the jointness of intellectual property and the critique of the extractive approach to social research that dominates the conventional social sciences.

To conclude, the moral of this story is well expressed in a famous section of an Argentinean Gaucho poem by José Hernández:

> Los hermanos sean unidos
> Porque ésa es la ley primera-
> Tengan unión verdadera
> En cualquier tiempo que sea,
> Porque, si entre ellos pelean,
> Los devoran los de ajuera.

> The brothers and sisters[3] must be united
> Because that is the first law.
> They must be truly united
> In any and all times
> Because, if they fight among themselves,
> they will be devoured by the outsiders.
>
> José Hernández, *El Gaucho Martín Fierro*, 1872

NOTES

1. The plurality of feminist approaches is widely known and the subject of regular discussion. The plurality of AR is less well recognized. There are diverse and divergent approaches to AR going under a variety of different names (see Greenwood and Levin, 1998). I personally shifted to using the term action research instead of participatory action research both because of complaints from colleagues about the appropriation of a term invented by "Southern" practitioners and because I agree with our European colleagues that AR without participation is inconceivable.

2. I am borrowing this term from a local colleague, George Ferrari, of Catholic Charities.

3. In Spanish, *hermanos* in plural is collectively masculine and feminine.

REFERENCES

Bloom, A. (1987). *The closing of the American mind*. New York: Simon & Schuster.

D'Souza, D. (1991). *Illiberal education: The politics of race and sex on campus*. New York: The Free Press.

Furner, M. (1975). *Advocacy: A crisis in the professionalization of American social science*. Lexington: University of Kentucky Press.

Gillespie. R. (1991). *Manufacturing knowledge: A history of the Hawthorne Experiment*. Cambridge: Cambridge University Press.

Greenwood, D., & Levin, M. (1998). *Introduction to action research: Social research for social change*. Thousand Oaks, CA: SAGE Publications.

Harrison, B., & Bluestone, B. (1990). *The great U-turn: Corporate restructuring and the polarizing of America*. New York: Basic Books.

Hernández, José (1872). *El gaucho Martin Fierro*. Buenos Aires: Editorial de la Pampa.

Herrnstein, R. J., & Murray, C. (1994). *The bell curve: Intelligence and class structure in American life*. New York: The Free Press.

Horowitz, I. L. (Ed.). (1967). *The rise and fall of Project Camelot: Studies in the relationship between social science and practical politics*. Cambridge, MA: The M.I.T. Press.

Kors, A., & Silverglate, H. (1998). *The Shadow University: The betrayal of liberty on America's campuses*. New York: The Free Press.

Krause, E. (1996). *Death of the guilds: Professions, states, and the advance of capitalism, 1930 to the present*. New Haven, CT: Yale University Press.

Lengermann, P. M., & Niebrugge-Brantley, J. (1998). *The women founders: Sociology and social theory*. New York: The McGraw Hill Companies.

Polanyi, K. (1944). *The great transformation*. New York: Rinehart & Company.

Ravitch, D. (2000). *Left back: A century of failed school reform*. New York: Simon & Schuster.

Ross, D. (1991). *The origins of American social science*. Cambridge: Cambridge University Press.

Young, I. M. (1990). *Justice and the politics of difference*. Princeton, NJ: Princeton University Press.

CHAPTER 10

Dilemmas of Power: Questions for All of Us

Rhoda Unger

Since the 1970s feminist criticism of the social sciences has focused on two major issues—one methodological and one sociostructural. Feminist critique of methodology questions whether social science research can ever be objective. Concerns about objectivity emerge in a number of areas including biases of researchers, biases in the selection of research participants, the impact of subjects' awareness of being studied, and the context-stripping nature of laboratory research itself (for a summary of this work, see Unger, 1998). Concerns also exist about the actual practice of scholarship. These include the lack of participation in research by members of marginalized groups, the greater probability of publication of research from individuals in elite institutions, and the occupation of various kinds of gatekeeping positions by dominant members of the social hierarchy (Unger, 1982, 1983). These latter criticisms can also be called dilemmas of power.

Although there has been much discussion of these issues by feminist scholars, most of the discussion has focused on the obstacles that feminist research has encountered in dealing with mainstream institutions. With few exceptions, there has been little discussion by feminists (or by other critics of mainstream social science) of issues involving objectivity and power when we ourselves are the decision makers. Such discussions have been left, therefore, to those outside of our communities and are often hostile in nature (cf. Patai & Koertge, 1994; Redding, 2001).

Sometimes, critical scholars deny the potential influence of their own subjective biases. For example, nearly 20 years ago I participated in a seminar on social construction led by a prominent feminist philosopher. Most of the other participants were in the humanities and not enthusiastic about any form of scientific research. At the time I was constructing a scale designed to measure personal epistemology (how people explain the way the world works) and its relationship to religious and political ideology (Unger, Draper, & Pendergrass, 1986). Members of the group permitted me to test the scale with themselves as respondents but vehemently denied the possibility that feminists, too, had biases. Even when I reported that the group, as expected, held very socially constructionist viewpoints, they admired my persistence but denied that any valid information could be explained by such positivist methodology. Many of the women in the group did not see feminism as a form of bias despite my empirical demonstration of the ideological tilt within the community.

The development of standpoint theory over the past 20 years has led to the growing acceptance by feminist scholars that all knowledge claims derive from some subjective perspective. We have been slower, however, to recognize that methodology is also inextricably linked to values. For example, the debate about the relative merits of qualitative and quantitative methodology continues within the feminist scholarly community as well as outside of it. There are many sides to this debate, but at least one important question is about where qualitative research works best. One view holds that qualitative research is good preliminary or ancillary work that "supplements" quantitative research, whereas another view argues that qualitative work addresses completely different questions than quantitative work, and one should not attempt to assimilate it into the experimental quantitative paradigm (Shields, 2002).

Of course, these viewpoints assume that qualitative research is a valid methodology for psychology. Both ignore the reality that most psychologists still regard studies that use numbers as more valuable than those that do not. Some perspectives are also more privileged than others. Some feminist scholars are now in a position to make a difference because they have, however improbably, become some of those who guard or open professional gates (Stewart & Shields, 2001). Therefore, feminists no longer have the luxury of examining issues of gatekeeping only from the perspective of those without power.

Feminists' neglect of concerns about power and the gatekeeping functions of previously marginalized critics is easy to explain. It is only recently that such critics have attained positions of power and authority such as departmental chairs, journal editors, and so forth. For a variety of reasons it is difficult for such individuals to acknowledge that they do, indeed, possess power. Perhaps we deny power because we also want to deny responsibility for the way things work (or do not work) within society as a whole (Unger, 2000). In any case, I have seen little discussion of these concerns within the social science community (for an exception, see Stewart & Shields, 2001).

ISSUES OF PROCESS

My concerns about these issues were reawakened recently by the questions provoked by an unsolicited manuscript submitted to a new on-line journal of which I am the first editor. *Analyses of Social Issues and Public Policy* (*ASAP*) is sponsored by the Society for the Psychological Study of Social Issues (SPSSI)—an organization that was established in 1936 in order to offer a "radical" critique of psychology, and which is sometimes called the "conscience of the American Psychological Association." This manuscript criticized a recent issue of the *Journal of Social Issues* (*JSI*, a print journal also published by SPSSI) on welfare reform (Zuckerman & Kalil, 2000). Briefly, the authors argued that the editors and authors involved in this volume had uncritically accepted governmental definitions of successful reform and had betrayed SPSSI's radical promise (Steinitz & Mishler, 2001).

As editor of the on-line journal, my responsibility was to find qualified reviewers for the paper and make a decision about publication based on their comments. What then were the dilemmas? Some were rather simple and could be resolved by a discussion with other gatekeepers such as officers of SPSSI and members of the editorial board. For example, should one journal publish critiques of another? Since the *Journal of Social Issues* (the print journal that has been published by SPSSI since the 1940s) is thematic and has no provision for commentary, the other journal editors had no objection to the paper's publication, assuming its scholarship was acceptable. The reviewers were enthusiastic and the paper was published in *ASAP* (http://www.asap-spssi.org). It also appeared in a print version of the journal the following year (Steinitz & Mishler, 2001).

Considering this outcome as unproblematic, however, assumes that scholarship is unbiased and uninfluenced by the values we bring to it. This is the view of those who take a positivist position on the objectivity and neutrality of the scientific method. This view is not always challenged by liberal feminists who believe that the practices of science work well once the gendered playing field is leveled. It assumes that the choice of reviewers and the content of their reviews are based entirely on objective merit and are not influenced by the ideological commitments of the gatekeepers involved.

As a critical feminist scholar I feel I have a commitment to question such norms even when they apply to me. For example, was I influenced in my decision to publish the paper by the previous scholarly critique of one of the authors whom I greatly admired (cf. Mishler, 1986)? Was I influenced by his elite affiliation—the Harvard School of Public Health? Was I influenced by the fact that he used some of my own work to bolster his case? Did I select reviewers based on their knowledge or their political viewpoints?

These questions might not have mattered so much if this paper had criticized scholarship in a more mainstream journal. But the target volume had appeared in a sister journal published by an organization whose values I share. I became concerned, therefore, with how I could be fair to the editors and authors of the volume on welfare reform. My concerns were heightened when correspondence with the senior editor of the welfare reform issue asking her to write a response indicated she was hurt and angered by the critique and, originally, wanted nothing to do with it. This produced another set of dilemmas.

Because the paper had received very positive peer review, the editors of *ASAP* were committed to its publication. However, publication without any response seemed unacceptable. What is the role of the gatekeeper in this process? My first reaction was to consult others. However, the president of SPSSI at that time was one of the people whose position had been criticized in Steinitz and Mishler's paper. And, although I consult *ASAP's* editorial board frequently, their role is primarily advisory. By definition, being a gatekeeper means making decisions and living with their consequences.

I decided to contact the senior editor of the welfare reform issue again by phone to attempt to persuade her to write a response. This may be a feminist policy, but my action was also influenced by the fact that I knew the individual and liked and respected her work. Obviously, the decision was facilitated by the existence of a mutual network. But, one can ask, is the existence of an "old girls' network" any fairer than the old boys' networks feminists criticized earlier? Networks imply unequal access to sources of power. And, although there have been attempts to create non-hierarchical structures for decision making, these are difficult to create when the power differentials are the result of informal networks rather than formal systems involving rules and policies.

I also decided to publish the original critical article in a special section of *ASAP* that we had discussed early in the journal's development. This section, "Point/Counterpoint," was designed to make use of the interactive and innovative nature of web publication. It permits the publication of articles that contain a more overt point of view than are found in articles termed as research in most mainstream journals. Readers of the journal have been asked, in particular, to write responses to articles in this section of *ASAP*.

However, the creation of different categories of articles is also problematic. Would readers see articles in Point/Counterpoint as less legitimate than those in the unlabeled part of the journal? A priori, how does one determine which manuscripts belong in each section? This is an important problem because many mainstream psychologists regard only quantitative data as meaningful. We have been trying to combat this perception in *ASAP* by publishing qualitative as well as quantitative studies. But, do we weaken the importance of historical analysis (an important component of Steinitz and Mishler's paper) by putting it into a separate category?

The senior editor of the original journal issue also called my attention to what she perceived as condescension and sexism in the original critical article, which both the reviewers and I had missed. It is difficult for most of us to distinguish between criticism of one's ideas and oneself. *ASAP* is committed to a policy of civil discourse and we urged the authors of the critique to be careful about personal attacks. I think we were partially successful, but hostility is sometimes in the "eye of the beholder," and it is difficult to ignore status differences produced by age, sex, and location within an elite institution. How can these differentials be addressed without sacrificing the commitment to open dialogue?

In order to reduce the one-to-one quality of the dialogue, I successfully solicited comments on the original paper from other members of SPSSI whom I knew to have an interest in the role of values in research and the impact of academic scholarship on the formulation of public policy. These attempts resulted in a set of four responses/comments that were also published in *ASAP* (Cherry, 2001; Fine & Barreras, 2001; Kalil, 2001; Zuckerman, 2001).

This seemingly positive outcome demonstrates yet again the power of collegial networks in the legitimization of scholarship. Although all SPSSI members and readers of *ASAP* were offered the opportunity to participate in another round of comments, only one uninvited commentator did so (Wilmoth, 2001). It is obvious that personal communications make such comments more probable. They call attention to the expertise of potential authors and make them feel that their input is desirable. In spite of good intentions, personal networks privilege some and neglect others and these processes are accentuated as the relevant scholarly community becomes larger.

Collegial networks are often communities that share similar values about the nature and quality of scholarship. It is probably not accidental that the one uninvited commentary was also the most supportive of the original volume on welfare reform. Even well-intentioned gatekeepers may not be able to avoid all the perils of intradisciplinary boundaries. What mechanisms exist for dealing with the dilemma of maintaining, simultaneously, scholarly excellence and open access especially when expertise is scarce and resources (journal space and time) are limited?

ISSUES OF CONTENT

The previous discussion is concerned with editorial decisions when so-called normative processes conflict with feminist principles of openness and collegiality. An examination of the content of these papers, however, also reveals intellectual dilemmas. Why did the contents of this journal issue on welfare reform provoke such an impassioned critique?

Examination of the original critique (Steinitz & Mishler, 2001) and the senior editor's response (Zuckerman, 2001) is quite illuminating. In many ways this controversy involves a "classic" radical/liberal confrontation. In brief, Steinitz and Mishler argued that

once the official definition of the problem is accepted as the primary research frame and the norms of neutrality and technical objectivity are assumed for analyses and presentation of data, the researcher gives up her option of directly expressing her personal concerns or allying herself with her subjects. (p. 164)

They wished to initiate a broad and critical discussion on the politics of research and whose interests are served by the dominant model of researcher neutrality and his or her role as an "honest broker." They also charged that the "mixed results" reported by most papers in the *JSI* special issue supports "the selectivity of policy makers and the media in what they choose to consider as relevant, which largely means they can discount any evidence of negative impact on poor women and their families of the new laws " (p. 168). Finally, they concluded that the possibility of producing studies that alleviate social injustice has

little to do with the rigor of their respective methods or their adherence to conventional standards of 'scientific' research. Rather...the likelihood of having an effect is a function of the type of alliance established between academic researchers and the groups whose struggles they wish to join. (p. 171)

In response, Zuckerman (2001), the senior editor of the *JSI* volume, who has worked for many years in the formulation and construction of public policy in Washington, D.C., pointed out that she too had a commitment to work for social justice. She argued that research can be used to change existing legislation and that "changing laws is radical, and the ultimate in political activism" (p. 188). She also noted:

In 1996, welfare reform was a train that had already left the station—the bill was going to pass, and the only question was how much structure the Federal government would impose and how much power they would give to the States. There was little relevant research on the likely impact of welfare reform, and what there was could be used by politicians from all across the ideological spectrum. (pp. 188–189)

Kalil (2001), the coeditor of the welfare reform volume, also recognized that the present welfare reforms could produce deleterious effects: "there are some who have traded a welfare check for a paycheck but who have also incurred additional stresses and may need additional supports, such as transportation and childcare, or help with dealing with a mental health problem" (p. 184). However, she believed that researchers are in a position to delineate those factors that make it difficult for some women to leave welfare and to help craft revisions to the law that will improve outcomes.

The final commentary in *ASAP* (Wilmoth, 2001) supported the position that evaluation researchers can be "honest brokers." He argued that "quantified, statistically representative information frequently has greater utility and perceived credibility than action research" (p. 195) and that it is also better for the information needs of policymakers. But, he also admitted that "even when the issue is not ideologically charged, policy makers frequently ignore hard data" (p. 200).

The parallels between the discussion of governmental gatekeeping as related by Wilmoth and academic gatekeeping as framed by this paper are compelling. Both discussions have to do with power and how power is exercised through collegial networks and through many small decisions over time that may have little to do with an evidential framework. Nevertheless, Wilmoth judges statistical findings as more important, even though he concedes that they may have no more impact on decisions than a well-told anecdote. Such comparisons do not make comfortable reading for those of us who would prefer to deny our own power.

As an "outsider on the inside," I believe the positions of all the participants in this Point/Counterpoint dialogue have merit and reflect their own commitment to social justice. But it also appears to me that some of the participants in this argument are talking past each other and have not addressed some of the fundamental sources of their differences. These include unexamined assumptions about causality (e.g., Is change the responsibility of the individual or the sociopolitical system in which individuals are embedded?); differing views about the definition and value of objectivity; and different assumptions about morality, fairness, and the role of the state. These values appear to extend well beyond beliefs about revolutionary versus incremental change.

Should editors attempt to extend an argument beyond the domain laid out by the original participants? This is an important question when, as in the present case, remedies are partial, are contingent, and cannot easily be dichotomized. The addition of other voices offers readers some ways to "evade" an either/or dilemma.

Two more papers that were part of the *ASAP* counterpoint discussion (Cherry, 2001; Fine & Barreras, 2001) are too complex to discuss fully here. Both, however, mapped out the large and complex number of strategies available to social scientists who are committed to both advocacy and scholarship despite the compromises they must make to work between apparently contradictory demands. Both highlighted the lessons of the past and the potential of the future to break down the walls of such problematic binaries as "knowledge and action, experts and the people, objec-

tivity and subjectivity" (Fine & Barreras, 2001, p. 176). These authors visu-
alize social research as a resource for social change, social change as a
process, filled with allies, coalitions, and the much-needed strategic application of rigorous social research.

LESSONS TO BE LEARNED

Problems with process appear to be more intractable than problems of
content. It is not easy to work with contradictory demands. It is even
harder to teach others to do so. Abigail Stewart and Stephanie Shields
(2001) have highlighted some of the problems encountered by a select
group of recognized senior feminist scholars in training their graduate
students. They speak of the problems of still having to advise women "to
do it all"—to acquire expertise in both qualitative techniques that give
voice to their participants and quantitative techniques that continue to be
favored by mainstream psychological journals. They contend "with the
difficult balance between being supportive and open to new ideas, and
being expected or required to identify and police 'quality,' particularly
when they perceive that the criteria for quality are contentious or arbi-
trary" (p. 313). In sum, they are concerned that even feminist gatekeepers
may reproduce the discipline that they/we are trying to change.

Content and process cannot easily be separated. In fact, it is the implicit
contradictions produced by the study of problems involving social justice
that create many of the personal and professional dilemmas discussed in
this chapter. What lessons can be learned from a consideration of the content of dilemmas involving advocacy and scholarship? I am assuming a
position that most knowledge claims have credibility for someone. There
is nothing to be gained by demonizing potential partners. However, credibility (believing something is useful or correct) is not the same thing as
legitimacy (the view that an idea has some kind of official or disciplinary
sanction) nor the same as a claim about truth. I take the position that all
problems and their solutions are socially constructed and defined.

Serious social problems are "highly political, in the sense that they
involve conflicts of interest between those who benefit from a particular
definition of the problem and those who do not." Consequently, "when
social scientists are called to help solve a 'problem,' they not only participate in a process that helps legitimate that problem as real, they also further a process that has already defined the problem in a certain way"
(Unger, 1986, pp. 224–225).

Moreover, the acceptance of all well-considered views as credible does
not mean that one must sacrifice either passion or politics. An examination
of the assumptions behind our scholarly commitments and an explicit
statement of these commitments would improve our ability to communi-

cate with each other. Unfortunately, many scholars interested in the application of their research are uninterested in conceptual discussion of these issues. They see them as tangential to their desire to "get things done." Conversely, those interested in the philosophy and sociology of science often have little interest in the "small" victories of empirical research with its mixed results and partial answers.

It might have been more discreet not to discuss openly this case history of a controversy encountered during the early stage of *ASAP*'s development. Or, I could have talked about the problems in more abstract and less reflexive terms. Some of the protagonists may not be pleased and I am concerned about how this chapter may affect personal and professional relationships. I have asked for more feedback on it than on most articles I have written (even those with similar themes). However, silence is another form of power. And, when we talk about power, we rarely recognize that we are talking about many little moments and the way in which power is in fact the accumulation of the ability to shape lots of microprocesses and tiny events (Stewart, 2002).

There are lessons to be learned from discussions about the use of power that are particularly important during a time when SPSSI has moved to Washington D.C. in order to become more involved in the formulation of public policy. One important lesson is that lack of information about gatekeeping processes does not serve the powerless. But lack of power is not necessarily a permanent condition.

As individuals from previously marginalized groups move into gatekeeping positions, it is important that we acknowledge our power and consider the responsibility that comes with it. Social mobility can confer the ability to see issues from both an insider's and an outsider's perspective. Remembering that one was once an outsider forces us to continue to question the sources of power, how it cannot be separated from the politics and the ideological position of the user, and how power functions even within communities committed to social justice. There is no virtue in ignorance. Scholarly articles are not published in an ideological limbo. To reveal rather than to conceal these processes may provide a useful teaching tool for those who are currently outside of the status hierarchy.

The failure to analyze and criticize our own work increases the opportunities for those who would tear down the edifices we have built. A good example of this process was provided recently by the author of a lead article in *American Psychologist* (Redding, 2001), which used our own discussions of inevitable biases in the research process to argue for the recruitment of more conservative psychologists whose viewpoint he believed to be absent from the discipline. If we have taught our opponents the necessity of questioning objectivity (even if it is ours and not their own), how much more important is this lesson for our friends?

REFERENCES

Cherry, F. (2001). SPSSI and activist science. *Analyses of Social Issues and Public Policy, 1,* 191–194.

Fine, M., & Barreras, R. (2001). To be of use. *Analyses of Social Issues and Public Policy, 1,* 175–182.

Kalil, A. (2001). The role of social science in welfare reform. *Analyses of Social Issues and Public Policy, 1,* 183–185.

Mishler, E. G. (1986). *Research interviewing: Context and narrative.* Cambridge, MA: Harvard University Press.

Patai, D., & Koertge, N. (1994). *Professing feminism: Cautionary tales from the strange world of women's studies.* New York: Basic Books.

Redding, R. E. (2001). Sociopolitical diversity in psychology: The case for pluralism. *American Psychologist, 56,* 205–215.

Shields, personal communication, June 4, 2002.

Steinitz, V., & Mishler, E. G. (2001). Reclaiming SPSSI's radical promise: A critical look at *JSI*'s "Impact of Welfare Reform" issue. *Analyses of Social Issues and Public Policy, 1,*163–173.

Stewart, A. personal communication, June 9, 2002.

Stewart, A. J., & Shields, S. A. (2001). Gatekeepers as change agents: What are feminist psychologists doing in places like this? In D. L. Tolman & M. Brydon-Miller (Eds.), *From subjects to subjectivities: A handbook of interpretive and participatory methods* (pp. 304–318). New York: New York University Press.

Unger, R. K. (1982). Advocacy versus scholarship revisited: Issues in the psychology of women. *Psychology of Women Quarterly 7,* 5–17.

Unger, R. K. (1983). Through the looking glass: No Wonderland yet! (The reciprocal relationship between methodology and models of reality). Presidential address to Division 35 of APA. *Psychology of Women Quarterly, 8,* 9–32.

Unger, R. K. (1986). Looking toward the future by looking at the past: Social activism and social history. *Journal of Social Issues, 42*(1), 215–227.

Unger, R. K. (1998). *Resisting gender: Twenty-five years in/of feminist psychology.* London: SAGE Publications.

Unger, R. K. (2000). Outsiders inside: Positive marginality and social change. *Journal of Social Issues, 56*(1), 163–179.

Unger, R. K., Draper, R. D., & Pendergrass, M. L. (1986). Personal epistemology and personal experience. *Journal of Social Issues, 42*(2), 67–79.

Wilmoth, G. H. (2001). The "honest broker" role and evaluation research affirmed. *Analyses of Social Issues and Public Policy, 1,* 195–205.

Zuckerman, D. (2001). Linking research to policy to people's lives. *Analyses of Social Issues and Public Policy, 1,* 187–190.

Zuckerman, D., & Kalil, A., (Eds.). (2000). The impact of welfare reform. *Journal of Social Issues, 56*(4), 579–586.

Conclusion

Mary Brydon-Miller, Yoland Wadsworth,
and Anmol Satiani

MARY BRYDON-MILLER LEADS OFF...

One of my favorite walks is along the South Downs Way. There is a point along the trail from which I can look out over the waters of the English Channel and across the green fields, hedge rows, and villages of West Sussex, back along the chalky path I've walked, and forward through the trees and along the ridge. Sitting down to write these concluding remarks for this volume, a project that has taken us many months and many miles, gives me an opportunity to appreciate the work we've done together and what I've learned through the process and to consider where I've been and where I might be heading next. It also affords me the chance to thank my traveling companions, chief among them Pat Maguire and Alice McIntyre, who've traveled with me the longest, and all of those who've shared the journey.

Why wander? I think for many of us restlessness, a certain dissatisfaction with where we were, is what first drove us out the door. Davydd Greenwood captures the frustration and sense of disillusionment many of us have felt when confronted by the realization that most of the work of social scientists within the academy seemed to be intent on "profiting from a passive role in the face of injustices that it documented without confronting them politically." But at the same time he reminds us of some of the trailblazers who, although their work might have been forgotten for a time, have left an important legacy of the potential role of the social sciences in democratic social reform. He also reminds us that this legacy might well have been lost had it not been for the efforts of feminist scholars who have so doggedly challenged the supremacy of the positivist elite. And he suggests we remain restless, not getting too settled in our comfy academic homes lest we find at some point that we are no longer able to move at all.

Angela Shartrand and Mary Brabeck's discussion of ethics reminds me of the immense responsibility inherent in calling myself a feminist participatory action researcher. This is not a title one can claim without demonstrating an active and abiding commitment to working for social justice. It is not untroubled by issues of power and privilege and must be constantly reexamined and renegotiated. It is not the kind of learning that is ever completed. As Jill Chrisp says, "My challenge is to continue knowing that I am not going to get it right." One aspect of this challenge is in the willingness to acknowledge the limitations of my own worldview and to continue to try to explore and, perhaps, even to embrace new perspectives. Nimat Barazangi's discussion of the difficulty of reconciling existing feminist and participatory action research rhetorics with the values and aspirations of the Muslim women with whom she works is an example of the importance of learning to respect the multiple locations of the communities within which we might practice. Kalina Brabeck considers similar issues and offers us a means for bridging differences without pretending to assume to ever truly know the experience of the Other. Issues of representation, of voice and authority, continue to challenge our practice whether we locate ourselves as insiders within the communities we study, as in Jill Chrisp's work with mothers of adolescent boys, or as outsiders, as was the case with both Alice McIntyre's collaborations with women in Northern Ireland and Brinton Lykes's work with Mayan women.

Among the contributors to this volume are deans of schools of education, full professors, journal editors, well-known and well-respected scholars in the fields of psychology, anthropology, and education. Feminist scholars and action researchers, despite years of feeling marginalized, we have begun to fill positions of power within the academy and within our disciplines. This role as gatekeepers and as decision makers is not always a comfortable one and presents constant challenges to our attempts to maintain an ethical stance. As Rhoda Unger points out, "when we talk about power, we rarely recognize that we are talking about many little moments." Sue Noffke and Marie Brennan warn us of the dangers that might lie in the intersection of our newly found institutional power and our good intentions. They describe the potential for university researchers to "walk all over the community" in their efforts to do good. "They do not usually do so maliciously, but by continuing to use existing relations of power, they do not make it possible to interrupt those power relations." Drawing on feminist theories, critical race theory, and postcolonial theory, I try in my own practice to remain mindful of the ways in which power can seduce us into believing that we are helping when perhaps we are not and to continue to try to find ways of using the power that I do possess to promote more democratic processes of achieving social change. In her discussion of her work in teaching action research from a feminist perspective, Pat Maguire mirrors my own conviction that training a new generation of committed practitioners is the best means of translating this new power into effective action.

Certainly, the most enduring lesson and the most cherished gift of working on this volume are the friendships that have grown out of the process. Old friendships have been deepened; new acquaintances are now companions. I know that I can count on these friends to call me back if I wander off the trail, to provide me a welcome if I end up on their doorstep one night, and to send me on my way again if it seems as if I've stayed too long in one place. In the introduction to this volume, we cite Jill Morawski's encouragement to attend to building relationships within our own workplaces and research sites. This project has been an example of trying to live up to that ideal. Of course we have had differences of opinion, sometimes outright disagreements, but overall we've been successful. I think it is a testament to the power of collaboration that we have managed to challenge one another to reconsider long-held ideas and to deepen our commitment to our work as educators and scholars while maintaining these friendships. We hope that readers of this volume will feel welcome to join us.

YOLAND WADSWORTH, COMING FROM OUTSIDE THE ACADEMY, PICKS UP THE THREAD

In a way, this book and the small focused international conference in Boston that was part of its process seemed to me to emerge from an irritation about a silence observed by feminists in the participatory action research (PAR) field. Pat Maguire had asked "Where were the women?" "Where was the acknowledgement of women's PAR and feminism?" particularly in men's—including prominent men's—writings about PAR. On the other hand, my own journey (until recently, outside academe) had commenced in 1972 in London with urban community development-based PAR and the critique of positivism and uncritical interpretivism. Subsequently in the 1980s, in a Feminism in Social Theory reading group, I recall being impatient with my academic sisters not acknowledging the decades of applied critical theory and PAR that had preceded their "discovery" of, for example, Anne Oakley's "contradiction in terms of interviewing women." I'd hear them marvel at how the women research subjects "really enjoyed being asked their opinions," but I was sensitive to the colonizing still taking place as the feminist researcher went off and still asked "her" questions, performed "her" analysis, developed "her" theory, and drew "her" conclusions. I was seeing the lost opportunities for coconstructing more grounded, valid analyses and conclusions *with* those whose lives were being theorized about and represented, not to mention with and by whom propositions and conclusions could have been tested in the hard yard of practice.

It has been marvelous, through the Traveling Companions project, to find so many feminist researchers who have clearly pushed past this standpoint and, as Davydd Greenwood has observed, deeply challenged the academy.

On the other hand, underlying my own practice of PAR was nevertheless a humanist feminist understanding of the base communities with which I worked. I cut my teeth in the 1970s on issues central to the lives of women—young mothers and their children and men at the community level—such as "suburban neurosis," playgroups and child care, neighborhood houses, refuges, adult and higher education "living and learning centers," and consciousness-raising reading groups (such as of Betty Friedan's "this book changes lives" *The Feminine Mystique,* organized by the radical local church). Although my work later focused on general community, health, education, and welfare issues, I also lived my life as a feminist (rejecting subordination in marriage, campaigning for child care and against compulsory childbearing, and getting an education, a profession, and my own home—the latter all denied my foremothers and considerable achievements of my foresisters).

Yet late in my life I too encountered the surprise of finding that even my hard-won democratic "homeland" of PAR was still able to render women PAR practitioners unimportant—most surprisingly at the Cartagena World Congress (where 40 out of 49 conveners, rapporteurs, chairs, and panelists were male) but also in the constant practice of honoring only male "forefathers," male authors, and male thinkers.

Yet despite these salutary experiences, there were and are feminist women (and men who are explicitly profeminist PAR practitioners) who speak up, and slowly the changes get made.

So the year of e-discussion and the meeting in Boston made for a marvelous journey with feminists who do understand and embrace the PAR epistemology and apply it to their work with women, alongside PAR practitioners who understand and embrace feminism while working on projects that may not primarily be about women (e.g., most recently in my case regarding mental health consumer/staff collaboration—involving both women and men across that divide). (And it helps to stay in touch to maintain this.)

Consequently in this journey we focused less on the matters that had hitherto divided PAR and feminist PAR and more on what we all shared. In a sense the metaphor shift reflects how "bridging the gap" gave way to us becoming "traveling companions" around shared issues, importantly:

- the daily ongoing concerns around issues of power relations (and constructing mutually empowering ones),
- issues of insider/outsider or us/them (and constructing you/me/we collaborations), and
- issues of divisions between "inside"/academy and "outside"/community (or how the production, organization, and legitimization of knowledge takes place in theory/practice).

What I personally took from this journeying with my traveling companions has been closely related to my own move from a lifetime "outside" the academy to a new life inside it. My explicit hope is to formalize an AR postgraduate education program to help a new generation of people to confidently and effectively practice and facilitate action research and to know how to speak to (and not default to) the positivist "standard operating system." I want to create a vibrant environment in which to "teach learners" and have "learners teach" from and about all the various PAR "strands, streams, and variants" including feminism, human services, community development, management and organizational development, agriculture/farming, environment, evaluation, and so on. As I struggle to find start-up funds for an academic program of this nature (while others around me snaffle large research grants and lucrative consultancies!), I am reminded of the personal price we pay if we want to travel this ethical journey of a noncoercive science, determined that all of us speak our truths, particularly those of us with truths long-rendered undiscussable. Yet while we struggle, I am reminded also of the ongoing need for our own self-critical consciousness—particularly regarding our nevertheless relative privilege and the part this plays in our working relations. In Boston— on the eve of entering the academy myself—I was particularly aware that we are not all academics, tertiary educated, researchers, or university students; interested in the published literature or in publishing more books ourselves; or having the capacity to choose to leave a community research site, and so on.

To conclude my thread in this final piece, I want to offer the observation that sometimes in PAR it feels like "we do everything on high heels and backwards." We not only must know all that a conventional researcher knows (and everything a community development or culture change agent knows too), but we must then also ensure that all this is effectively shared with others in the situation so that everyone is both researcher and actionist, and we (if facilitating) take a back seat!

Valuable indeed is the journey on which one finds so many traveling companions who are all dancing backwards on high heels, running into the same frontline issues: the representation of multiple (even contradictory or conflicting) tellings of the "same" story—whether by ourselves or by any other participant in the research; the consequences of surfacing or disappearing various valuable or destructive "truths"; or the essential paradoxes of coconstruction with base communities.

Suitably refreshed by each other's company, we now head back out onto the road.

ANMOL SATIANI CONCLUDES (FOR THE TIME BEING)...

As I think about the pieces included in this book and of my experience of the Bridging the Gap conference I am reminded of the multiple ways in which feminisms and PAR have been critical for me in imagining possibilities for social change.

Feminisms have offered me many gifts and challenges. I remember that one of my first experiences of feminism was in my Psychology of Women course as an undergraduate. I remember feeling that, as the only Woman of Color (a Pakistani-American woman) in the class, I had important opportunities, coupled with many challenges. I was clearly identified as the Other and felt pressured to conform to particular stereotypes of Asian women. I was constantly asked to explain *the* "Third World" perspective and often was dismissed when I challenged individuals' stereotypes. Issues related to race and culture were not integrated into the course discussions and gender was assumed to be the most salient aspect of identity in all contexts for members of the class. Some of my encounters were difficult and painful and I often wondered if I wanted to be a part of "feminism" as defined by my classmates. I learned a great deal from these experiences and came to realize that there are a variety of ways to engage with feminisms.

I continue to try and think critically about issues in my own communities related to gender and power. As a graduate student in counseling psychology, I continue to struggle with these issues. As I am developing my professional identities, as researcher, therapist, supervisor, teacher, and consultant, I am reflecting on how power intersects with issues of gender, race, and other aspects of identity. These are complicated issues and can be overwhelming to consider, particularly when, for multiple reasons, one is in a low-status position within a system.

I am still beginning to learn about PAR. The theme of multiple positions and multiple identities in these chapters has prompted me to think about issues of power and privilege as very dynamic and complex. It has made me think about my own clinical work, teaching, and research and the ways in which I hold power in particular contexts and simultaneously feel powerless in others. Contributors to this book continue to grapple with questions related to power and privilege and the potential for "colonization." This level of honesty and openness is refreshing and critical. I am struck by how powerful the message of humility is in these chapters, including Jill Chrisp's statement, "My challenge is to continue knowing that I am not going to get it completely right." The contributors who have been practicing feminist-oriented PAR for decades are still grappling with important questions related to power and privilege. Those who are practicing feminist participatory action research have not "arrived" at any comfortable place. I am energized and full of hope when I learn about individuals who are honest about living in spaces of discomfort. This discomfort seems to be a reality for many of the contributors but does not lead to inaction. Embedded in these chapters is also the idea that one must take action and not be paralyzed while grappling with important questions. As a graduate student and as a human being interested in social justice, this is an important message. I think of Tandon's words, "Participatory research principles are not purist. You can't sit and wait for the ideal situation. Waiting to do it right is paralyzing" (Tandon, 1985, cited in Maguire, 1987, p. 134).

These chapters help me to imagine possibilities. They challenge me to think beyond what I think that I "know" and remind me that I need to remain open to a variety of possibilities, both professionally and personally. Both PAR and feminisms (and their intersections) have helped me to consider future possibilities for myself as a future counseling psychologist and as a human being interested in social justice. I am constantly learning that there are a wide range of opportunities and activities with which I am capable of engaging. The contributions of this book also make me think of the challenges of thinking of individuals in contexts (rather than context-stripping with which my field has been historically engaged) and holding multiple levels of context simultaneously. I also have been thinking more about multiple levels on which one can act and how these levels are connected with one another.

An appealing aspect of these chapters involves knowing that there are others on similar paths, struggling with similar questions and concerns. Finding community seems to be a critical part of practicing feminist PAR. Although the contributors come from different areas of the world and different life experiences, and they may differ along lines of gender, race, sexual orientation, class, and other factors, these chapters make me think about the importance of finding communities in which one feels supported. Having these communities makes the "travel" easier to bear and can help to energize individuals and communities to engage in social action. I am grateful for the opportunity to be connected with many of the contributors of this book. I hope to continue to imagine possibilities for social justice and to choose to act.

NOTE

This chapter was equally co-authored by Anmol Satiani, Yoland Wadsworth, and Mary Brydon-Miller.

REFERENCES

Freidan, Betty. (2001). *The feminine mystique.* New York: W. W. Norton & Co. (Original work published 1963).

Maguire, P. (1987). *Doing participatory research: A feminist approach.* Amherst: The Center for International Education, University of Massachusetts.

Index

Academia: and activism, 98, 111, 159–61; complicity of, in social injustice, 87–88, 158; conservative backlash in, 162–64; and counter-insurgency efforts, 160–61; critiques of, 179–80; definition of, 80; disciplinary boundaries in, 161, 164; diversity in, 29; and feminism, 34–36, 98, 161–62; Muslim women's experiences in, 26–27, 29–30; pressures on researchers from within, 85, 90, 139–40, 165; power dynamics in, 3–4, 80, 171–73; relationship to local communities, 79, 87–88; status of Women's Studies programs in, 90, 164; teaching of PAR in, 183; view of Islam in, 25, 28, 31–33; view of storytelling in, 6; women's experiences in, 3–4, 160. *See also* Graduate students; Intellectuals; Research; Social Sciences

Action Research (AR): and community formation, 97–98; and feminism, 99, 108, 118–19, 130–32, 157–58, 167; focus on community in, 108–9; need for community involvement in, 107; place of, in academia, 166; and recognition of social power dynamics, 125; teachers' projects using, 127; use of, in education, 101–3, 107, 120–21; varieties of, 157. *See also* Feminist Participatory Action Research (FPAR); Participatory Action Research (PAR); Teachers

Activism: and academia, 4, 13–16, 100, 111, 159–61; and community formation, 97; feminist theory as resource for, 109–11; by Muslim women, 21, 26, 28; need to continue with, despite inevitable mistakes, 15–16; and PAR, 141, 182; role of family in encouraging, 100; *testimonio*'s role in, 47–48

Addams, Jane, 160

Adolescent boys, relationships with parents, 82. See also Mother-adolescent son relationship

African-American men, relations with police, 9–10, 13. *See also* Men; Race

Age: feminist views of, 8; and activism, 4, 15

About the Contributors

NIMAT HAFEZ BARAZANGI is a Research Fellow at The Feminist, Gender, and Sexuality Studies at Cornell University who specializes in curriculum and instruction, Islamic and Arabic Studies, and adult and community education. She received the Glock Award for her 1988 Ph.D. dissertation from the Department of Education at Cornell; a Visiting Fellowship from Oxford University; a scholarship from The International Council for Adult Education; a three-year Serial Fulbright Scholarship; and the United Nations Development Program 1999 and 2002 Fellowships. She published *Islamic Identity and the Struggle for Justice* in 1996, and has authored over twenty-five additional articles and essays.

KALINA BRABECK is a fourth year doctoral student in the Counseling Psychology program at the University of Texas at Austin. The focus of her current clinical and research work is intimate partner abuse in Mexican origin communities. She has published on feminist ethics, community trauma, testimonio, and participatory action research and is currently conducting her dissertation research on the help-seeking of battered Mexican origin women within their sociocultural contexts.

MARY M. BRABECK is Professor of Applied Psychology and Dean of the Steinhardt School of Education at New York University. A licensed psychologist, and fellow of APA (Division 7, 35, 52), Brabeck has published more than eighty book chapters, books, and journal articles, including *Practicing Feminist Ethics in Psychology* (Washington DC: APA, 2000) and (with M. Walsh and R. Latta) *Meeting at the Hyphen* (Chicago: University of Chicago Press, 2003). Her daughter is Kalina Brabeck.

MARIE BRENNAN is currently Dean of Education and head of the School of Education at the University of South Australia. She has been involved with action research in education settings for 25 or so years.

MARY BRYDON-MILLER is Associate Professor of Educational Foundations and graduate program coordinator for Urban Educational Leadership in the College of Education, Criminal Justice, and Human Services at the University of Cincinnati. She is co-editor (with Deborah Tolman) of *From Subjects to Subjectivities: A Handbook of Interpretive and Participatory Methods* and (with Peter Park, Budd Hall, and Ted Jackson) of *Voices of Change: Participatory Research in the United States and Canada*. She is also a member of the editorial boards of *Action Research* and *ASAP*.

JILL CHRISP has been active in women's movements in Aotearoa New Zealand since the early 1980s. She currently works with the Human Rights Commission, Te Kähui Tika Tangata. Her key research areas have involved cultural diversity and social change, the impact of socio-economic policy and public discourse on the family, and women and education. She is particularly interested in change-based research and has been facilitative in creating connections between feminisms and participatory action research in her country.

DAVYDD J. GREENWOOD is the Goldwin Smith Professor of Anthropology and Director of the Institute for European Studies at Cornell University where he has served as a faculty member since 1970. He has been elected a Corresponding Member of the Spanish Royal Academy of Moral and Political Sciences. He served as the John S. Knight Professor and Director of the Mario Einaudi Center for 10 years and was President of the Association of International Education Administrators. He also has served as a program evaluator for many universities and for the National Foreign Language Center. His work centers on action research, political economy, ethnic conflict, community and regional development, and the anthropological study of contemporary universities.

M. BRINTON LYKES is an activist researcher and Professor of Community-Social Psychology at the Lynch School of Education at Boston College. From 1999 to 2001, she held a chair in Psychology at the University of the Witwatersrand (South Africa). Her research explores the interstices of indigenous cultural beliefs and practices and those of Western psychology, toward collaborating in the design and development of community-based responses to state-violence in contexts of transition and transformation. She has published extensively about this work, is co-editor of three books, and co-author, with the Association of Maya Ixil Women/New Dawn, of *Voces e* *imágenes: Mujeres Mayas Ixiles de Chajul/Voices and Images: Maya Ixil Women of Chajul* (2000).

PATRICIA MAGUIRE is a Professor of Education and Counseling and Chairperson of the Gallup Graduate Studies Center of Western New Mexico University. Since 1988 she has been working with others to develop an extended university graduate center relevant to the needs and strengths of northwest New Mexico. Her research interests parallel her work as an activist educator and long time advocate for the lived interface of feminisms, participatory action research, and education. Her ground-breaking book, *Doing Participatory Research: A Feminist Approach* (1987), is in its fourth edition. She has written many chapters and articles on feminist-informed action research.

ALICE McINTYRE is an Associate Professor and Director of the Elementary Education Program at Hellenic College. She is a feminist educator and psychologist who has been engaged in activist research and education for many years. She has written a number of articles and book chapters about whiteness, education, and the use of participatory action research (PAR). In addition, she has explored the relationship between PAR, the racial location of white teachers, and their teaching practices in *Making Meaning of Whiteness: Exploring Racial Identity with White Teachers* (1997, SUNY Press). Similarly she has examined the use of PAR as an approach to collaborating with urban youth in the development of action/intervention community-school programs in *Inner-City Kids: Adolescents Confront Life and Violence in an Urban Community* (2000, NYU Press). Alice was recently engaged in a PAR project with women in Belfast, the North of Ireland, exploring the meaning of identity, violence, and community in the contexts of struggle and possibility. She describes that project in a forthcoming book: *Women in Belfast: How Violence Shapes Identity* (Greenwood Press).

SUSAN E. NOFFKE is Associate Professor of Curriculum and Instruction at the University of Illinois–Urbana/Champaign. Her work on action research has appeared in Educational Action Research, and Curriculum Perspectives, and Review of Research in Education. She is co-author (with Kenneth Zeichner) of the chapter, "Practitioner Research" in the Handbook of Research on Teaching (4th ed.). Her current work is with a university-school partnership, and involves working directly with children, school staff, and community toward educational improvement.

ANMOL SATIANI is a doctoral student in Counseling Psychology at Boston College. She is interested in issues of race, gender, class, and power. Anmol is also interested in Asian American mental health issues, concerns of Asian American women, and racial identity development.

ANGELA SHARTRAND is a doctoral candidate in developmental and educational psychology at the Lynch School of Education at Boston College. She received her Ed.M. in human development at Harvard Graduate School of Education and is completing a grounded theory study of urban adolescent women engaged in a youth philanthropy program.

RHODA UNGER is a resident scholar in at the Women's Studies Research Center of Brandeis University and a professor emerita of psychology at Montclair State University where she taught for over twenty-five years. She has a Ph.D. in experimental psychology from Harvard University, but has specialized in the study of women and gender and in social issues for many years. She has held a number of gatekeeping positions including the presidency of Division 35 (Psychology of Women) of APA and the Society for the Psychological Study of Social Issues (SPSSI). She is the inaugural editor of *ASAP-Analyses of Social Issues and Public Policy*—SPSSI's new on-line journal.

YOLAND WADSWORTH has worked in human services as a research and evaluation practitioner, facilitator, and consultant for 30 years. She authored national best-sellers *Do It Yourself Social Research* and *Everyday Evaluation on the Run* and has won both the Australasian Evaluation Society's ET&S award for a career contribution to evaluation and the Caulley-Tulloch Pioneering Evaluation Literature Prize for a co-authored study of how to "build in" consumer evaluation to acute psychiatric hospital practice (published as *The Essential U&I—Understanding and Involvement*). She is establishing an action research teaching program in the Institute for Social Research at Swinburne University where she is an Adjunct Professor.